THE LAN
OF TOWNS

THE LANDSCAPE OF TOWNS

MICK ASTON & JAMES BOND

SUTTON PUBLISHING

First published in 1976 by J.M. Dent & Sons Ltd

First published by Alan Sutton Publishing, an imprint of Sutton
Publishing Limited in 1987

This revised edition published in 2000 by Sutton Publishing Limited
Phoenix Mill · Thrupp · Stroud · Gloucestershire GL5 2BU

British Library Cataloguing in Publication Data
A catalogue record for this book is available from the British Library

ISBN 0 7509 2489 6

Cover illustration: Smithfield livestock market, *by Sidney Thomas Cooper
(1803–1902) (photograph Bridgeman Art Library, London)*

Printed in Great Britain by
Redwood Books,
Trowbridge, Wiltshire.

Contents

List of Plates

List of Figures

All plans in this book are to three constant scales for ease of comparison, with the exception of Figs. 2, 3, 4, 6, 8, 9, 24, 26, 27, 28, 33, 38, 40 and 41

Preface

This book is about towns, and is therefore concerned with the
environment in which most of Britain's population either live or
make frequent visits for work, shopping or recreation. Despite the
fact that urban living forms such a large part of most of our daily
lives, there is a great lack of understanding or appreciation of our
urban environment on the part of both the man in the street and the
officials responsible for organizing and developing that environment.
There is also a sad lack of curiosity about how towns have evolved,
although there are many general and specific books on the archaeology,
geography, history and architecture of towns.

As there are already so many books on towns, is there much point
in writing another one? Can we cover any ground which is not dealt
with adequately elsewhere? We are particularly concerned to discover
how towns have acquired their present appearance, what the different
elements contributing to their total impression are and how these
have first appeared and subsequently changed through time. This
involves some explanation of why towns developed where and when
they did, and what has happened to them since their first foundation.

Most people's concern with towns is as consumers of the
goods and amenities available in them. Any appreciation of the town
which has some historic dimension is likely to be dominated by the
aesthetic aspects of the buildings. Asked to name a historic town,
many will think of Bath, York or Chester. A suggestion that Birmingham, Hartlepool, Goole or Scunthorpe may also have historical
significance is likely to be met with surprise, as might be the idea
that Kilpeck, Bishop's Castle or Stoford could even have been considered as towns. It is one of our chief aims to show that a town's
historic framework amounts to more than just fine buildings. All
towns have an essential unique character which is much more besides;
this character is increasingly fragile and vulnerable as the pressures of
present-day redevelopment tend to make everywhere seem more alike.

If we can show that Barnsley is in its own way as significant historically as Bury St Edmunds or that Dudley rates consideration as seriously as Dunster, we shall have achieved some of our objectives.

The size of the topic is enormous, and we can offer no more than an introduction in which many omissions and irregularities of coverage are unavoidable. There is an inevitable bias towards areas of our own greatest personal experience, the Midlands, Wales and the South-West. However, we hope that the examples we use will be of service over a much wider area and that we have made some contribution towards a better understanding of and care for our urban environment.

M. A. and C. J. B.
Taunton & Woodstock
1976

Acknowledgements

Many people have contributed to this work. Our particular thanks must be expressed to Alison Smith, who read the text; Tom Hendey, for all his patience and care with the maps; Bob Mills, for work on Figs 6 and 8; Geoff Roberts, who did most of the photographic work; Alan Wilson, for Plates XI, XVI, XVII and XVIII; Ron Tandy and the staff of the Bodleian Library Map Room, Oxford, for providing easy access to plans; David Bromwich of Somerset County Council Local History Library, Taunton Castle, for much valuable help with sources; and Sue Woodley and Denise Elston for much of the typing. Our thanks are also due to numerous other people who have helped in various ways.

We are also grateful to the following: Professor J. K. S. St Joseph, Director in Aerial Photography, University of Cambridge, for Plates I, II, VI, VII and XIV (copyright reserved); Philip Rahtz for his help; Hunting (Aerofilms Ltd) for Plates XV and XX. Peter Addyman, Peter Tillott and Richard Hall of the York Archaeological Trust for Fig. 1; Alan Carter, Director of the Norwich Survey Project for Fig. 2; Public Record Office for Fig. 3 (ref. MPC/35: Crown Copyright reserved); Royal Commission on Historical Monuments (England) for Fig. 4 (National Monuments Record, Crown Copyright reserved); Fig. 24 is based upon original drawing by Dr W. Urry, 'Canterbury under the Angevin Kings' published by the Athlone Press of the University of London, 1967; Roger Leech and the Committee for Rescue Archaeology in Avon, Gloucestershire and Somerset provided Figs 20 and 42; and the Council for British Archaeology gave permission to base Fig. 41 on plans in *The Erosion of History* edited by Carolyn M. Heighway, 1972.

We have made extensive use of the published works of many authors, which have been acknowledged, wherever possible, by references in the text. It has proved difficult, however, to do this comprehensively, and a fuller list of sources used will be found in the

Bibliography. Any errors are the responsibility of the authors.

Finally, our greatest debt is to our wives, Linda and Tina, for their invaluable contributions at all stages of our labours, from the initial field-work to the onerous task of compiling the index; for making many gallons of tea; and for generally keeping the rest of life on an even keel in the meantime. To them this book is dedicated.

Chapter I

Introduction

It was in 1955 that Professor W. G. Hoskins, in his pioneer work *The Making of the English Landscape,* suggested that 'the landscape of towns, indeed, requires a whole book to itself'. Despite the many advances in the study of landscape history which have been made since then, that book has still not been written. In preparing this present book we have become painfully aware of the fact that this is a subject for not one, but many books. All we can hope to achieve here is to sketch in some of the major features of town development in Britain over the past two thousand years or more, to suggest ways in which the urban landscape can be further investigated, and to indicate the general relevance of such work in the present day.

Our title is *The Landscape of Towns,* and perhaps we should begin by defining our terms. What do we mean by a town? Many definitions have been produced in the past, most of them emphasizing the administrative and legal aspects. In so far as any attempt has been made to relate the definition of the town to its physical attributes, perhaps the only general measure of agreement is that size and appearance are unsatisfactory criteria. Certainly the purpose and qualities of towns have varied at different times, and we shall find many examples of places which have been regarded as towns during some periods but not in others. Similarly the features which have been regarded as essential items of urban equipment have changed through time, and have made various impressions on the present landscape. In the opening paragraphs of *The City in History* (1961) Lewis Mumford says of the origins, purposes and functions of cities that 'no single definition will apply to all its manifestations and no single description will cover all its transformations'. Emrys Jones in *Towns and Cities* (1966) asks 'What is a town? How best can we define it? Strange though it may seem the city defies a universal definition which would be acceptable to everyone. Is it a physical conglomeration of streets and houses, or is it a centre of exchange and commerce? Is it a kind of society, or even a frame of mind? Has it a certain size, a specific density? The difficulties involved in definition are countless.'

Faced with such problems, we have avoided any universal definition, and have preferred to adopt a more flexible approach, covering places which in their day were reckoned to be towns, regardless of their present status. We have not attempted to distinguish between the town as a settlement form and the essentially legal and administrative concepts of the borough or the city.

The second term to consider is 'landscape'. Since the word conjures up a vision of rolling hills, green pastures and woods, to use it in the same breath as 'towns' with their associations of busy streets and industries may itself seem something of a paradox. We shall later examine in more detail the elements which comprise a town's landscape; here we shall consider anything which contributes, or has contributed, to the town's overall appearance. Some of these elements, such as the street plan, are likely to be extremely persistent, and features surviving today may be many centuries old. Others are quite ephemeral but may be visually dominant in their day—anyone looking at photographs of towns early in the present century cannot fail to be struck by the large areas of shop walls given over to painted advertisements. Today most of these have faded almost beyond notice, having been replaced at shop-window level by hoardings and advertisements which may prove equally short-lived. We have decided to concentrate on the landscape of towns in the present day, tracing back those elements which have endured over the centuries and ignoring the ephemera of which all trace has now gone, rather than to attempt to reconstruct the landscape of towns at different periods in the past. We are concerned to show the value of field-work (again an inappropriately rural term) and observation in towns, rather than documentary or archaeological methods which might provide more evidence of the transient features. Nevertheless, looking at urban relict features without recognizing their original context would be not merely sterile but misleading.

Towns have attracted attention from more than one academic discipline in the past, and it may be asked whether any new approach is capable of producing significant new information. Before we attempt to answer this it may be useful to review briefly the contribution of different studies to the landscape of towns.

Historians

Historians, both professional and amateur, have perhaps had the longest experience in looking at the evolutionary aspects of towns.

(In view of the doubts expressed earlier about using words like 'landscape' and 'field-work' in an urban context, we hesitate to say that historians were first in the field.) Their work has been both general and specific, concerned both with the town as a countrywide institution and with detailed local studies. Much of it, however, has been concerned primarily with the judicial, administrative, social and economic aspects of towns. Such work is often of great value in its own right, but for anyone interested in the landscape of a town it can be infuriating to pick up a book purporting to be a definitive history and find it goes into intricate details about borough organization in the thirteenth century and notable mayors in the eighteenth century, but tells little about its physical appearance at any date and does not even provide a plan. The existence of a standard book of several volumes on a town's history does not mean necessarily that all aspects of its development will have been adequately covered.

A further drawback with some published local histories is their inadequacy of information-content and understanding. While some local historians have displayed a sound grasp of current research and ideas on the origins and development of towns and have arranged their work allowing comparison with other towns, others have been content merely to amass an indigestible array of miscellaneous parochial facts and fit them together in chronological order. This is extremely unfortunate if, as in many towns, such works, even when they date back to the last century, remain the most readily accessible single source on that town's history.

In spite of these generalizations the research of some historians has greatly enhanced our appreciation of the topography of some towns. Some of the most important works on urban topography have been the result of detailed and extensive documentary studies applied to plotting out maps of medieval properties in towns like Hull, Oxford, Canterbury and Kings Lynn (Bilson, 1928; Salter, 1934; Urry, 1967; Parker, 1971). Similar work is currently in progress in Bristol (Neale, forthcoming), and it is an encouraging sign for the future that some of the new archaeological units have historians on their staff, part of whose work is to provide historic development maps as an essential background to excavation sites.

Geographers

Studies of different aspects of the landscape and the interrelationship between the various physical and human factors which comprise it have formed much of the work of geographers in the past. Historical geographers have considered towns from the point of view of their historical development and as dynamic systems, using both field-work and documentary material as well as applying techniques of their own. Of particular importance is the work of Professor M. R. G. Conzen (Conzen, 1960, 1968), whose analysis of town plans has established the standard for this type of work. A different approach has been well demonstrated by Professor H. Thorpe in his classic study of Lichfield (Thorpe, 1951). Unfortunately, geographers have generally failed to follow up and develop these types of study. The techniques of their discipline have been changing rapidly and are becoming more scientific, but one cannot help regretting that, in grasping the statistical and model-building methods currently in vogue, few geographers now appear to take much interest in townscapes.

Architectural historians

Buildings cover a large area of any town and many studies of them are available, ranging from extremely detailed surveys of individual buildings to brief descriptions in popular reference works such as Professor N. Pevsner's invaluable *Buildings of England* series. In general, however, to qualify for inclusion in a description of town buildings, a structure must be either old, built by a famous architect, or attractive enough aesthetically to overcome the lack of the first two qualities. Thus in most towns it is not difficult to find out about the church, the castle and the guildhall; but of the host of shops, houses, workshops and factories which make up the vast proportion of town buildings little is usually written. It is only very recently, for example, that working-class housing in towns has begun to attract the serious attention it deserves (Chapman, 1971).

Even if some sort of survey of the buildings in a town appears to have been done, one finds all too frequently that it is concerned mainly with the architectural detail of the façade, whereas, historically, the roof and the rear of the building may tell us much more. It is found again and again that an apparently eighteenth- or nineteenth-century frontage encases a structure of the seventeenth or sixteenth century or even earlier, and if an assessment of the date-range of buildings in a town street is made from the evidence of façades alone, a totally misleading picture will be produced (Plate IX).

Archaeologists

Archaeologists have begun only relatively recently to make an important contribution to the study of towns (Heighway, 1972). In the past, on the rare occasions when excavations were carried out at all in towns, the effort has been concentrated on the recovery of Roman remains underneath the later town, or on some specific and specialized medieval site within it such as a castle or abbey: St Mary's Abbey, York, was excavated as long ago as the 1820s.   The first realization that towns themselves had information to offer perhaps dates from the excavation of blitzed sites in London after the 1939–45 war (Grimes, 1968).   In the 1960s, with the gradual realization by archaeologists that major redevelopment of town centres was damaging or irrevocably destroying the archaeological source material beneath, a new emphasis on 'rescue' archaeology appeared in historic town centres.   The first large-scale excavation programme to attempt to deal with the topography and growth of a major city as a whole was that of Winchester in 1961–71.   Imitations of this scheme were slow in gathering momentum, for the organizational structure of archaeology in Britain was still basically part-time, and it was unable to cope immediately with the scale of the operations involved.   In 1968 Martin Biddle was still making pleas for more work on British urban archaeology before it was too late (Biddle, 1968).   In due course the example did spread to some other major cities.

The results of the response to these 'rescue' situations have often been very impressive, and there has been a great increase in our knowledge about those towns, and, by inference, about towns in general.   Along with their own increasing professionalism, archaeologists have perhaps been more ready than some practitioners in other aspects of urban studies to appreciate the value of the complete interdisciplinary approach.   Nonetheless excavation to adequate modern standards is extremely expensive, and is only a practical possibility on a limited number of carefully selected sites.   If our interest is in town A, it does not help us much to know that the nearest site receiving active archaeological investigation is town B, thirty miles away.

Planners

The interest of planners in towns differs from that of the groups previously mentioned in that their concern is essentially practical rather than academic.   Planners are involved with the management of a town as a working organism, with traffic flow and population growth, rather than with the problems of the town's origins and historic development.   Until quite recently, in so far as their work had a historic dimension at all, it often tended to be solely of a cosmetic nature: efforts would be made to ensure the aesthetic enhancement of cobbled streets with overhanging timber buildings, but medieval street plans were a nuisance to be removed or bypassed, and the rear of medieval tenements were handy spaces for further development rather than of historic interest in their own right.   Now, however, a new emphasis on conservation of historic townscapes can be detected as a result of Conservation Acts, but again the concern is largely with appearances and atmosphere rather than origins, developments and historic worth (Cullen, 1961, Worskett, 1969, Sharp, 1968, Johns, 1965).

In this extremely brief and general résumé it has obviously not been possible to give more than the broadest of outlines of the work carried out on towns by various disciplines in the past.   If we have given the impression that all town historians are interested only in charters, geographers in theoretical models, architects and planners in façades and archaeologists in holes in the ground, we must offer our apologies for the injustice to those workers in these fields who have taken a broader view.   The discipline which combines elements from all these different approaches to study the landscape of towns is still relatively under-developed, lacking the cohesion afforded to other studies by the existence of university departments or learned societies, and lacking even a satisfactory polysyllabic name.

The topographical approach

The leading exponent of landscape studies in Britain has been Professor W. G. Hoskins, who many years ago set out the central thesis of much of his own work and that of his many followers when he wrote 'the English landscape itself, to those who know how to read it right, is the richest historical record we possess' (Hoskins, 1955a).   His own work on Exeter and Leicester (Hoskins, 1955b, 1960) has demonstrated the value of his approach in towns.   A somewhat different but equally influential approach has been used by Professor M. W. Beresford, whose work on medieval town plantations (Beresford, 1957, 1967a) was at the time revolutionary in its scale.   More recently he has been one of the leading figures in the study of industrial housing in towns. The influence of these two men has formed the basis for much urban landscape research, and we would like to acknowledge with gratitude the debt that this book owes them for its inspiration.

A quite different approach to the study of urban topography has been the recent international programme of producing atlases of towns as they were in 1800, showing all their medieval features.   So far two British volumes are in print, dealing with some twelve towns, and coverage of a further 118 towns is projected. Nothing of this sort has been attempted before. The project uses detailed coloured maps to show streets, boundaries, lines of former fortifications, sites of razed monastic and secular buildings, and diverted streams, with an accompanying historical account and investigation of the development of the town's topography. The ultimate value of the completed compendium will be immeasurable.

Let us now examine in more detail the elements which make up a town landscape.

The siting of towns

The reasons for the growth of towns at particular points have attracted a great deal of attention in the past. There are two main aspects of their location which must be considered. The first of these is the position of the town in its regional setting, its relationship with the surrounding rural area and the intervals between itself and neighbouring towns. The second is concerned with the local site, the ground upon which the town stands. Both aspects have been the subjects of much misunderstanding in the past arising from the failure to interpret correctly the relationship between human activities and the physical background. Towns have been labelled 'gap towns' or 'river-crossing towns' as if the existence of a break in a range of hills or a fording point over a river was enough to generate a town on that site. A glance at any map showing gaps and crossing-points where there are no towns should be enough to dispel this idea. Towns are built by and for people. Their regional and local sitings are the results of decisions taken by people and not of some inevitable physical control. Towns will be founded for specific reasons which are related to the requirements of the community at that point in time. The needs and customs of the contemporary society and the ways in which they change through time are all-important. The landscape provides town founders with innumerable possible choices of site, but the actual place chosen will reflect the socio-economic context and values of the founders, set against the capacity of their contemporary technology to overcome problems posed by the physical nature of the site. Hilltops and steep cliffs which were major defensive attractions for medieval town builders proved a considerable nuisance at a later date when such needs had ceased (Fig. 25). Marshy areas which were avoided in earlier periods could later be reclaimed and settled. Flat coastlines with wide sandy beaches but no harbours may have been deserted in medieval times but have proved ideal sites for nineteenth-century resorts. Isolated tainted springs shunned before the eighteenth century suddenly gave rise to booming spa towns. Wild heaths and moorland, unoccupied earlier, became sprawling mill towns in the nineteenth century.

When examining the site of any town of any date, it is important for us to envisage the landscape as it was at the time of the first settlement and throughout all later stages of expansion. Rivers and streams may have been of very different volume in comparison with the present day, or they may have been canalized, diverted or culverted. Areas of marshland and meadow may have been drained and reclaimed. Coastlines may have undergone considerable erosion or silting in the space of only a few centuries, as can be illustrated by the great medieval town of Dunwich, now almost entirely washed away, or Winchelsea, once a seaport but now a mile inland. Even small breaks or changes in the slope, barely apparent in the present townscape, could have exerted some influence in the planning decisions at the time certain areas were developed. We must therefore always look at the landscape from the cultural, psychological and technological standpoint of the initial settlers in order to gauge what aspects of the site were of particular importance to them.

The effect of the original landscape on the appearance of an existing town is considerable. Even if they were alike in all other respects, Sheffield and Ely, Great Yarmouth and Torquay would still be very different in character because of the underlying contours of the ground on which they stand. The physical nature of the site must, however, be seen as a background against which human activities take place and not as a causal framework.

As well as change there is also persistence. The concept of 'continuity' of an occupation site has been a recurrent theme of archaeological and geographical research. Continuity can refer to site, to functions or to institutions—the word is often loosely used. However, the fact that some town sites have been occupied for a very long time, and that some of their landscape features may have persisted for centuries, is increasingly being recognized. Whatever the initial reasons for a town's foundation on a particular site, once established it generates its own infrastructure, transport network and so on. Even if the reasons for the original siting had ceased to play any active part in the town's existence many centuries earlier, it will usually remain on the same site and either adapt itself to new functions or suffer lingering decline. The role of momentum is powerful.

It is useful to examine a group of towns which are close to one another and yet very different in character. This will quickly remove any remaining theories that the distribution or siting of towns is caused by a set of physical desiderata which are constant through time. Three Worcestershire towns which lie within a few miles of each other will illustrate the point. Kidderminster's name suggests a Saxon origin, and somewhere near it is the site of an eighth-century monastery. The town grew as a minor medieval market centre with a textile industry, but its most distinctive features developed only as a result of a historical accident in the eighteenth century when the carpet industry settled there. Most of its present landscape of mill chimneys and terraced housing dates from the mechanization of that industry after the 1850s. Neighbouring Bewdley looks an older town but is in fact of much later origin, developing as a late-medieval river port. It enjoyed a heyday of prosperity in the seventeeth and early eighteenth centuries but then stagnated in the nineteenth century so that its rich heritage of timbered and brick Georgian buildings remained relatively undisturbed. Stourport underwent rapid development as a boom town in the 1780s–90s through its canal and killed Bewdley's trade, but itself suffered a long period of stagnation after the mid-nineteenth century, when the coming of the railway to Kidderminster allowed the oldest of the towns to regain its original supremacy. These three towns are totally different in the reasons for their origins and their choice of sites, and in their townscapes they retain evidence of that difference to the present day.

The physical elements of the townscape

The townscape is made up of a number of different features—buildings, boundaries, streets—arranged in a particular way in the town plan and each put to a particular use.

(i) Streets are areas reserved for the use of various kinds of surface traffic. They may be major through routes accommodating all kinds of traffic, much of which may not be related to the direct function of the towns they pass through. They may serve a purely residential function in giving local access. They may be subsidiary roads, providing access to the rear of properties or have some particular use, such as a market-place. They may cater for specialist traffic, for example, pedestrian precincts, stepped streets, or narrow lanes. Other communication features, like railways and canals, could be included, but although of great social and economic importance they do not occupy a large proportion of total urban space. Two aspects of streets affect the townscape. On the one hand their surfacing, whether of cobbles, granite setts, paving or tarmac, is of visual importance. More subtle, but perhaps of greater significance, is their arrangement within the town plan. The shape, size, length and pattern of the streets are indications of their historic origin and function, and abrupt changes in width or direction may be evidence of other vanished historic elements such as town walls or gates.

(ii) Property boundaries may enclose plots of particular shape which are characteristic of a particular period or function. Plot boundaries divide up the spaces confined in whole or in part by the street lines and appear to have a relatively high survival-rate over long periods of time, often reflecting older, long-vanished features such as former defences or the agricultural fields over which the town has expanded.

(iii) Buildings within the plot boundaries form the individual units of occupation and function, and the landscape historian is interested in their structure and use only in so far as it affects their appearance. Thus the general size and shape, architectural style and building material can be used as clues to the building's origin, function and date, but the processes of manufacture going on inside a factory, the ritual of the church service, or the life-style of the inhabitants of a house are of interest only where they affect the form of the building.

(iv) The use to which areas of towns or individual buildings within them are put often has quite an effect on the townscape. Market stalls, shops advertising their wares by means of signs, factories emitting smoke and storing raw materials or finished products in the open may be cited as examples.

(v) The people who make use of the town are the most impermanent, and yet in some ways the most important part of it, because they represent the living element within the framework. The abiding impression of a town today is of large numbers of people and motor vehicles, almost to the exclusion of the town's plan or buildings. In this book we shall be concerned rarely with this last aspect, concentrating on the investigation of the first three elements. These tend to be more long-lasting and of greater historic significance, but we must remember that the people and the uses to which they put their towns are in no sense a negligible part of the landscape.

Some towns owe much of their character to one particular period. A basically Saxon, or medieval, or Georgian plan provides the framework within which later buildings and land uses have been incorporated. In other cases the origins of a townscape are much more complex, including contributions from many different periods. Careful topographical study can, however, enable us to analyse the present plan, to separate out the individual elements making up the complex whole, and to isolate the specialized precincts and the units developed

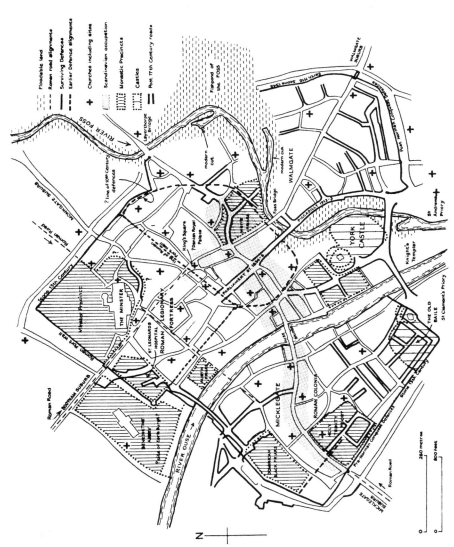

Floodable land
Roman road alignments
Surviving Defences
Earlier Defence alignments
+ Churches including sites
+ Scandinavian occupation
Monastic Precincts
Castles
Post 17th Century roads

Flatpond of the FOSS

RIVER FOSS

? line of 10th Century defences

Layerthorpe Bridge

modern cut

Ouse Bridge

modern cut

WALMGATE

PICCADILLY 1912

WALMGATE SUBURB

EARTH 1115 STONE 1345

FOSSGATE BRIDGE 1157

Post NORMAN COLONIZATION

St Andrew's Priory

NEWGATE SUBURB

Roman Road

King's Square

?Danish Royal Palace

Siege 1300-1315

Stone 13th Century

PARLIAMENT ST 1836

YORK CASTLE

Knights Templar

THE MINSTER

Minster Precinct

ROMAN LEGIONARY FORTRESS

St LEONARDS HOSPITAL

Roman Road

BOOTHAM SUBURB

Roman Fort Wall

THE OLD BAILE

St Clement's Priory

RIVER OUSE

BISHOPHILL

?site of early church

MICKLEGATE

ROMAN COLONIA

Post NORMAN COLONIZATION

Stone 13th Century

Roman Road

MICKLEGATE SUBURB

N

0   250 metres
0   800 feet

1 York: The development of the townscape.

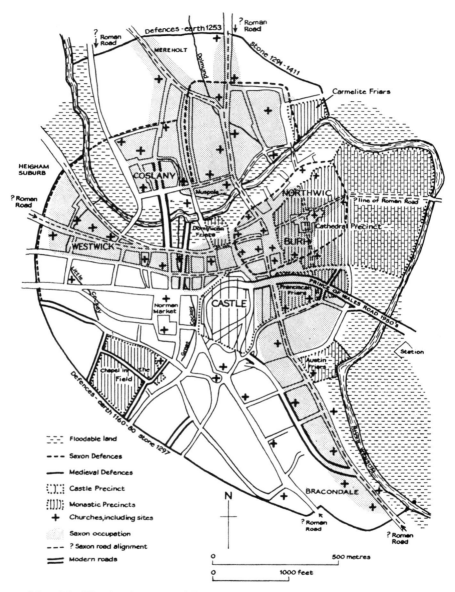

Floodable land
Saxon Defences
Medieval Defences
Castle Precinct
Monastic Precincts
Churches, including sites
Saxon occupation
? Saxon road alignment
Modern roads

0   500 metres
0   1000 feet

2 Norwich: The development of the townscape.

at different dates.   Two attempts are illustrated here, distinguishing different townscape elements in two great medieval towns, York and Norwich (Figs 1 & 2).   The characteristics of townscape elements of different periods will be examined in later chapters.

Chapter II

Documentary Sources

Throughout the greater part of this book we shall be concerned with what can be seen in the town on the ground, rather than with what can be discovered about it from the documents in a muniment room. We hope to show that the plan, buildings and general appearance of a town are themselves a very potent source of information, often providing details unobtainable from written sources. However, documentary evidence can add immeasurably to the understanding of what we see on the ground, and should always be taken into account.

We cannot here cover all the available sources which are of any relevance to the townscape, but in the absence of any single handlist of documentary sources for urban topography, it is hoped that the following summary may be of some value. For further guidance the reader is advised to consult general works on the subject (Hoskins, 1959, 1967; Palliser, 1976) and the various specific works referred to below.

(i) CLASSICAL REFERENCES: It is generally true that the later the period, the greater the amount of documentary material available, although this is not always matched by its accessibility. As one would expect, sources for towns before the Saxon period are very limited, and provide little information. Perhaps the earliest reference to a British 'town' is the description of an 'oppidum', possibly Wheathampstead, by Caesar in 54 BC. Later references to Roman towns in Britain occur in the third or fourth century Antonine Itinerary (Rivet, 1970) and the seventh-century Ravenna Cosmography (Richmond and Crawford, 1949), but these are little more than road-books listing contemporary place names.

(ii) LITERARY REFERENCES: For no small number of towns the earliest reference will be pre-Conquest and may be located in the Anglo-Saxon Chronicle or other Saxon texts (Garmonsway, 1953). Usually these do little beyond establishing the existence of a place at a particular date, or indicating fortifications where they occur.

From the twelfth century onwards there is an increasing number of literary references to towns (Hyde, 1966), some of which are brief descriptions only, such as those of William of Malmesbury (Stubbs, 1887). For individual towns there may be longer passages, for example for London (1173–4) and Chester (c. 1195) (Stenton, 1934; Taylor, 1912). The most detailed of all was William of Worcester's famous street-by-street portrayal of Bristol in about 1480 (Harvey, 1969; Neale, forthcoming).

After the sixteenth century there are accounts by an increasing number of travellers and topographers describing how towns appeared to them on their visits. The first to approach a blanket coverage of England was John Leland (Toulmin Smith, 1910), whose prime intention had been to make a survey of the libraries of the doomed monasteries. He began recording topographical observations for a proposed 'Description of the Realm of England', but it remained unwritten at his death in 1552. Fortunately his notes survived, to be reassembled in the eighteenth century. His comments on towns are often disappointingly laconic: many times we are told only that a town 'stondith much by Clothing' or was 'a good, quick Market town', though elsewhere he gives valuable detail.

Later in the same century another major topographer, William Camden, was writing his *Britannia* (Camden, 1586), an attempt to reconstruct the geography of the Roman province. Valuable snippets of information can be extracted, although his notice of contemporary towns was somewhat superficial.

The most entertaining and in many ways the most valuable of the nationwide travellers of the seventeenth century was Celia Fiennes who, between 1685 and 1703, covered an astonishing area of England and Wales on horseback. She kept an account of her observations as she went, apparently purely for her own amusement rather than for publication or on behalf of anyone else. Unlike Camden she was not much interested in antiquities, but despite occasional inaccuracies was a keen observer of contemporary town life. (Morris, 1947).

The first major topographical writer of the eighteenth century to show much interest in towns was Daniel Defoe (Defoe, 1726). He travelled widely during his life, but his book does not pretend to be a record of an actual journey. Unlike Celia Fiennes, he describes some places from distant memory of them and others he had probably never visited. His main interest was in trade and commerce in the towns, and here he is of great value, although his purely topographical content is not high.

After Defoe the number of travellers' diaries and topographical descriptions continues to increase, and we cannot list them all here. Before leaving literary sources, however, we should return briefly to the purely local topographical surveys of the post-medieval period. The pattern of county surveys set by Lambarde for Kent and Carew for Cornwall (Hoskins, 1959) was soon followed by more detailed town descriptions. Examples are Stow's superb *Survey of London* (1598) and Hooker's survey of Exeter compiled at about the same time, but not published until much later (Stow, 1598, Hooker, 1919). Surveys, usually with a historical emphasis, followed of Great Yarmouth (1599), Canterbury (1640), Stamford (1646), Newcastle (1649), Scarborough (1660) and many others (Hoskins, 1959). These all have some topographical value, even if their approach is a historical one. Despite these early leads, most English towns had to wait until the eighteenth or nineteenth centuries for their first published descriptions, and in all but a few the topographical element is limited.

(iii) STATE RECORDS: The earliest documents classifiable as state records are also pre-Conquest. Amongst the most significant is the Burghal Hidage, which has recently received a great deal of attention (Brooks, 1964; Hill, 1969). This is a list of places in the early tenth century credited with defences. It covers only the royal estates in Wessex, but is a valuable source of information. The earliest document to cover almost all the towns then exisiting in England is the Domesday Book of 1086, although even this omits London and Winchester. It describes over a hundred places as containing burgesses and more than fifty places as having markets, but it needs to be used with extreme caution.

For all its problems the Domesday Book is invaluable, if only because there is no comparable later medieval source. The nearest approach is perhaps the Hundred Rolls of 1279, which furnish useful descriptions of a few towns, including Oxford and Cambridge.

The great mass of crown records beginning in the twelth to thirteenth centuries includes much relevant material, but it is impossible to list here all the many classes of documents which may prove of value. Of particular note are the Patent and Close Rolls, which contain many murage grants and crenellation licences referring to town defences, and the Charter Rolls which contain many grants of markets.

(iv) ECCLESIASTICAL RECORDS: Towns in which much property was held by ecclesiastical corporations in medieval times are sometimes rich in documentary sources for topographical information. Deeds, rentals, surveys and other ecclesiastical records have been used to great effect in some towns, including Lincoln (Hill, 1948), Oxford (Salter, 1960, 1969) and Canterbury (Urry, 1967). Published material of a similar nature is available for others such as Winchester (Biddle, 1972) and London (Hodgett, 1971).

(v) CORPORATION ARCHIVES: Corporation records naturally date back only to the beginning of municipal liberties, and may vary considerably from town to town. A recent survey (Martin, 1963), counted eleven English boroughs, including London, with original administrative records preserved from the period before 1272, and another eleven with records from before 1300. One of the important functions of a corporation from the outset has been the registering of property transactions, so enrolled deeds have survived for Wallingford from 1232, London from 1252, Ipswich from 1255 (Martin, 1973) and Norwich from 1285 (Rye, 1903–15).

Another important block of documents relates to the corporation's own properties. Few of these are yet published. An exception is Bridgwater, for which all the thousand or so medieval deeds are now in print (Dilks, 1933–48, Dunning and Tremlett, 1971). Rentals and surveys of corporation property may exist from medieval times, and examples are published for the mid-fifteenth century for Gloucester (Stevenson, 1890) and Southampton (Burgess, 1974).

In addition there are many special categories such as records concerned with bridges, walls and defences, markets and rebuildings after fires.

Among the vast amount of post-medieval material likely to be found in corporation archives are the inherited records of Improvement Commissioners, a primary source for details of street and housing development, and the records of street and sanitary committees which succeeded them.

(vi) COMPANY AND PRIVATE ARCHIVES: A further wealth of post-medieval information can be traced in the private records of estate agents, auctioneers and charitable organizations, and in company records of industrial firms concerned with housing, water companies and so on.

(vii) MISCELLANEOUS POST-MEDIEVAL SOURCES: A vast quantity of deeds, rentals and leases remain in private hands, as do building contracts. Inventories are a valuable source for buildings in towns. Directories (Norton, 1950) and local newspapers are all of topographical value, though it is time-consuming to search the latter.

(viii) MAPS: The sixteenth century saw the first appearance of the town map, almost unknown in medieval times (Fig. 3). Early maps are often far from accurate, and it is often difficult to draw a clear distinction between the map and the prospect. Such maps were not true plans, but simply a vista which happened to take a more or less vertical bird's-eye view instead of an oblique one. The earliest plan of any town is always worth searching for. The first atlas of European town plans, by Braun and Hogenberg (1572–98), *Civitates Orbis Terrarum* (Skelton, 1966) contains the earliest corpus of British town plans, and this was soon followed by John Speed's *Theatre of the Empire of Great Britain* (1612), which contains no less than seventy-three plans of different towns.

Some caution must be exercised in their use, for there is a frequent tendency to publish new plans based closely on Speed or some other predecessor but redrawn in contemporary style, so that the information they contain may be a hundred years or so earlier than their own publication date. The middle and later seventeenth century saw relatively few new town plans, but there was a great spate of them in the eighteenth century, improving steadily in quality. The fine maps of the London cartographer John Rocque are outstanding (Bristol, 1742; Exeter, 1744; Shrewsbury, 1746; London, 1746) (Harley, 1967). It was in the nineteenth century that the first large-scale Ordnance Survey plans appeared (Harley, 1963).

(ix) DRAWINGS, PRINTS AND PHOTOGRAPHS: The eighteenth century saw a great vogue for publishing 'prospects' of towns, often from several viewpoints. The finest series contains the eighty-three views of the main cities and towns of England and Wales engraved by Samuel and Nathaniel Buck in the 1730s–40s. In the nineteenth century there were many more prints and engravings, showing street scenes or individual town buildings, such as Shepherd's views of London (1829). Amongst the innumerable paintings and drawings is the collections of drawings by Buckler in the British Museum and Bodleian Library, Oxford (Barley, 1974). Photographs begin to appear in the nineteenth century, and are again a source of immense topographical value; collections have been published for many towns.

(x) SECONDARY SOURCES should not be neglected, for although they often lack an adequate appreciation of urban topography, they may supply the first clues to the existence of possibly significant features. On no account should the section in the Victoria County History be missed where it exists. Although these vary widely in quality

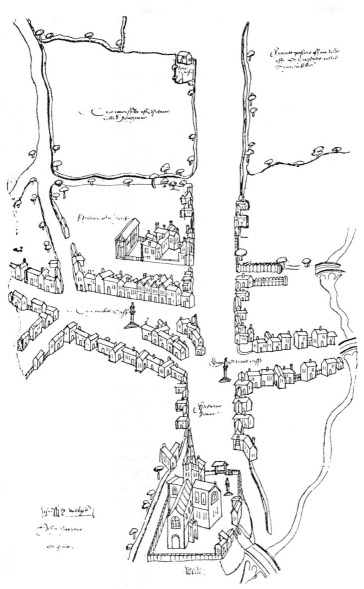

3 Ashbourne, Derbyshire, in 1547: contemporary plan.

according to their date of publication, for many towns they will be the most recent authoritative summary of their historical development.

There is no short cut to finding documentary material relevant to urban topography. For some towns documentation of all sorts is very full from an early date, for others there seems disappointingly little. Much of what exists is unpublished, and quite a large proportion of that is not even catalogued or listed. The total amount of medieval and post-medieval documentation is voluminous, and major urban sources can still be expected to come to light. Important unpublished material may be scattered in any number of repositories and record offices, and its discovery will often be a matter of sheer chance.

Chapter III

Prehistoric and Roman Towns

It has usually been assumed that towns were an introduction of the Roman occupation. However, it is becoming increasingly apparent that there were settlements in Britain which possessed many of the attributes of urban life a hundred years before. These were large permanent settlements with communal defences containing streets and regularly laid-out densely-packed buildings. They engaged in trade, commerce and industry, and acted as religious and administrative centres.

One of the key types of site in the study of town origins in Britain is the hill fort (Jesson and Hill, 1971). There are several thousand of these, widely distributed over most parts of the country except for eastern Britain and the Pennines, and varying considerably in size, siting and the nature of their defences. At present the earliest of them appears to date to about 800 BC, but they were continually being built and altered right up to the Roman invasion.

Until relatively recently, most of them were seen as isolated settlements occupied only in times of emergency during intertribal wars. Even where traces of huts were evident on the surface, it was assumed that such high and bleak sites could have been inhabited only temporarily.

However, this interpretation was a direct result of the limited archaeological techniques which had been applied. Most sites had been examined only by means of trenches cut across the defences. Very little of the interior plans of hill forts was examined before the idea of stripping large areas had been developed. Interpretations from archaeological evidence always need to be seen in the light of the limitations of contemporary techniques, quite apart from the limitations resulting from the variable survival of physical evidence. Similarly the development of aerial photography has permitted the discovery of large numbers of probably contemporary farmsteads in the vicinity of many hill forts, thus removing the impression of isolation which they give in the present day.

The most recent reappraisal of the function of hill forts in the pre-Roman Iron Age (Cunliffe, 1974) suggests that many of them may 'be regarded as the towns of the Iron Age'. It is now becoming clear that in southern Britain at least, dense and ordered internal settlement within hill fort defences was widespread. In the South-West, for example, Hod Hill in its ultimate pre-Roman phase was densely packed with circular huts, fairly haphazardly spaced but with several well-defined streets. The part which remains unploughed gives the 'impression of a heavily built-up urban complex as it would have been at the time of the Roman attack in AD 43' (Fig. 4). Maiden Castle

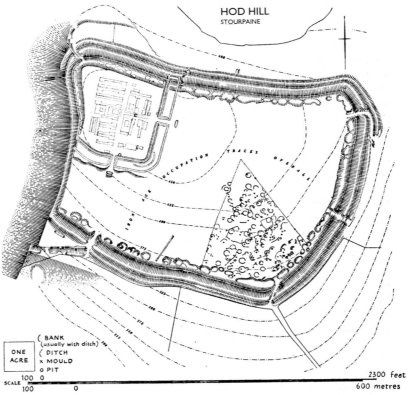

4 Hod Hill, Dorset: An Iron Age hill fort densely packed with huts (surviving as earthworks in the unploughed sector); Roman fort in north-west corner.

(Wheeler, 1943) and South Cadbury (Alcock, 1968–70) similarly display evidence of internal streets and densely-packed buildings. On the Welsh border Croft Ambrey (Stanford, 1974), Credenhill (Stanford, 1971) and Midsummer Hill, display regularly-planned internal occupation, with rectangular buildings in rows along streets. Dense settlement of a less regulated nature is also evident in certain hill forts in north Wales and southern Scotland. However, 'town' implies more than simply density of building within the defences. In many of these cases it is difficult to assess how many of the individual huts visible today were actually occupied at any one time.

Let us now leave hill forts and examine another type of proto-urban settlement of different character. During the four or five decades before the Roman conquest south-eastern Britain had been settled by groups of peoples from northern Europe known as the Belgae, who were characterized by a strongly organized social structure and warlike attitudes. One of their achievements was the introduction of coinage, for coins were certainly being minted in Britain by at least 70 BC. This coinage gives us the names of a number of the rulers of the Belgic peoples, who each seem to have ruled from a central seat of government. These tribal centres were quite different from the hill forts, usually being found on low-lying ground beside streams, overlooked by nearby hills, often hidden within woods and occupying much larger areas (Fig. 5). Relatively little is yet known about them, but among the sites which have received some investigation, the successive capitals of the powerful Catuvellauni in Hertfordshire and Essex are notable. Their earliest centre seems to have been at Wheathampstead, where an area of nearly 100 acres is surrounded by earthworks of massive proportions. This is probably the site protected by forests and marshes, well fortified and filled with men and cattle, captured in 54 BC by Caesar. He noted that such densely-wooded spots protected by a rampart and trench were referred to by the Britons as 'oppida', the term now generally applied to them. Wheathampstead was replaced by a site at Prae Wood, much closer to the modern St Albans (Wheeler, 1936). This has a more dispersed plan with several satellite settlements, one of which includes the Belgic mint. Its central area was enclosed by a series of ditches which are slight compared with Wheathampstead, but a defensive system of linear dykes seems to have been started further out. The third capital of the Catuvellauni was at Colchester, previously the centre of the Trinovantes, who were taken over around AD 9. This is a complex site with a densely-occupied centre and various satellites, surrounded by a complicated system of linear dykes enclosing a total of 12 square miles of country. A good

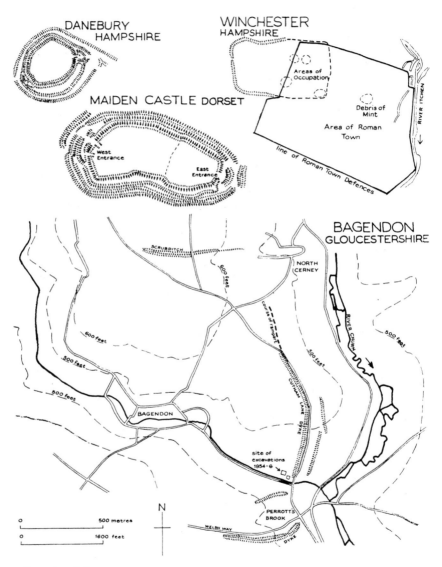

DANEBURY
HAMPSHIRE

WINCHESTER
HAMPSHIRE

Areas of
Occupation

Debris of
Mint

Area of Roman
Town

line of Roman Town Defences

RIVER ITCHEN

MAIDEN CASTLE DORSET

West
Entrance

East
Entrance

BAGENDON
GLOUCESTERSHIRE

SCRUBDITCH

NORTH
CERNEY

500 feet

course of rampart

RIVER CHURN

500 feet

500 feet

500 feet

CUTHAM LANE DYKE

500 feet

BAGENDON

site of
excavations
1954-6

PERROTTS
BROOK

0   500 metres

0   1600 feet

N

WELSH WAY

DYKE

5   Iron Age hill forts and oppida.

deal of pasture and agricultural land was included within the complete defence system.

Similar sites have been discovered elsewhere in Belgic territory. In Kent, for example, oppida have been recognized beneath the present Canterbury, and probably at Rochester, where there is evidence of another Belgic mint. Three oppida are known in the territory of the Atrebates, centred on Hampshire. The largest appears to have been at Selsey, now substantially destroyed, while the others are under the Roman cities of Silchester (Boon, 1957) and Winchester (Biddle, 1963–75) (Fig. 5). In areas peripheral to the South-East several tribes seem to have been dominated by a Belgic aristocracy. In the territory of the Dobunni in Gloucestershire there are two large oppida, at Bagendon (200 acres) (Clifford, 1961) (Fig. 5) and Minchinhampton Common (600 acres), both defended by dykes. In Oxfordshire the Grims Ditch in Wychwood may be an oppidum. At Old Sleaford in Lincolnshire there is evidence of a mint, although clear proof of an oppidum is lacking. The only remaining comparable site is Stanwick in Yorkshire, where a simple 17-acre hill fort was supplemented by additions of 130 acres and 600 acres. This is a long way from centres of Belgic influence, and the development is late compared with the oppida of the South. The construction of its enormous defences has been linked with the events preceding the Roman conquest of the Brigantian Kingdom, and Stanwick has been suggested as the site of the stronghold of Venutius, leader of the anti-Roman faction. It is thus not of truly urban character, being rather the reaction to exceptional circumstances of a people who had previously been of semi-nomadic character (Wheeler, 1954).

In contrast to the sites described above hill fort construction was not often undertaken by the Belgae in Britain, although they occasionally seem to have occupied and refortified pre-existing hill forts in the South-East during the early phases of their settlement. Bigbury in Kent, probably the hill fort stormed by Caesar's VIIth legion in 54 BC, is one example. In Dorset pre-existing hill forts like Maiden Castle and Hod Hill were reused and refortified by the ruling Belgae, and probably fulfilled similar functions to the oppida which served as centres in the South-East.

Further away from the South-East it is less easy to identify tribal centres. The Wrekin, Burrough Hill, Leicester, and Almondbury Hill, Huddersfield, have been put forward as possible capitals of the Cornovii, Coritani and Brigantes respectively, but the evidence of any proto-urban character is unclear. We have to move to southern Scotland before tribal centres can again be identified with reasonable certainty. Eildon Hill North, Roxburghshire, the 39-acre capital of the Selgovae, was captured and slighted by Agricola in AD 79. At Traprain Law, East Lothian, the 40-acre centre of the Votadini, dense occupation was maintained throughout the Roman period. It has been suggested that this settlement 'has a unique place as a "free" British town in Roman times' (Feachem, 1963) (Plate I).

By the time of the Roman invasion there are quite a large number of settlements which have many urban features. Within a framework of well-defined tribal units we can identify a number of centres of defence, trade and administration, commanding the allegiance of the inhabitants of the surrounding countryside. They contained a substantial and permanent population, show evidence of organized internal planning, and some evidence of monumental architecture in the provision of temples and religious centres. They also accommodated specialist functions like mints, and metal-working quarters such as that recognized at South Cadbury. The general nature of an appreciable proportion of British society was becoming stratified, imperialistic and capitalistic, with its economy money-based and market-orientated. It is difficult to escape the conclusion that many of these settlements were truly urban in appearance and function.

Nonetheless their influence on the landscape of present-day towns is extremely limited. Hill fort sites have become isolated earthworks, and only a very few are occupied by later town centres (Crawford, 1933; Barker, 1973). Lowland oppida may still retain impressive defences in places, which elsewhere may be represented only by field and property boundaries. Apart from a few centres like Colchester and Winchester, none of them seem to have been occupied continuously to the present day. A few oppida in Durotrigian territory (Dorset) where resistance to the Roman invasion was strong, were occupied by Roman forts, a parallel to Norman castles added to Saxon towns. Hod Hill, Dorset, is by far the clearest example (Fig. 4), but excavations at South Cadbury (Alcock, 1972) and Ham Hill, Somerset, have produced similar evidence of early Roman military buildings. Also there is increasing evidence of post-Roman reoccupation of some sites (Fowler, 1971; Rahtz & Fowler, 1972), although not yet recognizably of urban character. Perhaps we should see in such sites parallels to some of the small villages now occupying failed Roman, Saxon and medieval town sites.

Roman towns

On the whole the period of the Roman occupation is a relatively well-studied area of British history and archaeology, and Roman towns have received particular attention (Fig. 6) (Collingwood and Richmond, 1969; Rivet, 1958; Frere, 1967; Wacher, 1966 and 1975; Rodwell and Rowley, 1975; Todd, 1970). Despite this, however, a tremendous amount of work still remains to be done on many apects of Romano-British urban life. The initial stages of urbanization and the processes

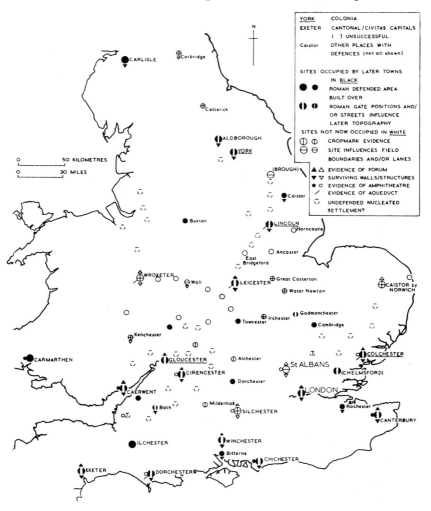

6 Roman towns: Contemporary and surviving townscape features.

of abandonment or eviction from hill forts and oppida are far from fully understood. There is, no doubt, considerable regional variation in the speed and success with which the native British were seduced into a Roman way of living.

As is the case with pre-Roman sites, investigation by competent archaeologists is our main source of information. The study of documentary evidence and of upstanding remains has made a limited contribution; field-work and aerial photography have augmented this considerably; but it is to decades of excavation that we owe most of our present knowledge of Roman towns in Britain. Even so, excavation has generally been limited to 'keyhole' views of fragments of the overall situation. Only at Silchester has there been anything approaching total excavation of a town. The greater part of this work took place before the 1914–18 war, when archaeological techniques and standards were inferior to those of today, and much potentially crucial evidence was probably lost without recognition (Boon, 1957 and 1974).

During the Roman occupation towns fulfilled an increasingly wide range of functions and can be stratified into a meaningful hierarchy for the first time. Variations in the origins and functions of Roman towns, and therefore of contemporary townscapes, were considerable. In four centuries of Roman occupation some towns would certainly have changed their character enormously from the time of their first foundation, much like a comparison between fifteenth and nineteenth-- century towns.

For the first time a true capital emerges. Immediately before the Roman conquest Colchester had held the position of chief trading centre in England, and it seems to have remained the hub of the Roman imperial cult. By about AD 100, however, London had risen rapidly as a thriving merchant settlement and soon became the seat of provincial administration. It remained in all senses the chief town of Britain throughout the Roman occupation, even after the division of the province into two by Severus in 212 with a second capital at York, further subdivision under Diocletian creating two more provincial capitals (probably Lincoln and Cirencester), and the designation of a fifth capital (probably at Carlisle) in c. 370.

Apart from provincial capitals, it is clear from contemporary sources that a number of different administrative categories of town were recognized. The most important towns were the coloniae, the municipia and the cantonal or civitas capitals. The coloniae were deliberately planted as an act of government policy. Building plots within them and land grants outside were systematically allocated to communities of Roman citizens, usually retired soldiers who provided both a reservoir of loyalty and a centre for civilizing influence. The first colonia to be founded in Britain was Colchester (AD 49), followed by Lincoln (c. AD 90) and Gloucester (c. AD 96–8). York was promoted to the same status early in the third century, when extensive replanning seems to have taken place. The municipium was a town governed by its own charter, the first and clearest example in Britain being St Albans. Certain other major towns may have acquired this status later.

The civitas capitals made up the majority of the higher-grade towns, being established as administrative and marketing centres for districts which were, for the most part, based on the pre-Roman tribal areas. Thus Wroxeter served as the centre for the Cornovii, Leicester for the Coritani, and Cirencester for the Dobunni. Several districts were artificially created by bringing together small tribal areas or by separating off parts of large territories. Winchester, Chichester and Canterbury were founded as centres for such districts early during the occupation, and Ilchester, Carlisle and, perhaps, Water Newton acquired similar status later. Trade and industry contributed to the growth of such towns, but their role was as much social and political as economic. Not all cantonal capitals succeeded as towns even during the Roman occupation, Chelmsford and Brough-on-Humber being examples which failed to achieve lasting urban status.

By modern standards even the largest Roman towns in Britain were small. London, the largest, contained only 330 acres within its walls; Cirencester, 240 acres; Wroxeter and St Albans 200 acres each. The average, represented by Leicester, was about 100 acres, while the smallest civitas capital, Brough-on-Humber, centre of the Parisii, was just 13 acres. Only in the more important towns described above was there much evidence of regular grid planning. Even where regularity exists it may have been a result of replanning in the late first century, the final result falling far short of original expectations. Except for the coloniae which were of military origin, the shape of even the large towns was very variable, tending towards irregular ovals and polygons rather than squares or rectangles (Fig. 7).

Below the level of the major towns was a large number of smaller centres with little or no sign of regular planning (Plate II). Their appearance resembles rather that of unplanned villages, and they are only called towns through having acquired defences late in their existence. Some of them had their origins as settlements outside the gates of military forts (Catterick Bridge) or as posting-stations (Godmanchester, Wall); many seem to have originated as uncontrolled ribbon development on main roads (Great Chesterford; Kenchester).

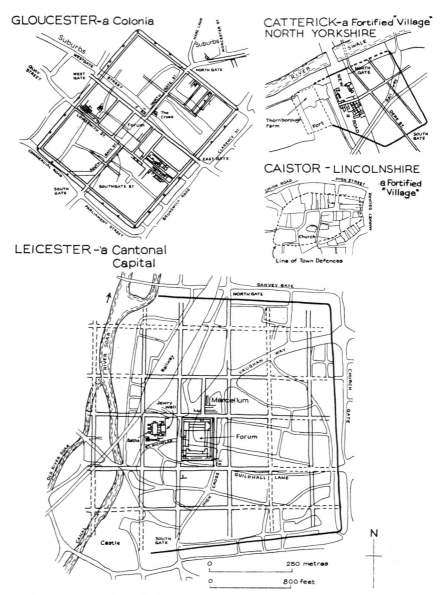

7 Roman towns: detailed plans.

A few had specialized industrial functions (Weston-under-Penyard, Charterhouse-on-Mendip, Wilderspool, Droitwich) or served as spas (Bath, Buxton), or ports (Sea Mills by Bristol, Rochester). How far such places were of true urban character is a matter of definition. There is no essential difference between them and undefended 'villages' such as Swalcliffe, Bourton Bridge or Dragonby.

The problems of definition require us to turn back and look at some of the characteristic features of the more important Roman towns, and to examine how their particular functions were reflected in the contemporary landscape.

Site

It is striking that, in contrast to pre-Roman centres, so many of the major Roman towns remain important settlements in the present day. Of the principal towns only Wroxeter and Silchester have failed to continue as urban sites, while St Albans has moved its centre a short distance (Fig. 14).

There is a growing body of evidence to suggest that, almost without exception, major towns were preceded by military forts which were later handed over to the civil authorities. Thus the site was the choice of a military commander influenced by strategic and tactical considerations seen against the possibilities of the physical character of the area. The sites chosen were rarely on the tops of hills, but on well-drained land with a readily available water supply, and invariably on or adjacent to well-defined routes or river-crossings. After the initial settlement had been established, expansion sometimes resulted in the taking in of less favourable land (as at Winchester and Cirencester), but the technological level of the Roman engineers was high enough to overcome most of the physical difficulties. When the population expanded beyond the capacity of the original water supply, this could be supplemented by aqueducts, often transporting water considerable distances (nine miles in the case of Dorchester, Dorset).

Street plan

The central feature of most large towns was the *forum*. This was normally a square or rectangular area serving as a market-place and surrounded on three sides by porticos, shops and offices. On the fourth side the *basilica,* a large aisled hall similar in function to a modern town hall or civic centre, contained the administrative offices

45

and law courts and provided space for public meetings. The size and complexity depended on the needs of the city. At Caerwent it was 'small and compact, while at St Albans it was unusually elaborate for Britain and included a religious complex in addition to the administrative and commercial centre. At Wroxeter and Exeter the *fora* were built over the sites of earlier legionary bath-houses.

Around the forum the street plan was laid out in a grid dividing the town into rectangular blocks or *insulae*. These tended to be between 200 and 400 feet square, but varied considerably in shape and size from town to town and within each town. Grids of any form probably did not become general before the late first century. Some of the anomalies in individual town plans may be explained by reference to features which existed before the grid was developed.

A few of the smaller towns, such as Catterick (Fig. 7) and Alchester have a regular street pattern indicating deliberate planning. More commonly, apart from a single main-road axis, the subsidiary streets of the small towns are most irregular and haphazard in their alignment (Plate II).

Public buildings

Besides the forum and basilica most towns had a variety of religious buildings and centres of entertainment. Such buildings had prestige value, and their origins and subsequent development and their scale at various times are important clues to the fortunes of the town.

The chief commercial centre was normally the forum but a supplementary market hall or *marcellum* was sometimes provided in a different location, as at Leicester (Fig. 7).

Baths ranked high on the list of civic amenities, but in many towns, as for instance Winchester and Chichester, the site of the first public baths remains to be identified. Compared with military bath-houses, relatively few early public ones are yet known. Only at Silchester, Caistor-by-Norwich and possibly Canterbury are there first-century baths. By the mid-second century there is more evidence, with baths built at Leicester, Wroxeter and Caerwent. The continental prototype was adapted to the vicissitudes of the British climate, with the *palaestra* (exercise courtyard) being placed under cover in an enormous hall.

The provision of a large bath-house demanded a constant supply of running water, and there is clear evidence of aqueducts at Wroxeter, Dorchester (Dorset), Lincoln and Leicester. Similar aqueducts have been inferred from the evidence of internal distribution pipes in other towns, as at Colchester (Crummy, 1974).

Public lavatories are known at St Albans and in the baths at Silchester and Wroxeter, and sewers have been discovered at York, Lincoln and Cirencester.

Amphitheatres were present at most towns, and their impressive earthworks survive at Cirencester and Dorchester. Their size dictated that they should be constructed towards the edge of the built-up area; if the town was walled later they were often left outside the fortifications. Only at Caerwent does the amphitheatre appear to post-date the defences, and there it was built within them, houses being demolished to make room for it. Theatres are less common in Britain, the bulk of those known being semicircular. Tacitus describes one at Colchester, destroyed in the uprising of AD 60, while at St Albans the theatre remains an impressive monument.

Religious buildings were by no means restricted to urban situations. However, most towns had several temples within their environs. At Silchester there was a religious quarter near the east gate, where a number of temples was concentrated. Interestingly the present parish church, is in the same area. Amongst the relatively few visible religious sites is the Mithraeum in London, excavated in 1954 (Grimes, 1968) and re-erected in Queen Victoria Street. There is evidence for Christianity in a number of towns during the later Roman period, including a mid-fourth century building at Silchester which was almost certainly a Christian church.

One further type of structure present in some Roman towns but not reappearing in Britain until the seventeenth century is the public monument. The newcomer to the province was confronted at Richborough, the normal port of entry, by a great four-way marble arch with large bronze statues. At St Albans there was a great triumphal arch, and monumental columns are known from Cirencester, Chichester and Catterick. Many places seem to have been embellished with commemorative statues, of which only disembodied heads or hands are normally discovered.

Domestic buildings

The shops and houses of Roman towns form the bulk of their buildings. The most common urban house-type seems to have been a long narrow building on a strip up to 100 feet long at right angles to the street and entered directly from it. The front part probably served as a shop or workshop, with the living quarters on an upper floor. In many towns these seem to have been concentrated in the insulae closest to the forum. Usually they were separated from their neighbours by a narrow passage, but at St Albans before the destruction of the town in the revolt of AD 60, block planning, with a continuous row of timber shops fronted by a portico, had already begun.

The town houses of officials and wealthy merchants were more elaborate in plan, with rooms grouped along a corridor, or ranged in wings around a courtyard. This classical plan is known from Colchester, Caerwent and Wroxeter. At Silchester there was evidence for courtyards and other plots being used as gardens and orchards.

Before the end of the first century practically all urban domestic buildings were of timber, wattle and daub, cob and clay. During the second century, however, there was an increase in the use of brick, flint and stone. The more prosperous buildings began to acquire central heating, mosaic floors, painted frescoes, and even, in a minority of cases, private bath suites. Cirencester had a particularly high proportion of distinctive tessellated pavements, and was the centre of a recognizable school of mosaic artists in the early fourth century.

Amongst the most impressive domestic buildings were the *mansiones* which served as hotels for official travellers, such as those of the Imperial posting service. No doubt there were many lesser lodging-houses, more difficult to identify, being less distincive in plan; a brothel has been identified at the seaport of Caister-by-Yarmouth (Rivet, 1958).

Industrial quarters

Some of the smaller Roman towns appear to have had an economic base which was heavily industrial in character, but most towns contain some evidence of industrial activity within them. Tileries and potteries occurred in the vicinity of most principal towns, and there were kilns actually inside Gloucester, Canterbury and Leicester. Tanning, fulling, copper-, bronze- and iron-working were widely represented.

Cemeteries

Romano-British cemeteries are known around most towns, usually occurring just outside the periphery. They are potentially an important source of demographic and pathological information, but have rarely left much surface trace in the landscape. Tombstones have been encountered in many towns and are normally to be found in the local museum. At Canterbury the Dane John Mound has been suggested as a Roman burial-mound, perhaps reused as a motte in Norman times.

Defences

Fortifications had been constructed around almost all important Roman towns by the end of the fourth century, and, because they often comprise the most impressive visible remains, have been the subject of much examination, although many problems still exist (Corder, 1955; Wacher, 1962 and 1966). At a town like Cirencester, where the defences have been examined at many points, only now is the full complexity of their structural history being appreciated. The relationship between defences and street plan is worthy of further study. There are cases where a grid of streets has been laid out over an earlier line of defences (Silchester) and where later defences have excluded an earlier part of the street system (Caistor-by-Norwich). Complicated sequences of defences on quite different alignments have been known for some time at St Albans and Silchester, and there are increasing hints that these towns may not be as unusual in this respect as was once thought.

Although more work needs to be done, a very general picture of the development of Roman town defences is now fairly clear. In the first century few towns were fortified, although St Albans, Silchester and Winchester clearly were. In all three cases their early earthwork defences seem to have been obsolete by the early second century. The coloniae of Gloucester and Lincoln reused the old legionary fortress ramparts, refacing them with narrow walls in the late first or early second century.

The early second-century defences at Brough-on-Humber are now believed to be connected with a naval base rather than with the civitas capital of the Parisii, and it is not until the end of the second century that more defence-building occurred. Almost all the major towns of Britain were surrounded at that time with earthworks, and some included masonry gates. London may have been provided with a complete stone wall at this time incorporating an 11-acre fort in the north-west corner dating from c. AD 100, which accounts for the salient west of Cripplegate (Grimes, 1968). It has been suggested that much of this activity may be associated with the attempt of the governor of Britain, Clodius Albinus, to usurp the emperorship in AD 193–7.

At various times through the third-century stone walls were being built round many towns which had previously only been embanked, and also round towns such as Canterbury which seem to have been previously undefended. An increasing concern for security may be indicated by the much smaller and less ostentatious gateways.

The fourth century saw Britain increasingly on the defensive against barbarian incursions from all directions. In 367 the defences gave way and the whole country was overrun. It was recovered by Count Theodosius, who was probably responsible for the programme of reinforcing defences of even the smallest towns which becomes evident after the mid-fourth century. External projecting bastions were built onto the front of existing walls in order to carry defensive artillery. The bastions were spaced so as to provide a covering fire along the entire face of the wall and new ditch systems had to be dug further out. These late additions may be appreciated most at Caerwent, where parts of the wall survive to a considerable height.

Suburbs

A number of towns, both large and small, show evidence of suburbs, which are, in effect, areas of settlement excluded by the walls rather than extensions developing in extra-mural positions. In some towns they appear quite extensive, as at Winchester and Gloucester. The ribbon development along the Silchester road at St Albans, and the suburbs of Canterbury on the west bank of the Stour, both show some evidence of abandonment when the walls were built.

Roman towns in the period 400–600 AD

The re-establishment of the defences of the province by Theodosius in 369 was to be short-lived, and the growing power of the Picts, Scots, Irish, Franks and Saxons beyond the frontiers was aided by the drain on the military resources of the province. This occurred during the adventures of the usurpers Magnus Maximus (383) and Constantine III (407), who crossed to the continent with parts of the army to support their imperial pretensions. The demands of the central government in Italy, which withdrew further forces in 401 to use against the Goths, worsened the situation, and by AD 410 it had lost control of events in Britain.

The traditional picture of the legions leaving the towns of Britain to go up in flames at the next barbarian attack can no longer be supported. On present evidence few, if any, towns were brought to a violent end. Some of the evidence once used to support this, such as the skeleton of the old man at Wroxeter who had crawled into a hypo-caust to die with his life's savings, cannot now be interpreted in this light. It is now clear that most Roman towns continued to be occupied in one form or another long after AD 410, and that, in some places at least, organized urban life continued through the fifth century. The Saxon advance into Britain was not a single organized movement of deliberate conquest, but a slow and complex process, beginning with the official invitation and ordered settlement of Germanic mercenaries.

It would be wrong to suggest that the events of the fifth century are yet fully understood, although various recent works (Alcock, 1971; Morris, 1973) have thrown light on what was formerly the darkest of ages. The documentary evidence is scanty and confusing, but in AD 410 the towns of Britain received a letter from the emperor Honorius permitting them to look after their own defence. An urban aristo-cracy certainly remained in control, and when St Germanus visited St Albans in AD 429 he was met by a large and well-dressed assembly who retained sufficient culture for a theological debate. Even in AD 446, a generation after the official abandonment of the province, there was sufficient administrative machinery in working order to organize a last appeal to the imperial authorities for aid.

The archaeological evidence is even more difficult to assess. The late and sub-Roman archaeological levels, being uppermost, are most liable to disturbance by ploughing on abandoned sites and by Saxon and later occupation elsewhere. The centralized pottery industry of the late fourth century broke down completely in the fifth, denying archaeologists the use of a crucial source of evidence. Similarly hardly any imperial coinage reached Britain after the end of the fourth century, and while for some time worn coins continued in circulation, the money economy appears to be broken down completely by about AD 430. On the other hand, it is archaeology which offers the only hope of further understanding this period, for the chances of any relevant new documentation being discovered are slim. Despite the difficulties of interpretation, considerable evidence has been forth-coming from excavations over the past twenty years.

There are dangers in the assumption that continuity of occupation on the same site also implies continuity of function. The discovery of a few early Saxon huts or fragments of fifth-century metalwork does not warrant the inference that town life continued. However, on several sites the evidence is sufficient to demonstrate that some urban organiza-tion survived well into the fifth century. At St Albans a sequence of late fourth- to early fifth-century buildings was succeeded by a wooden water-pipe laid across the site showing that the town aqueduct was still functioning after about 450 (Frere, 1972). Silchester has produced a large number of extremely worn late-fourth century coins, indicating a continuing money economy well into the fifth century, while a system of linear earthworks to the north and west of the town has been interpreted as British frontier dykes against the Saxon settlements in the Thames valley. At Wroxeter, over the ruins of the palaestra, evidence of large timber halls and shops of fifth-century date has been found (Barker, 1973), and occupation probably continued into the seventh century when Shrewsbury replaced Wroxeter as the main local centre. At Cirencester the forum was being subjected to continuous heavy wear until after AD 430.

The role of the Church through this period is not yet clear. In some areas its organization probably collapsed altogether, but at Carlisle it has been suggested that the continued presence of a bishopric may have been associated with the continuity of urban life through to the seventh century. The interpretation as a church of a fifth-century building, excavated at Caerwent in 1923, is now doubted, but Bede records one of Roman origin at Canterbury.

While some towns seem to have survived as Romano-British enclaves in the early fifth century by looking after their own defence, elsewhere there is clear evidence of Saxon settlement contemporary with occupation by late-Roman townspeople. At Canterbury Saxon huts of the mid-fifth century are known from one *insula* and appear to be neatly and regularly arranged. At Dorchester, Oxfordshire, a number of Saxon huts have been found beside Roman buildings along Roman streets. Peaceful coexistence with mercenaries is surely implied (Frere, 1962). Exeter appears to have been in premature decay during the late fourth century, but Britons were still living side by side with Saxons within the town in the early ninth century.

The uneasy quiet of the first half of the fifth century was disrupted by a return to the offensive on the part of the Saxons after AD 440. This was halted by the British victory of Mount Badon in the 480s, but by the end of the century there is little evidence that the towns retained many of their former functions. The steady breakdown of the villa estates had created food shortages in towns, thus increasing their vulnerability to disease. Urban life in the Roman sense had probably more or less disintegrated and refugees from the towns began to reoccupy some of the old hill forts (Fowler, 1971). What is really meant by the entry in the Anglo-Saxon Chronicle for AD 577, claiming that, after the Battle of Dyrham, the West Saxons killed three British kings and captured 'three of their cities, Gloucester, Cirencester and

Bath'? Can these places have retained any shreds of their urban character by that date?

The reassertion of Saxon power from the mid-sixth century met with more permanent success, and by about 600 their domination was complete over most of England and the scene was set for a new generation of towns.

Survival of Roman townscape elements (Fig. 6)

We have seen how the end of most Roman towns was a protracted devolution rather than catastrophic destruction. Therefore the nature of their contribution to the later landscape is related very largely to how rapidly and successfully they regained their urban momentum. Of the major towns, Silchester and Wroxeter were virtually abandoned, apart from a small village nucleus, and some of the smaller towns were completely deserted.

One might expect the most substantial structures to stand the best chance of survival, and it is indeed the defences which often survive in vestigial form when all else has vanished. At Silchester and St Albans there are massive chunks of masonry wall from the Roman defences, while elsewhere earthworks of the banks and ditches remain in varying stages of degradation. Major features such as these provided an obvious framework for later field and property boundaries, and this has usually contributed to their preservation.

Stone and brick from decaying Roman buildings was widely reused, and St Albans Abbey and the parish churches of Wroxeter and Silchester contain considerable amounts of such material. At Wroxeter two Roman columns provide the gate-piers to the churchyard and the capital of another has been hollowed out to form the font. Another pillar from Wroxeter travelled twenty-five miles to Wolverhampton where it was ornamented into a fine Saxon cross-shaft.

Road alignments heading for such abandoned towns are also often to be seen, either still in use or fossilized as footpaths or hedge lines. However, of the detailed internal road plan and the town buildings there is normally little to be seen at ground level. Most of what we know of such sites has come from the techniques of aerial photography over the last fifty years.

The reason for aerial photography being a source of new information lies in the effect buried features have on crop growth, even if there is no identifiable variation in the ground surface. After the surface of the earth is dug into, the soil in the fill never regains the consistency of the surrounding earth. It is different in texture, in moisture-holding capacity and in humus.   Certain crops, particularly barley and wheat, grow more vigorously and ripen more slowly where their roots penetrate into such features.   The anomalies in crop ripening can be clearly seen from the air, pits showing up as dark patches, and ditches marking defences, drains or aqueducts as dark lines.   Conversely over the stony matrix of a road or foundations the crop will ripen sooner and become stunted with the lack of moisture and nutrient available during its growing season (Plate II).   The value of this principle in the identification of the plans of abandoned Roman towns from the air is self-evident.   Ideal recording conditions vary enormously according to local soil and subsoil types, weather conditions, season and land use; but with the increasing acreages which are being ploughed, crop marks are now being recognized which relate to Roman towns whose very existence was previously only suspected. Examples where our knowledge of sites has been revolutionized include Dorn on the Fosseway, Whilton Lodge (Bannaventa) on Watling Street, and Irchester in Northamptonshire (Plate II).   Charterhouse-on-Mendip, a lead-mining town previously known only from finds, has revealed its street system in recent photographs, while at Corbridge, just south of Hadrian's Wall, there is evidence of a medium-sized town around the impressive remains of the military compounds. At Caistor-by-Norwich, the basic street system, with roadside drains and some internal buildings, has been shown by crop marks to be cut by later defences.   In contrast to the grid system there, aerial photographs have revealed very irregular street patterns at Irchester and Kenchester.

One example of the value of continuous aerial photography carried out over many years in all seasons and weather conditions is provided by Wroxeter.   The many photographs, taken principally by Arnold Baker, have enormously increased our knowledge of the plan, layout and development of the town, without excavation.   It has been possible to plot on detailed plans not only the main streets and defences but also the intricacies of house plans, individual bastions on the town walls, the ditches of the underlying military fortress, and even flimsy traces of Saxon huts (Baker, 1968).   It could be argued that the greatest single contribution of abandoned Roman towns to the later landscape is their effect on the growth of the crops which we plant over their sites!

How much has remained of the larger Roman towns, which were successful and returned to their former importance?   Again we must reckon with the surviving remains of the most substantial Roman structures such as the defences.   Recognizable fragments of Roman town wall survive today at Lincoln (Plate III), York (Plate V), Colchester and Caistor (Lincolnshire). When such towns were re-defended in Saxon or medieval times, most of the Roman circuit was usually reused, and even after these later defences too have disappeared, their influence is still to be seen in property boundaries fossilizing their courses. Even where all surface trace of Roman masonry defences has completely disappeared their course can often by detected by their effect on the present landscape. The mapping of breaks of slope often shows up the line of lost town defences. Parallel street or property alignments will often mark the inner and outer perimeters of defences, while road junctions may indicate gate sites. At Dorchester, Dorset, the line of the defences is laid out as a pleasant walk around the edge of the town.

The key positions on the defence alignments were the gates, and impressive standing remains of Roman town gates are still to be seen at Lincoln (the Newport Arch, Plate III) and Colchester (Balkerne Gate). Moreover eighteenth- and nineteenth-century engravings and prints suggest that much of the Roman masonry may have been incorporated into the now vanished medieval South Gate of Exeter and West Gate of Chichester. As the earliest means of access through the barrier of the walls, the gate positions were most likely to be fossilized by the subsequent street pattern, and, because the most direct way through the town was from gate to gate, the original main-road axis of the Roman town was often also preserved. Such features do not in any way imply direct continuity of use, only a response to a major existing constraint. A comparison of the plan of any reasonably well-known Roman town with that of its medieval successor will clearly show just how little the later side roads have followed Roman alignments (Fig. 7—Leicester).

The effectiveness of the defences as a constraint poses interesting questions as to the effect on subsequent topography of other major ruined structures. Why have no substantial remains of any basilicae survived? Why of all the great and impressive public bath-houses have only two major upstanding remains survived in very different contexts, the Old Work at Wroxeter in the middle of the fields (Webster and Woodfield, 1966, Plate IV) and the Jewry Wall at Leicester (Kenyon, 1948) in the centre of a busy town? The magnificent baths at Bath itself are exceptional in their long-continued use. The only other major structures to survive in any form are the earthwork remains of the amphitheatres at Cirencester, Dorchester (Dorset) and Silchester.

There is more to continuity, however, than the passive survival of inanimate chunks of masonry. The continuity of religious traditions on the same site can readily be demonstrated throughout historic times, and in some instances it can be shown that medieval churches stand on earlier pagan religious sites. It may well be that some early churches outside Roman town defences have an element of continuity in them not previously suspected. What are their relationships with extra-mural Roman cemeteries? It would be natural to replace shrines or temples in such cemeteries with Christian churches. The example of St Alban's Abbey, the focal point of the medieval and modern town, is well known, standing on the reputed site of the martyrdom in the fourth century of St Alban outside the Roman city (Fig. 14). It has recently been suggested that two now vanished medieval churches outside the walls of Cirencester may be sited over Romano-British cemeteries (Reece and Catling, 1975). A particularly interesting site is the London church of St Bride, Fleet Street, where the visitor to the crypt can see the remains of a substantial Roman extra-mural building with a plain tesselated floor, succeeded by a small church whose earliest visible remains are perhaps of the sixth century (Grimes, 1968). The dedication itself is of significance, for St Bride was an Irish saint born in AD 453. At York several churches can be shown to rest on Roman buildings in a direct relationship to them. Churches outside Roman towns, alongside Roman roads and particularly in areas of extra-mural Roman cemeteries may sometimes prove to have very early origins indeed.

Less substantial transmissions from Roman times to later periods are place-names. It is well known that those incorporating the element 'castor' or 'chester' in some form are of Roman origin and refer to fortified towns or military sites. 'Stret' or 'strat' names indicate places which may or may not be of Roman origin but which stand on Roman roads. Some names like 'Wickham', 'Wick' and 'Wich' incorporate the Germanic element *wic* which is itself derived directly from the Latin *vicus* meaning village or small town, and themselves stand on the sites of Roman settlements (Gelling, 1967). However, such evidence needs to be used with caution for the later place names are often corrupted enough to be completely misleading. In addition to the above names (which indicate a knowledge in Saxon times of the existence of a Roman settlement), it is less frequently appreciated that the Roman name itself has often survived, transmitted into the new language: Londinium has become London; Lindum Colonia, Lincoln; and less obviously—Isca (Dumnoniorum), Exeter; Viroconium, Wroxeter; and Venta (Belgarum), Winchester.

It may be thought that in this somewhat distant period, which has been thoroughly investigated in the past, there may be little evidence left to discover without excavation. In more than one town, however, considerable fragments of Roman masonry have been identified in cellars and encased in later buildings, unrecognized for what they were in isolation, and only identified when they were seen to fit into a pattern. At Caistor, Lincolnshire, Philip Rahtz found part of the Roman town wall in a cellar and in gardens where it had lain unrecognized until the complete line of the defences was traced (Rahtz, 1960). At Canterbury the layout of the Roman theatre was derived from similar pieces (Frere, 1970). The recognition of such features must prompt the question of how much more evidence remains to be identified in towns which have received less attention. In abandoned sites field-work may also yield important evidence. At East Bridgford it has been possible to show by the collection of pottery that the occupied area of the town of Margidunum was far greater than the small area of the defended enclosure (Todd, 1969). There is similar evidence for Wall, Ancaster and Godmanchester.

Finally we must refer briefly to features in towns which are of Roman origin, but where excavation is the only means of identifying them as such. At both Chelmsford and Godmanchester some existing property boundaries have been shown by excavation to follow the exact lines of Roman property divisions (Drury, 1973; Green, 1961). This may be surprising in view of the loss of much of the street plan in other towns. Are they exceptional? How much of the rest of the townscape of existing towns with Roman origins does in fact reflect the Roman pattern? How much of Roman Britain are we seeing without realizing it in some of these places?

Chapter IV

Anglo-Saxon and Scandinavian Towns

We have seen that the Anglo-Saxon advance into Britain was halted during the early sixth century by a period of successful British resistance; but after about 550 it began with renewed vigour, and it was during this time that many of the Anglo-Saxon kingdoms gained their political cohesion.

Before about the ninth century there is evidence of urban life in only a few centres. Most of these had been centres of population during Roman times, and there was probably little break in continuity of occupation. Even if their strictly urban functions may have suffered temporarily during the sixth century, they were the first places to regain some of the characteristic functions of towns. London was quite clearly engaged in extensive trade in the seventh century, York by the mid-eighth century and Southampton, Canterbury and Rochester can be regarded as towns before the ninth century (Ordnance Survey, 1966 and 1973).

The later Saxon towns have been the subject of enormous advances in our knowledge since 1945. It is now possible to identify this period as a formative one in the topography of many towns, when the broad outlines of their development, their basic street alignments, and the allocation of specialized secular and ecclesiastical areas were being organized (Fig. 8).

There remain many difficulties. By comparison with the foundation processes of the larger Roman towns, the origins of new Saxon towns appear complex. They were brought into being over a long period and in areas whose social and political attributes were very variable: motives for their foundation therefore differed considerably. It is becoming increasingly apparent that there was often a greater specialization or fragmentation of functions in different centres. Within a small area one place might be the centre for defence, another the market town, and yet another the ecclesiastical focus of the district

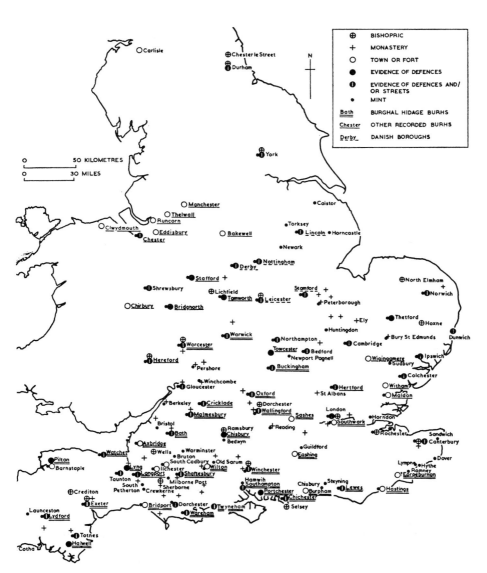

⊕	BISHOPRIC
+	MONASTERY
○	TOWN OR FORT
●	EVIDENCE OF DEFENCES
◐	EVIDENCE OF DEFENCES AND/OR STREETS
·	MINT
Both	BURGHAL HIDAGE BURHS
Chester	OTHER RECORDED BURHS
Derby	DANISH BOROUGHS

50 KILOMETRES

30 MILES

N

○ Carlisle

⊕ Chester le Street
◐ Durham

·◐ York

○ Manchester
· Caistor

○ Thelwall
○ Runcorn
○ Clwydmouth
○ Eddisbury
◐ Chester
·◐ Torksey
◐ Lincoln · Horncastle
· Newark

○ Bakewell

◐ Nottingham
◐ Derby

·◐ Stafford +
· Shrewsbury
⊕ Lichfield
◐ Tamworth ◐ Leicester
·◐ Stamford +
+ ⊕ North Elmham
+
·◐ Norwich
○ Chirbury · Bridgnorth
·◐ Peterborough
+ + · Ely
· Huntingdon
· Thetford
· Hoxne
·◐ Warwick
· Bury St Edmunds
◐ Dunwich
⊕◐ Worcester
· Northampton +
· Cambridge
◐ Hereford
◐ Towcester ·◐ Bedford
· Ipswich
○ Wigingamere
+ Pershore
· Newport Pagnell
· Sudbury
◐ Buckingham
· Colchester
· Winchcombe
·◐ Gloucester
·◐ Hertford
○ Witham
+ St Albans
·◐ Maldon
+ Berkeley
◐ Oxford
·◐ Cricklade
· Dorchester
London
· Hordon
· Bristol
·◐ Malmesbury
·◐ Wallingford
⊕◐ Southwark
◐ Bath
◐ Sashes
· Rochester
· Ramsbury
· Reading
◐ Chisbury
Sandwich
· Bedwyn
·◐ Canterbury
○ Axbridge
· Dover
○ Watchet
· Wells
· Warminster
· Guildford
Lympne
· Hythe
· Pilton
· Bruton
· Eashing
· Romney
· Barnstaple
◐ Lyng
· South Cadbury · Old Sarum
◐ Forpeburnan
·◐ Langport
◐ Ilchester
◐ Shaftesbury
· Wilton
·◐ Winchester
Taunton
Hamwih
Chisbury
· Steyning
◐ Lewes
South
◐ Sherborne
◐ Southampton
◐ Burpham
Petherton
· Milborne Post
· Crewkerne
◐ Portchester
◐ Chichester
○ Hastings
⊕ Crediton
· Launceston
◐ Exeter
◐ Dorchester
◐ Twyneham
⊕ Selsey
◐ Lydford
◐ Bridport
◐ Wareham
+
◐ Totnes
· Cotha
◐ Halwell

8   Towns, 600–1066 A.D.

(Fig. 9). These fragmented functions become increasingly concentrated in larger centres as we approach the Norman conquest.

What do we know of the old Roman centres in the seventh century before they were supplemented by the new Saxon towns? In London little is yet known of the city's Anglo-Saxon archaeology (Biddle and Hudson, 1973). There is documentary evidence for its choice by

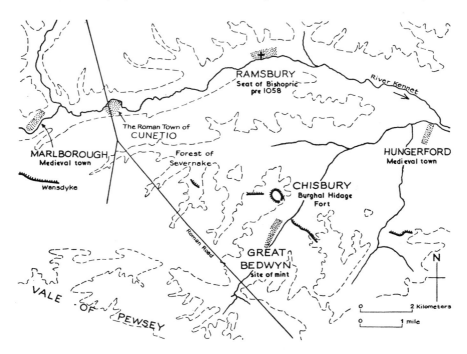

9   Segregation of late Saxon urban functions in north-east Wiltshire.

Pope Gregory in 601 as the primary see of England. As events transpired it lost this position to Canterbury, but the first St Paul's Cathedral in London was built in 604 to serve the diocese of the East Saxons. There was a royal palace in the city, which may well have occupied the south-eastern quarter of the Roman Cripplegate Fort, probably still a defensible entity in the early seventh century, and there was a mint by AD 640. Certainly by the eleventh century London was the largest and most thriving town in England, a position which it never lost.

York was the second city of Anglo-Saxon England, maintaining its position from Roman times (Fig. 1). It was already re-emerging in the seventh century, as the capital of Northumbria and a major centre of Anglian Christianity. Pope Gregory chose it in 601 as the site of England's second archbishopric (although in fact it did not achieve this status until 735). Excavations under the present Minster have suggested that parts of the headquarters building of the old Roman military fortress were still in use in the ninth century as the royal Northumbrian centre. However, when King Edwin accepted Christianity in 627 it is unlikely that any usable stone churches remained in York, for a small timber oratory dedicated to St Peter had to be specially constructed, soon to be replaced by a more permanent structure. This lay in or close to the old Roman headquarters and royal complex. Of the dozen other churches in York of pre-Conquest origin at least three—St Helen-on-the-Walls (recently excavated), St Mary Bishophill Junior and St Mary Bishophill Senior—are sited directly over Roman buildings. The last was on an almost identical alignment with an underlying Roman building, one wall of which was still standing when the Saxon church was built. There is slight evidence of a mint in York in the seventh century. The Anglian town probably relied largely on the Roman fortress walls for its defence, keeping them repaired where necessary. An interesting survival of this period is the Anglian tower on the north-west wall, built probably in the seventh century (Plate v). It represents one of the few visible monuments surviving from this period of any town's history. There are indications of a monastic community being attached to the episcopal centre in the eighth century, and the town was undoubtedly of considerable importance when it fell to the Danes in 867 (Cramp, 1967; Royal Commission on Historical Monuments, 1962 and 1972).

Of the other former Roman towns we know little. At Canterbury the see was established by Augustine in 597. His first church which, according to Bede, was of Roman origin was on the site of the present St Martin's, to the east of the city. It became the seat of the archbishopric and had a monastic house attached to it early in the seventh century. Lincoln, Bath and Carlisle were all described as cities by the late seventh century. Dorchester-on-Thames has produced some of the most conclusive evidence of continuity from Roman times and was chosen by St Birinus in the seventh century as the centre for his missionary activities amongst the West Saxons, probably because of the existence of a royal palace of the West Saxon kings. A short-lived bishopric was based there from 635 to c. 660 (Dickinson, 1974). The bishopric was re-established in the ninth century, but by then

Dorchester was in sharp decline as the late Saxon military towns of Oxford and Wallingford developed.

Even before 800 a number of new settlements had appeared, soon to become towns. The place-name element *wic* characterizes a number of these, meaning probably 'collection of dwellings', 'street' or 'town'. It is applied, for example, to Ipswich, Norwich, Sandwich, Hamwich (Southampton), and Dunwich. Their character in the early stages is obscure. At Ipswich the origins of the town seem to be related to the patronage of the East Anglian royal family, the Wuffingas, during the period 625–700; it probably had a marketing, servicing and trading function, and was certainly an extremely important centre of pottery production from the eighth century onwards. The basic outlines of the town were probably established at this time (Scarfe, 1972; Scole Committee, 1973).

Norwich (Fig. 2) is not a single foundation, but an accretion of several small settlements, each in existence before 850. Planned extensions and Norman additions have further confused the pattern, and it is only relatively recently that some of the topographical problems of Norwich have been unravelled (Green and Young, 1972; Carter, 1972 and 1975; Carter and Roberts, 1973). Of the early development of Dunwich little is known, for the site has been almost entirely swept away by the sea. It may have been the site of a bishopric as early as 630, and it suffered extensive damage at the hands of the Danes in 870 (Scarfe, 1972).

Perhaps the most interesting new Saxon town developing before the ninth century is at Southampton. Here, on the west bank of the River Itchen, opposite the fortified Roman port of Bitterne, an unfortified commercial nucleus was established. This is recorded by name as Hamwich, and was a market centre in 721. The mother church of Southampton, St Mary's, is in this area, and it may have been the site of a minster church of mid-seventh century origin. Hamwich suffered considerably from Viking raids in the ninth century, and this, no doubt, contributed to its decline. A more permanent handicap was the shallowness of the lagoon at the mouth of the Itchen which formed its harbour, because of the increasing size of trading vessels.

It is quite clear that Hamwich was in decline in the early tenth century, and that the St Mary's area was largely abandoned by about 970. Certainly by Norman times there were only a few houses remaining near the church. The site reverted to fields, was built over again in the nineteenth century, and became available for archaeological investigation in the present century through bomb damage and slum clearance. This work has clearly delimited the extent of Saxon

Hamwich, but its internal layout is as yet imperfectly understood. There are hints of made-up streets systematically laid out in at least two directions with buildings and property boundaries aligned on them. Two Saxon burial grounds have been discovered, in addition to the presumed site at St Mary's itself. There is ample evidence of considerable commercial activity, and there was a mint somewhere in the area during the tenth and early eleventh centuries (Addyman and Hill, 1968–9). Hamwich was replaced in the mid-tenth century by a new fortified town a short distance to the west on the shores of the river Test. This appears to have born the name Hampton, soon qualified as Southampton to distinguish it from Northampton. (Crawford, 1942; Burgess, 1964).

From the towns we have looked at so far, it is clear that in mid-Saxon times there were several different types. Contemporary sources recognized this, and distinguished between the *ceaster*, the town site inherited from the Romans, the *port* and the *burh*. The *port* was strictly a centre of commerce possessing market rights and was often unfortified. The earliest market centres tended by their very nature to be the seaports, but the word was rapidly applied to inland centres which had no connection with the sea.

A *burh* was essentially a fortified place. It might have been the residence of a king, bishop or ealdorman, but it was used loosely to mean a town from quite an early date, as at Canterbury, recorded by that name in the Anglo-Saxon Chronicle in 754. The main spate of *burh* construction was associated with the Danish invasion, but there is some evidence in Wessex at least of a network of fortified centres well before then. In the Midlands too some of the Mercian *burhs* may be of early origin. The name of Hereford means 'army ford' and it may have been fortified in the late eighth century by Offa during his campaign against the Welsh. Excavations there in 1968 revealed an earlier rampart underlying the documented tenth-century defences (Rahtz, 1968).

A further element in town creation from the seventh century onwards was the Church. When Pope Gregory advised Augustine to establish two metropolitan sees at London and York (AD 601) it was no accident that these had been the civil and military capitals of Roman Britain. In the event Augustine preferred Canterbury to London, where the see soon encountered political difficulties. By the mid-seventh century every major Anglo-Saxon kingdom except Sussex had its own bishop, and Kent had two, for a second see had been established at Rochester in 604. Five of the seven sees existing in 668 were based in old Roman towns—London, Canterbury, Rochester,

Winchester and York. So too had been the first see of Wessex, established at Dorchester-on-Thames. The work of evangelization might have been expected to proceed most easily from old-established centres where some continuity of urban life and tradition of civilization had persisted. The same feature is to be seen in the work of lesser missionaries such as Bassa and Cedd, who chose the old Roman forts of Reculver and Bradwell-juxta-Mare for their churches in the 660s. The only two non-Roman early sees were Dunwich, perhaps because in East Anglia the disruption of the old communities had been greatest, and Lichfield, founded only in 669. The site of the first cathedral there is now marked by the small church of St Chad, in an isolated position at the east end of Stowe Pool, near the Roman site of Wall and reasonably close to the Mercian royal palace at Tamworth. The cathedral site was moved a short distance westwards to its present location in 700, and for a short time in Offa's reign (788–803) Lichfield was raised to the status of a third archiepiscopate alongside York and Canterbury.

Between 668 and the tenth century new sees were created all over the country. However, they were not all associated with successful commercial or defensive centres. In 1075 Archbishop Lanfranc decreed that episcopal sites should be based in large towns and thus many sees were moved: Dorchester-on-Thames to Lincoln, Elmham to Thetford and then Norwich, Ramsbury and Sherborne to Salisbury, and Lichfield to Chester. Of all the Saxon cathedrals in towns only Winchester has, so far, been extensively excavated (Biddle, 1970).

Many monastic foundations were established in each English kingdom from the seventh century onwards. While many of these were in isolated positions and were never destined to become centres of urban activity, others, such as Gloucester and Bath, were located in old Roman towns and played a considerable part in their revival. Other still, like Winchcombe, Peterborough, and Bury St Edmunds, deliberately stimulated town development at their gates. At Canterbury the remains of at least three seventh-century monastic churches can be traced amongst the ruins of St Augustine's Abbey. On the whole, however, the new monastic towns are a product of the late Saxon period (page 74).

In 789 the Anglo-Saxon Chronicle records how three Danish ships landed at Portland and killed the reeve of Dorchester who came to find out their business. From then until the mid-ninth century there were sporadic Danish raids, during which many places were ravaged. In 865 a new phase began, with a great Danish army engaged on organized invasion. By 871 they had taken York, Nottingham, East Anglia and Wessex.

The initial phase of campaigning, when the Danish army threatened to overrun all England, was halted by Alfred's victory at Edington. The later years of Alfred's reign were fully occupied with the re-organization of the national defences, including a major programme of *burh* construction, which was carried on by his successors (Fig. 8). By the second decade of the tenth century no place in Wessex was more than twenty miles from a *burh* which formed a unit in a planned scheme of national defence. Many of these *burhs* are located close to Roman roads and at the lowest bridging-points of rivers. Although strategic and defensive considerations were the prime criteria for choice of site, accessibility for commercial activity was a factor not entirely neglected. Such places are listed in a document of about AD 919 called the Burghal Hidage (Hill, 1969; Brooks, 1964; Davison, 1972).

From the point of view of origin, some Burghal Hidage forts are simply reused Iron Age hill forts, such as Chisbury Camp in Wiltshire (Fig. 9). Others are old Roman towns or forts whose defences were similarly reused (Chichester, Portchester, Winchester (Fig. 10) and Towcester (Fig. 12)). The site named as Hampton in the list may well be the old Roman site of Bitterne, serving as the *burh* for the unfortified Hamwich. More than half were completely new Saxon foundations, of which some developed into key medieval towns and remain important today (Hastings, Lewes, Malmesbury, Oxford). Others were less important as towns and may have achieved their peak in the late Saxon and early medieval periods (Burpham, Wilton, Bridport, Langport (Fig. 12), Axbridge). Others again may have been only temporary emergency refuges without permanent habitation. Recent excavations at Lyng in Somerset have failed to show any evidence of permanent Saxon occupation within the defences. Several names appear in the list whose identity is not certain, and some of these, such as those tentatively identified with Sashes Eyot in Cookham and Newenden near Appledore, are probably of similar character.

Some of the shortest-lived *burhs* are amongst the smallest. Halwell is a simple tiny earthwork whose circumference exactly corresponds with the length of defences suggested by the document. Pilton is equally insignificant. Both may be reused prehistoric sites, which were never permanently occupied, and developed no functions other than defence. Of the newly-founded sites a high proportion occcupy promontory positions, where three sides are defended by natural slopes or marshland and only the neck of the promontory needed to be strengthened with earthworks (Fig. 12).

Perhaps the most interesting group of *burhs* listed in the Burghal Hidage are those larger towns where there was no topographical constraint on their development: they were either on open sites or

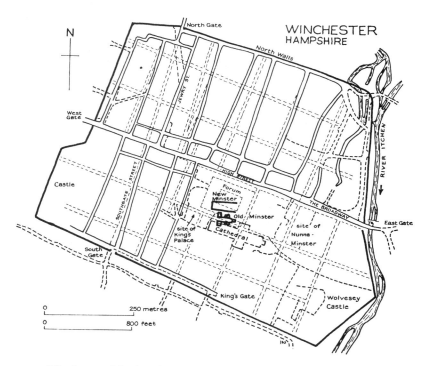

10 Winchester: The late Saxon street plan in relation to the Roman roads and defences.

on promontories so broad as not to interfere with their plan. Here the evidence of large-scale town planning in late Saxon times is now indisputable (Biddle and Hill, 1971). Wareham (Fig. 11), Wallingford (Plate VI) and Cricklade are the best-preserved examples. At each, massive earthwork defences were constructed around rectangular areas; the earthworks themselves survive in impressive form at the first two towns mentioned. Within the defences a regular grid of streets was laid out, dividing the interior into 'insulae', obviously based on Roman prototypes. However, at the *burh* of Winchester (Fig. 10), it has been shown that the present grid of streets within the reused Roman defences is quite different from the Roman one. The

11   Wareham, showing late Saxon street plan and defences.

east–west axis of the Roman road between the two main gates was retained, but a complete new system of side streets superseded the Roman pattern. The resulting arrangement of small rectangular blocks of land divided into long plots is very similar to that of Wareham or Wallingford. It seems most likely that this spate of new-town planning, which can also be identified in Chichester, Dorchester, Exeter, Bath and Gloucester within Roman defences, in Oxford on a new site and even in a small town like Lydford (Fig. 12), must be attributed to royal authority in Wessex around 900. A significant aspect of the internal street plan demonstrated at both Wareham and

67

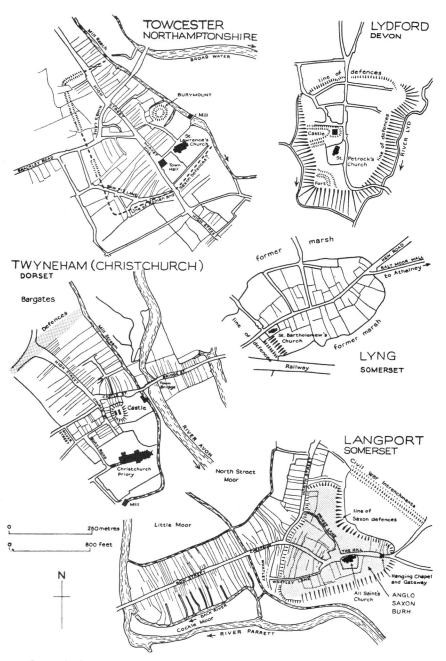

12 Saxon *burhs*.

Winchester is that two plot-types of considerably different size appear, implying different functions. It may be that the small plots were the original permanent building sites, while the larger plots were open areas serving as the refuge 'camping-sites' of the surrounding rural settlements. Another feature of the late Saxon grid-plan *burhs* is the absence of any distinctive open market-place: markets were simply held in the wider streets.

Minor property boundaries dating from the tenth century and continuing through to the present day have been demonstrated at Winchester and Lydford, and one suspects that many more internal boundaries in such towns are of equally early origin. Elsewhere surviving Saxon churches sometimes appear to be closely linked with gates to the *burh* (St Michael's at Oxford and St Martin's at Wareham) and it is quite probable that churches in similar locations, such as Lyng, without visible Saxon fabric, are in fact of Saxon origin.

The *burh* network developed in Wessex by Alfred and Edward the Elder was copied elsewhere. The Kingdom of Mercia had effectively been destroyed by the Danish invasions, with its north-eastern part completely under their domination and the remainder little more than a province of Wessex. There is some evidence of Mercian *burhs* at Worcester, Hereford, Gloucester, Chester and Shrewsbury before about 910. A new network was commenced by Aethelflaeda, partly aimed against the Danes from whom some of the old Mercian territory was slowly being won back, but also as a means of obliterating what little remained of Mercian independence. Aethelflaeda's *burhs* included two new towns soon to become county administrative centres— Warwick and Stafford. Old hill forts were reused at Eddisbury Hill and perhaps at Runcorn, while Bridgnorth displays the promontory location of so many Wessex burhs. Grid plantation is represented at the old Mercian capital of Tamworth. Aethelflaeda had also captured several fortified sites from the Danes before her death in 918. Her campaigns were continued by her brother, Edward the Elder of Wessex, who had already built new *burhs* at Hertford (911–2), Witham (912) (another site where impressive earthwork remains survive), Bedford (915), Maldon (916) and Towcester (917). He then moved northwards to found *burhs* at Nottingham (918–20) (Fig. 13), Thelwall (919), Manchester (919), Bakewell and Clwydmouth (Rhuddlan) (921), the last being the only Saxon *burh* in Wales.

After 920 no new Anglo-Saxon towns of major rank were founded as *burhs*. In Wessex Athelstan reorganized the system, keeping on only those *burhs* which were commercially viable; others were abandoned or replaced, such as Halwell by Totnes, Eashing by Guildford

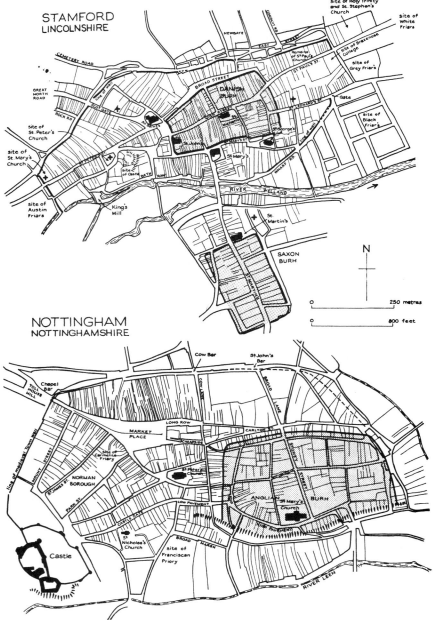

13 Stamford and Nottingham: Pre-Conquest *burhs* in relation to medieval towns.

and Pilton by Barnstaple. In the later tenth century attempts were made to throw some slight defences around a large number of small commercial centres in Wessex, such as Milborne Port, Crewkerne, Winchcombe, Warminster and Berkeley. Although their defensive needs were subordinate to commerce, few of these places ever succeeded as towns. Finally in the early eleventh century there was a reaction against such small, weak and indefensible *burhs*, and a return to a truly defensive function at the expense of all else. Some of the great Iron Age hill forts such as Cissbury, South Cadbury and Old Sarum were reutilized at this time.

Various references have already been made to mints in the larger towns, and although these do not leave any trace in the landscape, it has been said that 'Of all the possible tests of borough status . . . in many ways the most satisfying and complete' is the mint (Loyn, 1961). In Athelstan's time the coinage was reorganized, and money was permitted to be minted only in specified towns and the number of authorized moneyers gives some idea of their relative commercial importance. Apart from major towns, mints existed in a host of smaller places, including Newport (Shropshire), Bridgnorth, Pevensey, Bruton, Crewkerne, Ilchester, South Cadbury, and Horndon (Fig. 8).

Beyond the Danelaw frontier other towns were being developed by the Scandinavians themselves. If the first Viking raids were solely for plunder, their subsequent contribution to the development of trade and industry was enormous. York was captured by the Danes in 867 and Danish coinage was being minted there before the end of the ninth century. The Danish city was independent until 919 when it was taken by Norse Vikings, who, in their turn, set up a Norse kingdom which lasted until the expulsion of Eric Bloodaxe in 954. By the end of the tenth century a great concourse of traders, particularly Danes, was present in York and its monastic life had revived. It was probably the most populous city in England after London (Fig. 1). Perhaps the most striking feature of York to survive from this period is its exceptionally high proportion of street names of Scandinavian origin ending in 'gate'. The 'gate' element is widespread in the towns of the Danelaw, meaning simply a street. In most cases it now represents the only tangible evidence of Scandinavian occupation. It is most common in Yorkshire, in York itself and towns like Beverley and Richmond, but it also occurs in Leicester, Lincoln, Newark, Nottingham and Peterborough (Hutton, 1969).

Further south, the centre of Danish power in the north Midlands was concentrated in the so-called Five Boroughs, Leicester, Derby, Nottingham, Stamford and Lincoln, commanding territory acquired at the partition of Mercia in 877. Leicester and Lincoln were old Roman sites, and apart from the influence on street names the Scandinavian effect on their townscapes does not appear to have been great. Nottingham was a new town foundation, perhaps succeeding an earlier rural village. It had great strategic value, controlling a crossing-point over the Trent and having strong natural defences. The line of the defences of the pre-Conquest borough can readily be traced by parallel streets inside and out and by changes in level. It occupied the south-eastern quarter of the area of the medieval walled town, which included the church of St Mary. Within its defences there is some evidence of a rudimentary grid plan. It had a mint, and was an important centre of trade in the tenth century. When Edward the Elder captured it in 921 he built a second *burh* south of the river (Fig. 13). Derby lay half a mile downstream of a Roman fort on the opposite side of the river Derwent. A small Anglian settlement called Northworthy seems to have been engulfed by it. The existence of defences is implied by a reference in 917 (Turner, 1971), but there is no later evidence. A possible defensive line can be picked out in the present street plan. As at Nottingham there are some signs of a regularly-planned area of streets, and the market-place looks as if it lay outside the defences. At Stamford, (Fig. 13), after the decline of the nearby Roman town of Great Casterton, the centre of population shifted a short distance along the Great North Road to a crossing-point over the Welland, the 'stone ford' from which the town takes its name. The mother church of St Mary had been founded by the side of the road near the ford by the mid-seventh century. The Danish fortified borough left the church just outside its south gate, and diverted the line of the original Great North Road to pass outside its south-west corner. The area within the Danish defences again bears evidence of regular planning, the central spine of High Street having a number of lesser streets running back to the defences. This early defended area was completely engulfed by the later medieval walled area, its northern extent being delimited by Broad Street which became the main medieval market-place. An earlier market-place, now largely infilled, but equated with the place called 'Portland' in the Domesday Book, lies immediately outside the west gate of the borough. Presumably this is of late Saxon or Anglo-Norman origin and is comparable with similar features at Derby and Nottingham. Stamford retained its independence under its Danish rulers until about 920, when the West Saxon army of Edward the Elder received its submission. The Chronicle tells us that Edward 'had a fortress built on the south bank of the river, and all the people who owed allegiance to the more northerly fortress submitted to him and sought him for their lord'. The position of Edward's Saxon *burh* south of the river can be inferred from street alignments. Stamford's greatest importance as a town was in the late Saxon period. There were fifty-two moneyers there in the time of King Edgar, and it ranked as the fifth city of England. Just to the north-east of the town a group of pottery kilns were producing what was probably the finest glazed pottery of the time in the whole of western Europe, and it was widely exported (Rogers, 1965).

Of the other *burhs* and towns in the Danelaw we need take only passing notice. Northampton originated as the military and administrative centre of another Danish army, and was captured by Edward the Elder in 918. Its burh defences can be inferred from street alignments within the medieval walls (Lee, 1954). Cambridge, originally a small walled Roman town, was first occupied by the Danes late in the ninth century. During their settlement it developed rapidly as a commercial town and port with the defence known as the King's Ditch, hardly any traces of which now remain, cut in late Saxon times (R.C.H.M., 1959). Thetford, like Hamwich, is an interesting example of a once important Saxon town subsequently completely abandoned. It was agricultural land until quite recently, when excavations in advance of development have enabled archaeologists to record something of the late Saxon town before its destruction. It was surrounded by earthwork defences (Davison, 1967). The later medieval town was on a different site, north of the river. Of the other tenth-century fortified sites (Bedford, Hertford, Tempsford, Buckingham, Towcester and Huntingdon) little is known.

The initial effect of the Danish invasions on the organization of the Church was disastrous. Many sees and monasteries disappeared or were moved. The most significant move was the flight from Lindisfarne with the shrine of St Cuthbert in 875, first to a minor Roman settlement at Chester-le-Street in 882, and then ultimately in 995 to a commanding position in a meander of the River Wear, an unoccupied rocky spur opposite an existing village called Elvet. After the establishment of a new cathedral a small market-place was developed outside its northern precinct, forming the nucleus of the city we now know as Durham. The town was besieged by the Scots in 1006, and already by this date it was entirely protected by ramparts.

Most of the monasteries in the areas of Danish settlement were destroyed, many never to be refounded. However, during the tenth and eleventh centuries, when some of them were being replaced, the entire monastic movement in western Europe was undergoing a period of reform under the influence of Cluny Abbey. It is probably no accident that some of the most important centres of monastic reform in England, where they were not already sited in towns, were actively involved in town foundation during this time.

Pride of place as a pre-Conquest monastic town foundation must go to St Albans (Fig. 14). The Chronicle of the abbey preserves the tradition that in 948 Abbot Wulsin diverted the course of the Watling Street out of the Roman town, across the river, past the monastery gate on the north side of the precinct, and then back to its original course about a mile further south. Two new churches, St Michael's and St Stephen's, were built at the point of departure from and return to the original route. Outside the abbey's north gate a large triangular market-place was laid out, with a broad base along the line of the diverted main road to accommodate the maximum number of stall sites close to the abbey. At the far end Wulsin built a third church, St Peter's. The plots on either side of the market-place were offered to traders and settlers, who were tempted there with the offer of free timber and other materials to build their houses.

There is some evidence that Abbot Wulsin's new market town supplanted a small *burh* called Kingsbury, traces of whose eastern defences are still visible. A greater contrast with the tight-knit grid within the defences of a *burh* is difficult to imagine. As we shall see, this type of large open market-place, variable in shape but not infrequently triangular, outside the gates of an abbey, represents another most characteristic late Saxon town-type. In St Albans Wulsin's development still dominates the present layout of the town, and all three of his churches remain at its entrances (Toms, 1962).

Bury St Edmunds is another site where a similar, if more complex, development seems to have occurred. Around 630 a small minster or monastic site was established at a place called Bedericsworth. Here in 903 were deposited the remains of Edmund, King of East Anglia, who was murdered by the Danes in 869. Edmund came to be venerated as a saint, and the site was to become a popular place of pilgrimage. His shrine was temporarily removed to London in 1010 in the face of a renewed Danish onslaught, but returned three years later. It was probably at this time that a small town was founded outside the southern gates of the church along the west bank of the River Lark. The central point of this town was an open market-place, represented by the Eld or Old Market, now St Mary's Square. This lay within a small *burh* which gave the town its new name, and whose outlines are probably detectable in street alignments between the Rivers Lark and Linnet. Bury certainly had a mint by this time,

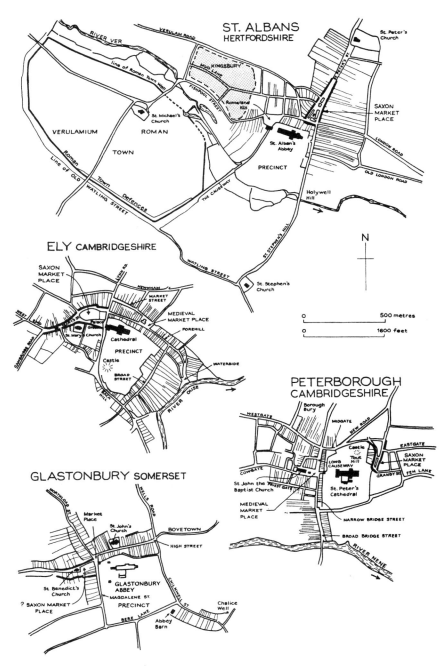

ST. ALBANS
HERTFORDSHIRE

RIVER VER

VERULAM ROAD

line of Roman Town Wall

Mud KINGSBURY Lane

FISHPOOL STREET

Roman and Hill

St. Michael's Church

VERULAMIUM

ROMAN

SAXON MARKET PLACE

St. Alban's Abbey

TOWN

Line of OLD ROMAN WATLING STREET Town Defences

THE CAUSEWAY

PRECINCT

LONDON ROAD

OLD LONDON ROAD

Holywell Hill

N

ELY CAMBRIDGESHIRE

SAXON MARKET PLACE

LANE RD.

WATLING STREET

NEWNHAM

MARKET STREET

St Stephen's Church

WEST END

Palace Green

St Mary's Church

MEDIEVAL MARKET PLACE

FOREHILL

CAMBRIDGE ROAD

Cathedral

PRECINCT

Castle

WATERSIDE

BROAD STREET

RIVER OUSE

0   500 metres

0   1600 feet

PETERBOROUGH
CAMBRIDGESHIRE

WESTGATE

Borough Bury

MIDGATE

NEW ROAD

EASTGATE

Castle Tout Hill

SAXON MARKET PLACE

COWGATE

LONG CAUSEWAY

GRANBY ST

FEN LANE

GLASTONBURY SOMERSET

St John the Baptist Church PRIEST GATE

St Peter's Cathedral

MEDIEVAL MARKET PLACE

NORTHLOAD ST.

WELLS ROAD

Market Place

St John's Church

BOVETOWN

HIGH STREET

NARROW BRIDGE STREET

BROAD BRIDGE STREET

RIVER NENE

St Benedict's Church

GLASTONBURY ABBEY

MAGDALENE ST.

PRECINCT

? SAXON MARKET PLACE

CHILKWELL ST.

BERE LANE

Chalice Well

Abbey Barn

14 Late Saxon monastic towns.

and there are records of burgesses. The town was transformed in
the 1070s by Abbot Baldwin, whose new planned town to the west of
the abbey was based on a regular grid of streets. The old market-
place, although most of its functions were now carried out in Abbot
Baldwin's new market square, retained its function as a horse-market,
and is shown under that name in Thomas Warren's map of 1748
(Lobel, 1935; Scarfe, 1972).

At Peterborough, too, the Saxon market-place was largely superseded in medieval times, but still leaves a trace of its presence in the
landscape today. Here the first monastery was founded in 657 in a
place then called Medeshampstead. After refoundation in 966 the
abbot proceeded to build a wall round the abbey and changed its
name to Burgh. To the north-east of the abbey a small town with a
market-place and its own church was laid out, and it was here that
the Norman castle was sited at the time of the Conquest. In the
twelfth century, however, as at Bury, a completely new town was
founded to the west of the abbey gate with a new rectangular market-
place (Steane, 1974).

Similarly at Ely, outside the west gate of a monastic precinct
originally founded in 673, a market-place was laid out with its own
church of St Mary some time in the late Saxon period. The later
medieval market-place was positioned on the northern side of the
abbey wall (Taylor, 1973).

At Abingdon the situation is complicated by the existence of an
earlier minster church, represented now by St Helen's, which is on a
different site from the Saxon abbey. St Helen's church lies close to
the confluence of the Thames and the Ock, and was the focal point
of at least three streets in medieval times. The abbey, founded
around 670, was originally situated two and a half miles north of the
town at a site called *Abendoun*. It soon moved downhill towards the
Thames, bringing its name with it, and displacing an earlier settlement
of *Seukesham*. It was destroyed by the Danes, but refounded in 954.
The later tenth or early eleventh century seems a likely time for the
laying out of the present roughly square market-place west of the
church, which is clearly a later feature than the streets leading towards
St Helen's. A new road brought into it from the west is significantly
called The Bury (Biddle, Lambrick and Myres, 1968).

The sites described probably represent only a fraction of the late
Saxon market-places which exist. A case could certainly be made for
others, such as Evesham (Bond, 1973) and Glastonbury (Fig. 14).
Although there is considerable variation and no standard plan, they
all have some elements in common. They tend to open out close to

the entrance to the monastic precinct, which itself, of course, may have been subject to modification at various later dates. They tend to be large and open, unless reduced by later encroachment, and are in considerable contrast to the confined market streets in *burhs*. Often they are associated with a separate parish church, and in several cases they seem to have been replaced and left as somewhat isolated backwaters by post-Conquest replanning. The activities of these late Saxon monasteries in town foundation are important for their own sake and for their legacy to the topography of the towns they created. Perhaps of even greater importance is their role as the instigators of a profitable fashion which was to be copied extensively after the Norman Conquest by ecclesiastics and laymen at many places up and down the country.

Chapter V

Medieval Towns

The consolidation of Norman power after the Conquest brought new vigour to commercial life, and the twelfth and early thirteenth centuries witnessed an unprecedented boom in urban growth. Most of the pre-Conquest towns revived, some four or five hundred completely new towns were created, and an even greater number of rural settlements were promoted to borough status. Some of the elements making up medieval towns, particularly street plans and property boundaries, have survived to the present and provide the framework within which modern towns are accommodated.

It is often assumed that new medieval towns can be divided into two groups: those growing 'organically' and those 'planted' at a particular date by a particular founder. However, a town is a type of settlement which appears only in a society which has achieved a certain level of sophistication and it is unlikely that such a complex structure could develop spontaneously without some degree of deliberate creation, promotion or support. Any simplistic explanation of 'organic' towns growing at 'natural route foci' should be rejected since innumerable 'route foci' have no town, and in some cases even deliberate attempts to found towns on such sites have failed. A late twelfth-century urban venture at Bretford, where the Fosse Way crosses the Warwickshire Avon is now only a small hamlet. Conversely the idea of towns being deliberately created is often an oversimplification of the actual processes. The number of towns which present an entire contemporary plan is a small minority compared with those showing successive accretions of different dates. Yet the latter group are no less 'planned' or 'artificial' than the former.

Professor Beresford has focussed attention on medieval new towns planted on previously unoccupied sites (Beresford, 1967a). He has examined the reasons, chronology and results of town plantation in England, Wales and Gascony, specifically excluding promoted villages and planned extensions to pre-existing settlements, although he took care to point out that they were all prompted by the same economic circumstances. It is certainly convenient to discuss new towns separately, if only because they show the most highly-developed medieval town planning; but it must be recognized that such places are not a distinct category of towns on their own, simply extreme examples of a more widespread phenomenon.

Medieval new town plantations

The earliest group of Norman foundations was dominated by royal initiative and military considerations, since most were adjacent to new castles. Subsequently there was a change of emphasis from royal foundations on strategic sites to commercial new towns, more dominated by their market-place than by a castle. Battle, the first important unfortified Norman town, had neither town walls nor castle, but consisted of a single main street running from the abbey gate to a triangular market-place. The royal interest in town foundation revived with the conquest of Wales. King John planned a spate of unsuccessful Welsh foundations but Henry III established eight new Welsh towns including Hay-on-Wye, Montgomery, Welshpool and Caerphilly. Of all the English kings, Edward I took the greatest personal interest in town foundation. He had had wide experience of plantations in Gascony before he came to the English throne, and in England was responsible for the major town-planning achievements at New Winchelsea (Fig. 21), Kingston-on-Hull and Berwick-on-Tweed (Plate VII). In Wales he established such classic 'bastides' as Flint, New Rhuddlan, Conway, Caernarvon and Beaumaris, and encouraged others in town foundation.

Even royal interest was not a guarantee of success. Henry III's new port of Warenmouth in Northumberland, established in 1247 on the common pasture of Bamburgh, had completely disappeared by the sixteenth century, and Edward I's Newton, founded in 1286 on the shores of Poole Harbour, was similarly abortive, now being remembered only by the place name 'Newton Cottage' (Bowen and Taylor, 1964).

The Black Death virtually marked the end of medieval town plantation and few new places were developed after the 1350s. The last medieval royal town plantation was Edward III's Queenborough on the Isle of Sheppey, founded with its castle in 1368. It never consisted of more than a single main street (Fig. 15).

More 'new town' sites almost certainly await identification. Although Professor Beresford's gazetteer states of Worcestershire,

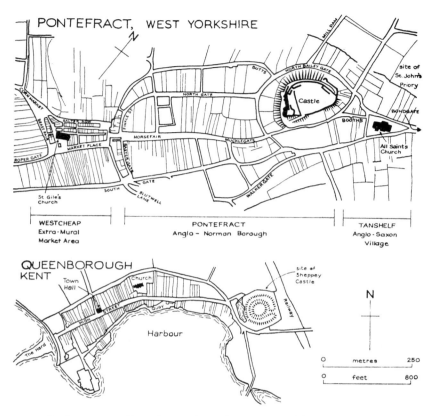

MILL DAM

site of
St. John's
Priory

BUTTS

NORTH BAILEY GATE

NORTH GATE

Castle

BONDGATE

CORN MARKET

BEAST FAIR

SHOE

BAXTER ROW

BAILEY GATE

HORSEFAIR

MUCKLEGATE

BOOTHS

MARKET PLACE

All Saints
Church

ROPER GATE

GATE

SOUTH

SLUTWELL
LANE

WALKER GATE

St Giles
Church

| WESTCHEAP
Extra-Mural
Market Area | PONTEFRACT
Anglo – Norman Borough | TANSHELF
Anglo-Saxon
Village |

QUEENBOROUGH
KENT

Town
Hall

Church

site of
Sheppey
Castle

Railway

N

HIGH STREET

Quay

Harbour

The Hard

| 0 | metres | 250 |
| 0 | feet | 800 |

15 Castle towns: Pontefract, eleventh century with earlier and later elements; Queenborough, the last Royal medieval town foundation (1368).

'No medieval plantations have been found in this county', subsequent work has shown that Halesowen, Alvechurch, Evesham, Pershore, Broadway, Upton-on-Severn, Tenbury and Bromsgrove all display symptoms of planned growth, although some of them certainly have pre-Conquest nuclei. Perhaps the most convincing example is Bewdley, whose name is clearly of Norman French origin. It does not appear in the Domesday Book, although its 'suburb', Wribbenhall, is recorded as a berewick of Kidderminster. The church stands on a constricted site in the middle of the town's main street, with no churchyard. For centuries it was a subordinate chapel to Ribbesford parish church a mile away, and therefore never acquired burial rights. In the fifteenth century there was uncertainty as to whether Bewdley was in Worcestershire or Shropshire, and it was regarded as a sanctuary for fugitives from either county. This type of marginal position was common in other medieval new towns. Examples include Newmarket (Suffolk and Cambridgeshire), Royston (Hertford-shire and Cambridgeshire) and Wokingham, where an iron bollard still marks the former division of Berkshire and Wiltshire through the centre of the town. Bewdley's plan is regular, with four of its streets laid out in an almost perfect square. Perhaps most conclusive of all is Leland's description in 1539, 'I gather that Bewdley is but a very new town, and that of old time there was but some poore hamlett. . . . I asked a merchant there of the antientness of the towne, and he assured me that it was but a new towne'. Leland's 'poore hamlett' was an earlier planned market settlement on Wyre Hill, half a mile to the west. The migration to the riverside seems to have begun after the construction of the bridge in 1447. Bewdley is therefore an unusually late development, post-dating even Queenborough, usually claimed as the last medieval new town.

Towns expanding by successive planted additions

Bewdley demonstrates that even late medieval planted towns can contain more than one distinct planned unit. In places with a longer history this is more common, and, although successive planned extensions may be poorly documented, they can often be distinguished in the town plan. Professor Conzen has shown how the changes in direction and level of blocks of properties and streets can be used for this purpose (Conzen, 1960, 1968). Certain significant street names, such as 'Newland', which occurs at Sherborne, Witney, Banbury and Pershore, are further valuable clues.

The degree of complexity which may appear even in a small town may be illustrated by the case of Eynsham, Oxfordshire (Fig. 16). Its plan at first seems confused, lacking any single main axis or regularity. Could this not be a candidate for 'organic' growth? If, however, we dissect the plan, looking at each street in turn, it is quite clear that the place has expanded by the addition of one new street after another and, though each unit is planned, they are not all contemporary and consequently the overall effect is irregular. The Domesday record of Eynsham suggests only a thriving agricultural community. The earliest axis of Eynsham is along an east–west route to the early crossing-point of the Thames at Swinford. The eastern part of this road is

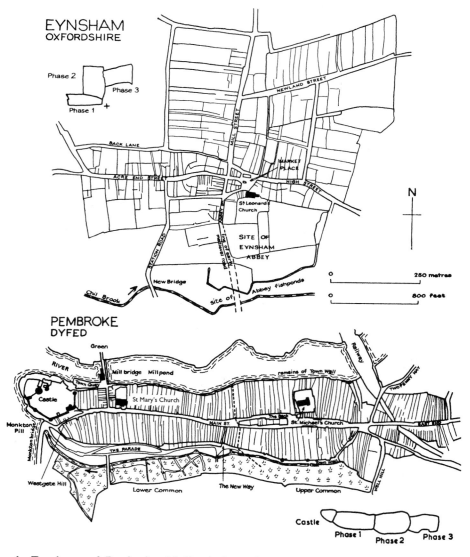

16 Eynsham and Pembroke: Medieval plan units.

called High Street but the western part, even more significantly, has long been known as Acre End. This was probably the earliest agricultural nucleus of the community. The market-place looks like an intrusion into the middle of the older east–west street alignment, and possibly some buildings were cleared away to accommodate it. It lies just outside the precinct of the Benedictine abbey founded in 1005, close to the parish church. King Stephen granted to the abbey the right of a Sunday market in 1135–9, and the privilege of burgage tenure.

Running northwards from the Market Square is Mill Street, whose western side is lined with burgage tenements and it is probable that it was not developed before the market was acquired. Moreover its tenements are demonstrably later than the properties on the north side of Acre End Street, whose back lane and garden alignments continue through to Mill Street.

The significantly-named Newland Street leads off at an angle from Mill Street, and its tenements lie, not at right angles to Newland itself, but parallel with Mill Street, indicating clearly that Mill Street was in existence before the Newland tenements were developed. Newland dates from 1215, when a charter was acquired for a borough extension.

Thus at Eynsham, a very minor town, three or four quite distinct units of settlement growth can be distinguished from the plan evidence alone and a hypothetical growth sequence can be built up, documentary evidence being used to date some of the phases. A similar exercise could be carried out for many other places, including Montacute (Fig. 20).

Pembroke is often quoted as a classic example of a simple twelfth-century castle-borough, laid out by Gilbert de Clare after 1110. A single street approaches the castle gate along a ridge, with tenements on either side. This simple plan-unit was walled (Fig. 16). But is it as simple as it appears? Why does it have two churches, one in either half of the length of the street? Is the 'waist' halfway along the walled area simply a reflection of a physical constriction in the ridge, or could it mark the limits of an earlier and more restricted town closer to the castle, later extended with an enlarged circuit of walls and a new church?

Promoted villages

There are very many cases where a simple one-phase planned layout is grafted on to an existing village centre. Sometimes the village, normally containing the parish church, is distinguished by a name like Old Town, as at Brackley, Chard (Fig. 19), Stratford-on-Avon or Moreton-in-Marsh. At Shipston-on-Stour, the earlier agricultural centre bears the evocative name of Husbandman's End (Fig. 22).

Failed urban promotions

Practically every county has places where attempts at urban stimulation failed, and all that remains is a village, sometimes with remains of abandoned streets and burgage tenements. Examples include Clifton-on-Teme and Feckenham in Worcestershire, Snitterfield and Aston Cantlow in Warwickshire, Stratton Audley in Oxfordshire, and Stoford in Somerset. In other cases the settlement has disappeared completely, leaving only earthworks or an isolated church, as at Burton Dassett, Warwickshire, and Bignell, Oxfordshire, or an empty castle-bailey extension, as at Caus, Shropshire, and Kenfig, Glamorganshire.

Thus, the line between new towns, multi-phase plantations and promoted villages is an arbitrary one. The element of artificiality, of personal intervention by a powerful individual and of planned development on the ground, is common to all. It is now clear that some degree of plantation and regular planning, far from being the exception, is in fact the norm in medieval towns. It becomes increasingly more difficult to find examples of an 'organic' town developing haphazardly from nothing through its advantageous 'geographical' position.

The medieval town plan

The plan of a medieval town is likely to stem from a number of factors—the physical nature of its site, plan elements inherited from earlier periods, and the needs of its medieval lords and inhabitants. The physical site has often been thought of as a dominant factor in the determination of the plan. Far more frequently, however, the site is not on its own a particularly significant factor. Although extremes of slope or waterlogging were usually avoided, one has only to look at the gradient of Gold Hill at Shaftesbury, or to read Celia Fiennes's bitter complaints about Ely ('the dirtyest place I ever saw . . . a perfect quagmire . . . tho' my chamber was near 20 stepps up I had froggs and slow-worms and snailes in my roome . . .') to appreciate that such adverse sites could be and were occupied if the need was there.

The founder of a town or its inhabitants may have had a variety of motives in mind when laying it out. The town plan is likely to reflect those motives, as will the choice of site. A town located in an area of political instability, where defence is likely to be an important consideration, will tend to look for a constricted site which is not too readily accessible. The significant point about Durham or Shrewsbury is not that the contours of entrenched river meanders have controlled the development of their plan, but that such sites were deliberately chosen in the first instance by people in whose minds the need for protection was uppermost. Similarly, a town whose basis for existence was commercial will tend to be readily accessible and well served by communications from without, and to contain ample market space within.

These original needs may well change over the centuries, and the original plan be altered and adapted accordingly: and on occasions the town may move altogether. Nonetheless once the original plan was established, certain elements tend to remain as identifiable relict features, and few medieval towns established on earlier sites have completely erased every trace of their predecessors.

The changing emphasis from defence to commerce is an important underlying theme in medieval towns. It is true that some important marketing centres existed before the Conquest, and equally true that town walls were being constructed round other places as late as the fifteenth century. While not denying the significance of such developments, we can probably regard them as exceptional.

Another important change is the increasing independence of towns from the castle or monastery. From the beginning of the twelfth century we can trace the emergence of a new autonomous burgess class, as one town after another freed itself from its feudal and manorial ties and became an independent self-governing community. The effect of these changes is clearly reflected in the topography of many towns. The castle or monastery gate ceased to be the focus it once was, and the market-place gained a new, central importance. Whereas the early foundations of Windsor, Arundel and Launceston were dominated by their castles, in Kendal or Penrith the town plan is completely divorced from the castle, and Boston, Watford and Dunstable have no castles at all. At Denbigh the walled town by the castle on the hilltop is virtually deserted, while later commercial development was concentrated on lower, more accessible ground (Fig. 25).

The increasing significance of market-places can clearly be illustrated. Many old towns were well established as *burhs* or castle-boroughs before they became important as commercial centres. It can repeatedly be demonstrated that the market-place is a latecomer to the plan, either being accommodated by internal demolition and alteration, or as an added marginal feature outside the earliest line of defences. At Hereford, Northampton, Nottingham and Stamford large open market-places had developed outside the tight-knit streets of the defended *burh*, becoming in effect new town centres, which were later included within the enlarged circuit of the medieval walls (Fig. 13). In Oxford markets were held in the streets around the central cross-roads of the *burh* till the late eighteenth century. However, the very wide northern entry into the town, St Giles, probably served a similar function as an extra-mural market-place, though it was never incorporated within the city defences. Also at Buckingham the market-place lies outside the *burh* defences, developing as the main centre of the undefended medieval town. Elsewhere areas were cleared inside the defences to accommodate an intrusive market-place, as at Wallingford (Plate VI), Warwick, Worcester and Langport (Fig. 12).

Such commercial reorientation was not restricted to towns of pre-Conquest origin. At Pontefract (Fig. 15) the pre-Conquest settlement was a rural village called Tanshelf, whose site today is represented by the ruined church of All Saints, south-east of the castle. The establishment of the castle in the early twelth century was closely followed by the laying out of a small walled area with one central-street axis, now represented by Micklegate and Horse Fair. The main street of this area, chartered in 1194, was just wide enough to serve as a market-place, but its military derivation is clear. Beyond the west gate of the walled Anglo-Norman borough is a very different area, a large extra-mural market-place, which received a separate charter in 1255–8 as the Borough of West Cheap; a new chapel, St Giles, was built to serve it. Today the extra-mural market-place, divided by infill into separate streets now known as Salter Row, Wool Market, Beast Fair, Shoe Market, and Corn Market, forms the town centre of Pontefract. St Giles's chapel was elevated to become the town's new parish church after the ruin of All Saints in the Civil War. The old walled borough has become a rather shabby backwater. Kidwelly (Fig. 25), Caernarvon and Cardiff are further post-Conquest military towns which developed extra-mural market-places.

Street-plan types

The classification of urban street plans is difficult, because form cannot always be equated with origin or function. However, some distinctive plan-types are so frequently encountered that they deserve closer examination.

1. OPEN TRIANGULAR OR IRREGULAR MARKET-PLACES:
This type frequently occurs as a distinctive feature of towns with great abbeys founded before and after the Conquest (Fig. 14). However, it is also a feature of other towns such as Market Harborough, Bampton (Fig. 17) and Alnwick where the focal point is provided simply by the meeting place of two or three roads, often pre-dating the town.

2. CASTLE-BOROUGHS:
A castle might serve as an urban nucleus in the same way as a monastery. At Windsor, Skipton and Taunton (Fig. 17) similar plans evolved, with a broad triangular or rectangular market-place outside the castle gate.

More commonly, however, a narrower, single-street plan is found with tenements on either side backing onto a lane running around the inner perimeter of defences linked to the castle. Many examples occur among the new Anglo-Norman foundations in Wales and the borders. These today are often very stunted settlements, like Richards Castle or Kilpeck, where only earthworks remain to show the line of the town walls and internal tenements. In some places, of both English and Welsh foundation, the borough amounted to little more than an outer bailey of the castle, and Cefnllys, Dryslwyn, Dolforwyn, Old Dynevor, Bere, Skenfrith and Whitecastle show little evidence today of their former urban functions.

Not all castle bailey boroughs were doomed to failure. Some English towns still have a distinctive semicircular orientation, which reflects their origin in relation to castle precincts. Perhaps the best-known example is Devizes (Fig. 18) where there are two separate market-places side by side, both curving slightly around the castle nucleus. The outer market-place is the earlier, the inner one representing subsequent colonization of the castle bailey. Richmond, Launceston, Wisbech, and, on a smaller scale, Pleshey and Tutbury are all influenced in their shape by castle nuclei.

3. UNDEFENDED LINEAR PLAN:
The undefended market town, with tenements on either side of a single main street, is by far the commonest medieval town street plan. The single-street axis is often, but not invariably, swollen into a cigar-shaped plan, in order to accommodate the market (Thame, Brackley, Henley-in-Arden, Chipping Campden, Ashford). This plan-type

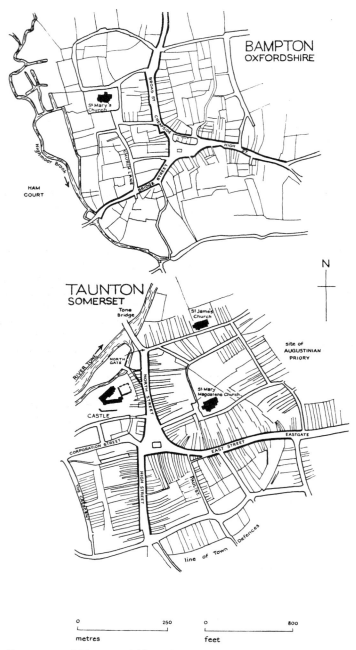

17 Bampton and Taunton: Triangular market-places.

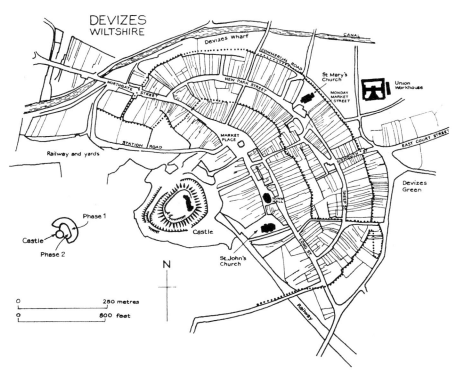

DEVIZES
WILTSHIRE

Devizes Wharf

CANAL

COMMERCIAL ROAD

St Mary's
Church

Union
Workhouse

NEW PARK STREET

MONDAY
MARKET
STREET

NORTHGATE
STREET

EAST COURT STREET

STATION ROAD

MARKET
PLACE

Railway and yards

Devizes
Green

Phase 1

Castle

Phase 2

Castle

TOWN
HALL

St John's
Church

N

0   250 metres

0   800 feet

Railway

18   Devizes, a two-phase castle town.

seems to be a product of the period after c. 1100, when the advantages
of market-street frontages were superseding defensive considerations.
Usually the market axis was related to a pre-existing route, and
clung closely to it. At Henley-in-Arden the new town was
founded along the Stratford to Birmingham road late in the twelfth
century by the lords of Beaudesert, on the opposite side of the river;
they had first attempted, unsuccessfully, to establish a market at
Beaudesert itself in 1141 (Fig. 19). Sometimes roads were purposely
diverted to pass through a new market town. In 1219 the Bishop of
Lincoln obtained permission to divert the Oxford-Aylesbury road into
his new market town of Thame, thereby adding a mile to the journey.
At Dunster, Montacute and Chipping Sodbury (Figs. 20 and 43) sharp
bends in the streets entering the towns tell a similar story.

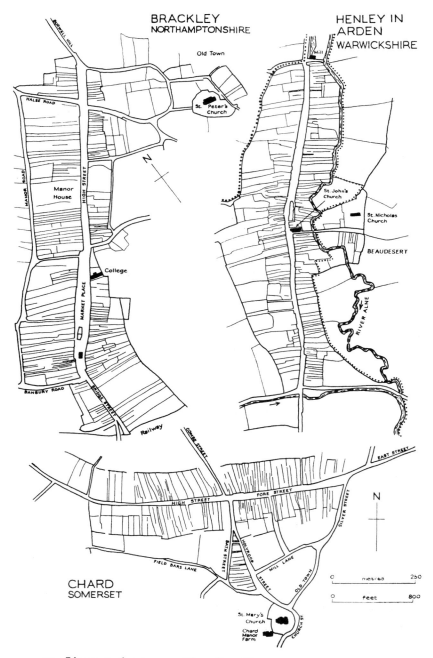

19 Linear market towns with earlier village centres.

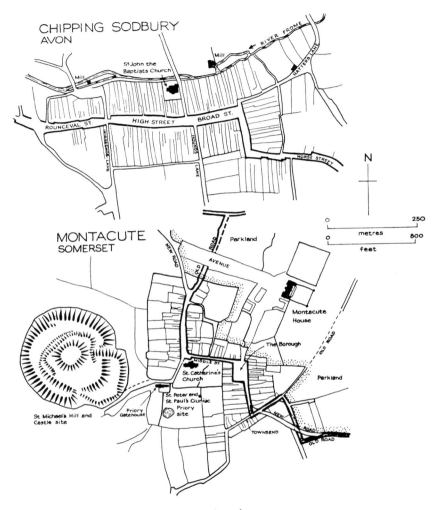

CHIPPING SODBURY
AVON

St John the
Baptists Church

Mill

Mill

RIVER FROME

HATTERS LANE

ROUNCEVAL ST.

HIGH STREET

BROAD ST.

SHRUBBERY LANE

HOUNDS LANE

HORSE STREET

N

0 ——— 250
metres
0 ——— 800
feet

MONTACUTE
SOMERSET

NEW ROAD

OLD ROAD

AVENUE

Parkland

Montacute
House

The Borough

OLD ROAD

MIDDLE ST.

St Catherine's
Church

St Peter and
St. Paul's Cluniac
Priory
site

Parkland

St Michael's Hill and
Castle site

Priory
Gatehouse

NEW
ROAD

TOWNSEND

OLD ROAD

20 Road diversions into new market-places.

Often the market-street axis was not the original centre of the settlement, and at Brackley, Chard (Fig. 19), Thame and many other towns
earlier nuclei can be identified clearly by distinctive street or district
names and somewhat isolated churches.

91

4. GRID PLAN:

The more ambitious medieval new towns sometimes used a grid plan, as at Ludlow (Hope, 1909), Salisbury (Rogers, 1969), New Winchelsea, Stratford-on-Avon and Abbot Baldwin's Bury St Edmunds, and this has sometimes given rise to the impression that it was more widespread than is the case (Figs 21 and 22). Some of the smaller towns for which a grid has been claimed, like Church Brough or Bishops Castle, amount to no more than a cross-roads with back lanes, and we must take care to distinguish these from the schemes using a dozen or more chequers. True grids are found in less than 10 per cent of all medieval new-town foundations.

Perhaps because it is one of the easiest types of street plan to lay out on the ground, the grid is one of the most consistent features of planning in new towns. We have already seen it in Roman and Anglo-Saxon towns and we shall meet it again in new towns founded up to the nineteenth century.

Medieval grids are more variable in shape and size than earlier examples. At New Winchelsea Edward I created an extremely regular

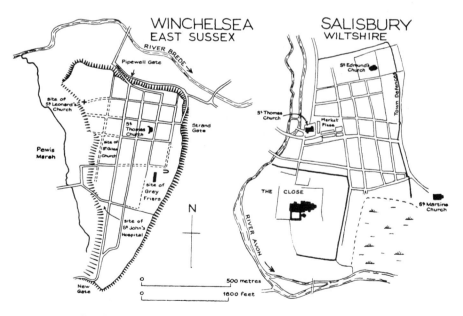

21 Medieval new towns planned on a major grid system.

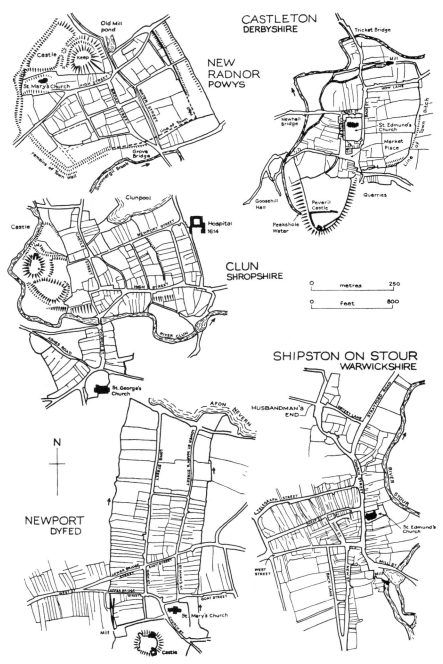

22   Medieval new towns planned on a minor grid system.

pattern with straight streets and *insulae* which were almost perfectly square (Fig. 21). This pattern still dominates the present very shrunken town, and can also be detected in the earthworks and boundaries representing its abandoned streets. At Ludlow, New Shoreham, Hedon and Caernarvon the *insulae* were rectangular, and at Flint and Bury St Edmunds they were even more elongated; further variations may be found at Stratford-on-Avon, Salisbury, Rye and many of the Welsh planted towns.

5. UNIQUE PLANS:
Occasionally a medieval town plan contains features which seem to be unique. Perhaps the most unusual example in Britain is Great Yarmouth (Fig. 23), whose medieval nucleus consisted of three parallel main streets running along a sand spit between the River Yare and the open sea. Crossing these there were over 150 narrow lanes known as The Rows, the smallest of which, Kittywitches Row, was just 27 inches wide at its narrowest point. This extraordinary pattern is clearly shown on the earliest plan of the town in 1588. Unfortunately many of the Rows received heavy damage in the air raids of 1942, though some traces remain. The origin of these rows has never been explained satisfactorily.

6. COMPOSITE PLANS:
Any number of permutations of different plan-types may be encountered in towns, many displaying more than one planned area. At Bridgnorth the early medieval town was confined within an extended bailey north of the castle, delimited by the roads now called West and East Castle Street. Later in the twelfth century a new borough with a pattern of rectilinear streets was added to the north. At Evesham the early extra-monastic market settlement of Merstow Green was superseded before the late twelfth century by a grid of streets (Bond, 1973). At Ashbourne the single main-street axis had a large triangular market-place opened off it by the late thirteenth century, at the far end from the church (Fig. 3), while a subsidiary trading settlement called Compton grew up on the opposite side of the Henmore Brook.

More difficult to detect is a planned layout which has been eroded by gradual changes to the point of being completely lost, or one which has subsequently been replaced by a new planned layout using different principles. One possible example is Henry II's New Woodstock. Throughout its recorded history the principal feature of the town has been its large, much infilled triangular market-place, but the pattern of back lanes is not what one would expect if this was the

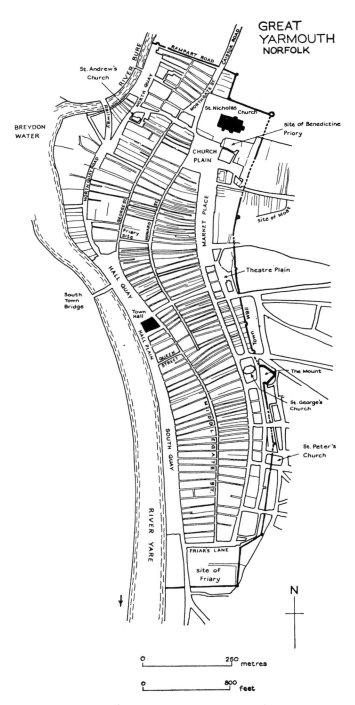

St. Andrew's
Church

RIVER BURE

RAMPART ROAD

CUSTOM ROAD

NORTH QUAY

MORTGATE ST

St. Nicholas Church

site of Benedictine
Priory

BREYDON
WATER

CHURCH
PLAIN

MARKET PLACE

NORTH QUAY ROAD

GEORGE ST

HOWARD ST

Friary
Site

Site of Moot

RAILWAY

Theatre Plain

HALL QUAY

South
Town
Bridge

Town Hall

Town Wall

HALL PLAIN

QUEEN STREET

The Mount

St. George's
Church

MIDDLE GATE ST

St. Peter's
Church

SOUTH QUAY

RIVER YARE

FRIAR'S LANE

site of
Friary

N

0   250 metres

0   800 feet

23   Great Yarmouth.

original plan. The borough boundary is almost perfectly rectangular in shape and from this, and various lane and property alignments, it is possible to suggest that the original intention may have been to lay out a tight-knit grid. This must have broken down at quite an early stage, perhaps because the population of the town did not increase as rapidly as expected.

Plan elements

1. THE MARKET-PLACE:
We have already seen how the shape and size of the market-place is closely related to its origin. Few medieval towns confined street trading to the market-place alone and markets were held in church-yards up to the thirteenth century. Other towns have subsidiary open spaces where extra market stalls could be erected. At South-ampton the High Street opens out at St Lawrence, New Corner and Holy Rood, and stalls were also put up before St Michael's church and north of the Bargate.

In the main market-place considerable infilling has often taken place (Figs. 3, 15, 16). Pressures on the open space came from several sources. Market stall holders tended, unless forced to do otherwise, to leave their stalls in position from one market day to the next, and in consequence many developed eventually into permanent inhabited structures. Frontagers on a market-place attempted to gain space by pushing their shop fronts foward, a practice still seen today where nineteenth- and twentieth-century shop fronts may be well in advance of the main building. The market-place was also accepted as the legitimate place for any structure likely to be of general public benefit, such as the church, market cross or market hall and today public conveniences and commemorative clock-towers tend to occupy such positions.

The process of encroachment was often well advanced by late medieval times. The sixteenth-century plan of Ashbourne (Fig. 3) shows considerable infill in the original market triangle. At Wantage in 1284 the Justices in Eyre ordered the removal of various stalls which had so narrowed the market-place and highway that carts could not pass; but the following year permission was acquired to re-erect them all. Today the market-place of Wantage, even after the removal of the Market House and Butchers' Shambles, is probably less than half its original size. In Thame the great early thirteenth-century cigar-shaped market-place of the bishops of Lincoln was being infilled only a few years after its creation. In 1221 the Bishop was said to

I. Traprain Law, East Lothian: An Iron Age tribal capital occupied throughout the Roman period.

II. Irchester, Northamptonshire: Crop marks of irregular Roman street pattern and buildings within line of town wall marked by hedges.

III. Lincoln: The Newport Arch: Remains of the Roman North Gate.

V. York: Town defences on the north-west side, showing the Roman wall of c. A.D. 300, the seventh-century Anglian tower and the medieval town wall above.

IV. Wroxeter, Shropshire: The Old Work: Remains of the Roman civil baths and excavations of late Roman levels in 1969.

VI. Wallingford, Oxford-shire: Town planning in the tenth century: A grid of streets within the de-fences of a Saxon *burh*.

VII. Berwick-on-Tweed, Northumberland: The Tudor town defences, with traces of the medieval walls, enclosing a larger area, visible to right.

VIII. Frome, Somerset: Cheap Street: A medieval lane with buildings of the seventeenth century and later.

IX. Hereford: A timber-framed building concealed behind a nineteenth-century façade in High Town.

X. Blandford Forum, Dorset: A new townscape of the 1730s: Church, market hall and housing built by the Bastard brothers after the fire of 1731.

XI. Warwick: North-gate Street and St Mary's church tower, rebuilt after the fire of 1694.

XII. Tunbridge Wells, Kent: The Pantiles: The promenade of a seventeenth-century spa town.

XIII. Taunton, Somerset: The Crescent, a Regency terrace built in 1807.

XIV. Stourport-on-Severn, Worcestershire: A late eighteenth-century canal port town.

XV. Bath, Avon: The medieval walled town (centre), the first Georgian expansion, with Queen Square, the Circus and Royal Crescent (top left) and Great Pulteney Street on the Bathwick estate (top right).

XVI. Birmingham: The Law Courts, Corporation Street: High Victorian civic architecture.

XVII. Birmingham: Superior by-law housing in Victoria Road, Harborne.

XVIII. Birmingham: Nineteenth-century blind-back housing in Heath Street, Winson Green.

XIX. Lincoln: Nineteenth-century waterfront and warehouses at Brayford Pool in 1967.

XX. Hendon: Inter-war housing estate.

have 'made on the king's highway in the Forum of Thame an encroachment where he raised houses to increase his rent, to the length of 100 feet in all'. Thirty years later another bishop erected eighteen stalls on the market-place along the royal way, and the encroachments were said to be 'augmented . . . from year to year'.

In some towns efforts to limit encroachment on the main street or market-place were fairly successful, but the side streets were less strictly controlled. In Winchester many of the side streets have a curious funnel-shaped plan and it has been suggested (Keene, 1972) that this was because the incentives for encroachment were greatest towards the main market street, and there was less pressure at the less desirable end of the street nearest the city wall.

2. STREETS AND LANES:

With the possible exception of certain towns of military origin, most early medieval towns were fairly spacious, the popular concept of great congestion being a truer picture of the sixteenth to seventeenth centuries than of the medieval town. Quite apart from the extensive areas of yards, gardens and orchards behind the houses, the main streets themselves were frequently wide and open. When William of Worcester visited Bristol he paced out several streets 50 feet wide and many more 35 feet wide (Neale, forthcoming) and when the Bishop of Worcester founded Stratford-on-Avon he laid out new streets 50 feet wide and made the main market street 90 feet across. Ludlow Broad Street, despite its Georgian frontages, probably gives a truer impression of the medieval town street than does the Shambles at York.

It is possible to detect changes in the street plan taking place in medieval times. Lanes and streets were sometimes truncated or completely closed off by the creation of monastic and ecclesiastical precincts. In Canterbury the Austin Friars enclosed two lanes in 1408, and the Grey Friars also truncated an old lane south of the High Street (Urry, 1967). In both Oxford and Cambridge the development of college precincts made considerable differences to the previous street pattern. Sometimes new streets were created to improve access after a town had developed and in Yarmouth some of the Rows seem to have been widened into streets (Fig. 23). Street names sometimes give an indication of a new medieval street as at New Gate in Stamford or New Street in Birmingham. The name alone is insufficient proof of medieval origin, for the same nomenclature has been used of new elements in street patterns right up to the present century. Elsewhere diversions can be found. In Eynsham the abbey precinct seems to

have been extended in the early thirteenth century, and there is documentary evidence for a new street and bridge being built in 1217
(Fig. 16). Abbey Street, which now comes to an abrupt halt, was
truncated and its traffic diverted round two right-angled corners into
New Bridge Street (now Station Road).

The repair of medieval town streets may originally have been the
responsibility of the frontagers but in the thirteenth century many
towns acquired grants of pavage, which allowed them to raise money
for proper paving. Flat stones, cobbles or gravel were used according
to local availability. Instead of being cambered, they usually sloped
towards an open drain along the centre. New Salisbury, which was
laid out on low-lying ground, had a system of open water-channels
running along most of its streets.

By the fourteenth century the tendency is increasingly apparent for
certain noxious trades such as butchering and fishmongering to be
confined to individual quarters or streets within the town. Long after
such trades have dispersed, street names such as Butcher Row or
Shambles, Fish Street or Friday Street, still remain.

3. PROPERTY BOUNDARIES:

The most characteristic medieval urban property form is the burgage
tenement, in which the house or shop stands at the frontage of a long
strip laid out at right angles to the street alignment. For medieval
new towns the tenement size is sometimes specified in the foundation
charter. At Stratford-on-Avon the Bishop of Worcester offered
quarter-acre plots measuring nearly 200 feet by 60 feet at a shilling
rent. At Salisbury the tenements were smaller, the average size being
about 115 feet by 50 feet, also at a shilling rent. At Thame they were
much bigger, a shilling rent being charged for acre plots, sometimes
between 650 and 700 feet long with original frontage widths of about
60 feet. The actual size of the plots offered may be a product of the
nature of the ground over which they were laid out. In the case of
Stratford and Thame the burgages are known to have been built over
land taken out of open-field cultivation, and their dimensions are
clearly related to local agricultural measurements. Such tenements
laid out over open fields can often be identified by their slight reversed-
S curve in plan, and may be common in other towns. Elsewhere the
dimensions are probably related to medieval house construction, such
as optimum bay width or span. At Alnwick nearly half the burgages
within the walls had a frontage width which equalled or was a recognizable fraction of 28 feet. Another third of them were similarly related

to a 32-foot width.   The smallest widths recorded were 14 and 16 feet, exactly half of both predominant units, which represent common lower limits of bay widths.   From this evidence Professor Conzen was able to suggest that the standard burgage frontage in Alnwick implied a row-house of two structural bays with its eaves facing the street (Conzen, 1960).

Medieval properties generally are a subject worthy of more detailed examination.   The plot widths suggested by some of the documentary records are much wider than the plots which actually exist on the ground in the present day.   Indeed, the abiding impression of burgage tenements in many towns today is of a very restricted frontage—in extreme cases as little as six feet, quite commonly between 10 and 25 feet.   On the most important thoroughfares every attempt seems to have been made to cram the maximum possible number of properties into a given length of street, and the only room available for the expansion of the individual premises was therefore down the strip at the rear.   There are found complete ranges of outbuildings, workshops and sheds at right angles to the main building.   Access to the yards is usually gained from the front by an arch under the main building range and from the rear by a back lane.

It may well be that the plots originally laid out were spacious, with a wide frontage, but there are documentary references to half- and quarter-burgages as early as the thirteenth century.   It seems that throughout late medieval times, reaching a peak in the sixteenth to the seventeenth centuries, subdivision of plots on the most important commercial frontages was commonplace.   It is this process of modification which has given us the very long, narrow strips seen in so many medieval towns today.

Despite the processes of subdivision and, occasionally, amalgamation, it has been shown by excavation that many tenement boundaries are of very ancient origin.   In Westwick Street, Norwich, many property boundaries remained virtually unchanged from the twelfth to the eighteenth century and in the heart of Viking York they seem to have been constant even longer (Radley, 1971).   Away from the main commercial frontages, however, the situation may have been more fluid.   In the cloth-working quarter of Winchester in Lower Brook Street there is clear evidence of the encroachment of some properties over their neighbours (Biddle, 1972).   In rare instances documents can be used to reconstruct detailed maps of the disposition and ownership of medieval properties.   Fig. 24 shows central Canterbury in 1200, as reconstructed by Dr Urry (Urry, 1967). Similar evidence is available for Oxford and Hull (Salter, 1960, 1969; Bilson, 1928).

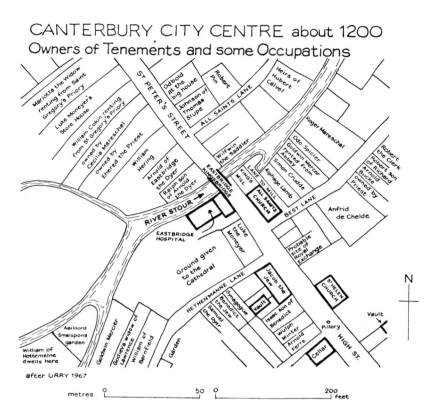

24 Canterbury city centre, c. 1200: Owners of tenements and some occupations.

Medieval town houses

The surviving buildings of the sixteenth century and earlier have not been adequately studied and recorded in most towns (Pantin, 1963) and those that do survive are often not the typical houses of the Middle Ages. For example the 'Jew's' or 'Norman' houses of Lincoln, Southampton, York and Bury St Edmunds are exceptions, being of good quality workmanship and built in stone. Most of the early town buildings were probably of wood and have not survived. Some have now been examined in archaeological excavations on redevelopment sites, but often the traces they leave are slight. Nevertheless such work usually provides the only evidence of buildings which rarely appear in the documentary record.

Medieval houses and shops can remain unrecognized behind later façades or encased in later buildings (Plate IX). Patient and skilful examination of interiors and roof spaces has led to the identification of many such buildings (Parker, 1971; Pantin, 1947; Laithwaite, 1973; Portman, 1966). Work on warehouses, workshops and other ancillary buildings of this period has been relatively neglected.

Despite study of the architectural and structural features of buildings, surprisingly little attention has been paid to their plans in relation to the plots on which they stand. Pantin, however, has distinguished two main types—the 'Parallel' type where the hall lies parallel to the street and the 'Right-Angle' type where the hall is at right angles to the street. The former may be 'extended' with attached solar and other rooms parallel to the street; such buildings may have courtyards and side wings, or the hall may occupy most of the frontage. Elsewhere 'double range' plans are apparent with shops or outbuildings and even courtyards between the hall and the street. 'Right-angle' buildings frequently occupy narrow plots and the conventional three-unit plan of hall, solar and services is strung out along the plot with an alley at the side.

The considerable variation in the plans of medieval buildings is to a large extent a reflection of the size of plot available to the builder. A wide-fronted plot would enable a building complex similar to a rural farm to be erected, while a narrow plot would clearly necessitate some variation or cramping of the normal arrangement. Except in the older, long established towns (Urry, 1967; Salter 1960 and 1969) most burgage plots were wide enough for a substantial farm-type complex. Even half-burgages of 25–30 feet could accommodate a hall and rooms parallel with the street. However, with the further division of burgage plots and competition for street frontages, this inevitably became difficult. Buildings with gables onto the street and halls behind became more common and this is the pattern frequently seen today.

Medieval town defences

The most recent study of town defences (Turner, 1971) has listed over 130 towns in England and Wales known to have had defences of some sort during the Middle Ages but the eventual total may well be about 200. In Scotland, where town defences have been little studied, a further dozen or so examples are known at present.

In its widest sense the term 'town defence' has been used to embrace everything from clearly defensive stone walls to simple bargates whose function was to control access to markets and the collection of tolls. Towns with complete circuits of stone walls range from major cities like York to the 33 acres of Cowbridge. Elsewhere stone walls formed only part of the circuit, the remainder being protected by timber stockades, as at Stafford, or open to river frontages, as at Chepstow. Earthwork defences which presumably carried timber pallisades, existed at Boston, Cambridge, Ipswich, St Albans, Tonbridge, Salisbury, Taunton and Lichfield. Gates without any other defences existed at Glasgow, New Aberdeen, Chesterfield, Bewdley, Tewkesbury and Henley-in-Arden.

The most elaborate part of the defences, the gates, were frequently the first element to be built. The simplest form was a rectangular tower with a passage through, used in York in the eleventh-century Bootham Bar. This returned to favour in the late fourteenth century at Winchester West Gate (c. 1390) and at Coventry in the surviving Cook Street and Swanswell Gates of the fifteenth century. D-shaped towers on either side of the gate were widely employed in the later thirteenth century, examples including the Upper Gate at Conway and the West Gate at Caernarvon (1283–6), while in the mid-fourteenth century circular towers were used at the Land Gate, Rye, Strand Gate, Winchelsea, and West Gate, Canterbury. Some town gates achieved additional protection by the existence of a projecting barbican, as at the Walmgate Bar, York. Elsewhere many town gates included accommodation of some sort over the entry. At Langport and the two surviving gates at Warwick the arches are surmounted by chapels. Gates also existed on bridges, detached from the main line of walls and in towns which had no other defences. Only two examples survive, at Warkworth and Monmouth, but they were formerly much more widespread, documented examples occurring at Bedford, Oxford, Bewdley, Bridgnorth, Holt, Shrewsbury, Durham and Newcastle-on-Tyne.

Apart from their gates most walls had mural towers. The earliest seem to have been shallow semicircular bastions, superseded after about 1260 by D-shaped towers. Later, horseshoe-shaped, circular, polygonal and square towers were used. Several towns had spurworks, usually to protect their harbours (Conway, 1282 and Chester, 1322), while another means of defence involved towers between which a boom or chain could be suspended across the water. At Norwich this arrangement was in use in the mid-fourteenth century and at Portsmouth it was introduced in the early fifteenth century.

Some medieval town walls were constructed along the course of Roman or Saxon predecessors without any change to the circuit as at Colchester and Chichester. Others reused the earlier alignments with very minor changes such as London and Leicester. At Chester, Rochester and Gloucester (Hurst, 1972–4) the area defended in medieval times was more extensive, with only parts of the Roman alignments reused in each case.

There is little documentary evidence for new town walls being built in Norman times, but in the thirteenth century a large number of murage grants indicates considerable activity. In some cases masonry walls were simply replacing defensive earthworks. The distribution of medieval walled towns underlines the insecurity of the Welsh border and the south and east coasts, but increasingly town walls were becoming a matter of prestige. As more and more towns acquired their independence through charters, the qualities of urban life which they possessed needed not only to be protected, but to be seen to be protected. Coventry, which had risen rapidly from total obscurity to the fourth largest town in England by the fourteenth century, acquired its first murage grant in 1328. Construction was not completed until 1539, by which time most town walls were obsolete, and the total circuit of over two miles can hardly have been defensible (Gooder, 1967).

Several towns enlarged their defended circuit during medieval times by taking in suburbs within extended wall alignments. At Bristol the walls of 1200 were totally replaced on all sides during the following centuries. At Lincoln the Roman defences continued in use, but extensive suburbs to north and south were enclosed within earthworks and gates. At Newcastle-on-Tyne there are two striking re-entrants along the course of the wall, which originally connected with the castle (Fig. 37). On the eastern side the wall was extended down to the Tyne between 1298 and 1307, to include the village of Pandon. The western re-entrant is now believed to represent a change of policy during construction (Harbottle, 1969). Such changes of area were not confined to large towns. At Carmarthen the area walled in 1233 was supplemented by a planned extension to the east, walled in 1415, which increased the defended area by over 200 per cent.

The survival of walls varies enormously. At Caernarvon and Conway the entire circuit of walls and gates survives virtually complete. Chester retains its walls almost complete, but has lost its gates. York (Fig. 1), Chepstow, Tenby and the abandoned town of Denbigh (Fig. 25) retain the greater part of their circuits. The walls of Oxford, Canterbury and Southampton are well preserved in some areas but

103

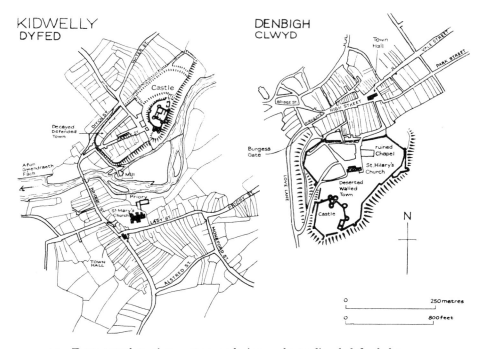

KIDWELLY
DYFED

DENBIGH
CLWYD

25   Extra-mural market centres replacing early medieval defended towns.

elsewhere have been lost virtually without trace.   Many towns have
small fragments remaining, often hidden in back gardens and under
later buildings.   In a few cases all trace of town walls known to have
existed have now gone, Barnstaple, Doncaster and Aberystwyth being
examples.   However the reconstruction of such vanished alignments
is possible using early maps, street names, documentary references and
detailed field-work.   Wall courses continued to function as parish and
property boundaries long after their defensive functions had lapsed
and their actual fabric decayed.   Odd fragments of medieval masonry
and reused stonework may be traced around their course.   There may
be sharp breaks of slope on the wall line because the best use was made
of natural slopes, the effect of which was reinforced by the build-up
of refuse and debris inside the town.   Street alignments may be very
informative, ring-lanes being found on either side of the wall course.
Culs-de-sac terminating inside the town wall also mark its course; and

knots of roads focus at gate sites. Where town ditches existed, they may be traced by strips of open ground which were shunned by later builders or by lines of buildings with subsidence cracks (Aston and Rowley, 1974). Even with all these possible clues a well-documented town wall may sometimes vanish so completely as to defy all attempts to trace its course, as at Haverfordwest.

There are probably a few cases where documentary evidence exists, but no wall was ever built. The borough charter of Bala allowed it to be defended and murage grants for Crickhowell, Ruthin and Overton are recorded but there is no indication that defence works were ever begun at these places.

Castles

In Saxon towns castles were latecomers and as the intent of the Norman conquerors was to dominate and subdue potential centres of trouble, their strongholds were superimposed on towns, regardless of what was there before. In Lincoln no less than 166 houses were destroyed to make way for the castle, in Shrewsbury 51. The Domesday Book records similar events elsewhere, and even today the course of roads such as Oxford's Castle Street, or Colchester's High Street, show evidence of diversion around this new feature of the townscape.

Some castles, such as Warwick, Alnwick and Windsor, developed into great residences which still occupy large areas of the town. Others disappeared at an early stage leaving little trace. They may be remembered by street names or by street alignments curving around their defences (Fig. 11).

In contrast to pre-Norman towns, many later medieval towns included a castle as an integral part. This is particularly evident in Welsh plantations such as Beaumaris, Brecon, Conway and Flint. The unity of town and castle is emphasized on sites like Old Kidwelly and Denbigh, where both are now forsaken (Fig. 25). Sometimes, however, the castle precedes the town. At Bala the small Norman motte has no relevance whatsoever to the fourteenth-century town standing alongside it, and at Caernarvon the Edwardian castle has a kidney-shaped plan because it incorporates the site of an earlier Norman castle.

Monastic precincts

Monasteries were an important element in many towns, the most powerful group being the wealthy pre-Conquest Benedictine foundations, although the Augustinian canons also possessed major houses in towns. Generally the later reformed monastic orders, such as the Cistercians, shunned urban sites.

The precinct of a wealthy monastery could occupy much of a town and at Durham the cathedral and castle occupy so much of the constricted meander-core site that there is little space available for secular development. In many walled towns ecclesiastical or monastic precincts had separate defences, as at Lincoln and Worcester and in some cases, such as Bury St Edmunds, Salisbury and Lichfield these were stronger than the defences of the town itself. In Reading, Ely and Evesham the monastic precinct was the only part of the town to have medieval defences.

The steady expansion of religious institutions often had considerable effects on the townscape, as secular institutions were reduced in importance. The area occupied by religious precincts in Canterbury, for example, was enormous and at Oxford collegiate growth dominated more than half the walled city.

The various orders of Friars did not gain a foothold in towns until the middle of the thirteenth century. At first they simply occupied whatever premises they could find, but as they progressed, they acquired their own sites on which they developed a simplified form of the monastic precinct. These sites are often cramped, and tend to be towards the town margins (Fig. 13). As friaries and hospitals relied heavily on the surplus wealth of the town population for their support, the number and size of such institutions can be used as a rough gauge of the town's prosperity.

Parish churches

The church in most medieval communities was the major public building and it reflects many aspects of the development of its community. It served as a place for business, public assembly, storage and a variety of other functions, in addition to its religious use. In towns they are usually the oldest buildings which survive, the site, and in some cases the actual fabric, having been used for the same purpose for more than a thousand years.

One of the most striking differences between medieval towns is the provision of many parish churches in some towns and only one in others. Within the walls of London there were no less than ninety-seven medieval parish churches; Norwich had fifty-six, York thirty-nine, Lincoln, thirty-four, Exeter sixteen, Oxford and Wallingford thirteen, and many other towns had ten or a dozen. In addition most had a number outside their walls. By contrast Grantham, Great

Yarmouth and Boston had only one church each. The number is not an indication of the town's prosperity or a reflection of its expansion but is related to its antiquity. Before the Gregorian reforms of the late eleventh century, churches had been attached to private estates and remained the personal property of the layman who had built them. Old towns partitioned amongst many landowners were therefore often furnished with many churches, some of them extremely small. Rationalization of parishes after the twelfth century tended to eliminate some of the smaller churches. The process was slow, however, and many towns are still over-provided. The present problem of what to do with the redundant churches is serious. In Norwich, for example, of thirty-one churches surviving within the walls, only six are now needed for ecclesiastical use (Jesson, 1973).

The church often indicates the earliest agricultural nucleus onto which new towns were grafted and the intrusion of a new town into an established parish pattern often created difficulties. At Kidwelly, for example, the parish church was four miles from the town. Chapels-of-ease could be built to serve the new communities, these being often identified by the lack of churchyards (because they never acquired independent rights of burial), or the 'encroaching' nature of their sites into market-places (Pontefract, Fig. 15; Henley-in-Arden, Fig. 19; and Bewdley, p. 80).

A further feature of town churches worthy of closer study is their date and dominant period. Because they provided an outlet for the surplus wealth of the feudal lord, the merchant class, or of the community as a whole, they will often mirror the fortunes of the town. At Henley-in-Arden the church of Beaudesert, the manorial centre, is solidly Norman, while the chapel-of-ease in the new town itself, less than 200 yards away across the River Alne, is mostly fifteenth century (Fig. 19). The magnificent perpendicular churches associated with the wool trade and medieval prosperity in the Cotswolds and East Anglia—Northleach, Fairford, Burford, Lavenham, Long Melford—are well known. The church will often also indicate the decay of a town. The magnificent naveless chancel with its ruined walls and blocked arches is an eloquent reminder of Winchelsea's former importance.

Medieval suburbs

Extra-mural development was well advanced before the Norman Conquest, and early suburbs in some towns like Hereford and North-ampton later became town centres. The eleventh and twelfth centuries saw a continuation of suburban growth along the approach roads outside town gates. Most suburbs were relatively poor, but there were a few conspicuous exceptions. Outside the west end of London an aristocratic quarter was already growing early in the Middle Ages, while in Bristol the magnificent church of St Mary clearly reflects the wealth of the Redcliffe suburb. In Lincoln and Canterbury, however, suburbs which were fashionable in the twelfth century were largely deserted by the rich in the thirteenth. The valuable privileges being acquired by intra-mural communities after c. 1200 hastened the decline of many suburbs.

Suburbs tended to be natural locations for activities requiring plenty of space and for trades which constituted a fire risk or health hazard. Thus from an early date we find horse- and cattle-markets such as London's Smithfield, held outside the walls. Increasingly sophisticated borough organizations often banished unpleasant activities such as tanning outside the walls, to leave traces in such street names as Tenter Banks at Stafford and Skinners Lane at Caernarvon. Potters, fullers, and above all, blacksmiths, also usually operated in the suburbs.

Because of the space they required, most religious houses founded after about 1100 had to seek suburban sites; and in the case of the Benedictine priory east of Cardigan or the Augustinian priory at Taunton, the monastic complex acted as a magnet, drawing out suburban development. Friaries were more dependent on the towns for their support, and although, as latecomers their sites were often marginal, they are frequently within the walls. Hospitals on the other hand, are usually suburban, often on the exit roads. Leper hospitals, which were widespread by the twelfth century, were for obvious reasons sited away from the built-up area.

Chapter VI

Tudor and Stuart Towns

By the end of the fifteenth century the basic distribution of market towns in Britain was substantially complete. Another three or four centuries would elapse before there was any further major change in the pattern of urbanization. After the last of the medieval new towns, Queenborough and Bewdley, there was a lapse of six or seven generations before another town was founded in Britain. The creation of Fraserburgh in 1570 was followed by a mere trickle of half-a-dozen further new towns before the end of the seventeenth century.

The most striking feature of Tudor towns in Britain was the phenomenal rise of London which by 1523 was already ten times wealthier than the greatest provincial towns. Its growth continued unabated in the seventeenth century, engulfing Westminster and Southwark, and also spreading northwards and eastwards. Its prosperity may readily be deduced by the rapidity with which it recovered from the Great Fire of 1666, which we shall examine in more detail later.

There was some fluctuation in the relative importance of the main provincial towns. York, which had retained its position as the second city throughout medieval times, was beginning to lose ground in the sixteenth century, and by about 1700 had fallen well behind. Norwich took its place for a time; although Leland speaks of its 'sad decay', it was given a new lease of life by the settlement of Flemish immigrant weavers. The most successful of the medieval 'new towns', Newcastle-on-Tyne, was almost certainly among the four main provincial towns, its chief trade being the export of coal to London.

The eastern side of England continued to be economically dominant during the sixteenth century, as it had been in medieval times, but the tilting of the balance westwards was increasing. By 1700, Bristol, profiting from the increase in Atlantic trade, had displaced Norwich at third place, while Exeter, Salisbury and Worcester had also risen rapidly from comparative obscurity.

In the towns below the rank of provincial capitals there was also considerable variation in relative prosperity during the sixteenth and seventeenth centuries. In Tudor times Southampton was booming as an outport for London, many ships preferring to land their wares there for transport overland to the capital, rather than attempt the awkward sea passage up the Channel and round the North Foreland. It had a large colony of Florentine and Genoese merchants. However, the changing pattern of European trade, with the decay of the Italian cities and the rise of Antwerp, led to an increasing amount of business being handled in London itself, and Southampton declined accordingly. It suffered severely from the Plague in 1665, and Celia Fiennes described it as 'almost forsooke and neglected'. (Morgan and Peberdy, 1968).

The effect of competition between neighbouring ports or market towns is often striking during this period. Chester, in Tudor times still an important border town and Irish port, was strangled by the silting of the Dee estuary. By the end of the seventeenth century its place had been taken by Liverpool, formerly a medieval new town but now a veritable 'London in miniature'. At Abingdon a new bridge over the Thames built in 1416 had drawn trade away from the older crossing-point at Wallingford, which Leland describes as in sad decay, its thirteen medieval churches reduced already to the three which remain today. Similarly Bewdley was beginning to overhaul its older rival, Bridgnorth, as the main Severn river port for the West Midlands, and Ware was eclipsing the trade of the old county town of Hertford.

Many other once important medieval towns were in decay. Changes in the organization of the woollen cloth industry had robbed a number of places of their chief medieval trade. Leland comments of Brackley which once 'was a Staple for Wolle, privileged with a Mayor', that it 'by Estimacion of old Ruines hath had many Stretes in it, and that large'. He paints a similarly graphic picture of Boston, while King's Lynn and Stamford were also declining through loss of their wool trade. In Lincoln the number of parish churches had fallen in two generations from thirty-four to eighteen. Silting of harbours was another adverse factor, with several of the medieval Cinque ports affected. New Winchelsea, severely damaged by successive French and Spanish raids during the fourteenth and fifteenth centuries, received its final blow with the silting of its harbour in Elizabeth's reign, and today remains an empty shell of a town (Fig. 21). Rye, which took on Winchelsea's role briefly after its decline, was in turn, according to Camden, beginning 'to complain that the sea abandoneth it'; Celia Fiennes reported its harbour as choked by sand and it relapsed to become a minor local market centre. Leland describes the same story at Hythe and Sandwich. In contrast, on the east coast, the ancient Saxon town of Dunwich was being washed away by the sea: five parish churches had gone in medieval times, two more in the first half of the sixteenth century, two of the town gates went over the cliff in 1570, and in 1677 the sea broke into the market-place. The last of Dunwich's medieval churches and the site of another town gate have been swallowed up in this century. Another Saxon town, in decline for economic rather than physical reasons, was Thetford, where Celia Fiennes noted that it had been 'formerly a large place but now much decay'd and the ruines only shews its dimensions'. Yet another cause of decay was the removal of the military significance of a place. Flint, although still a shire town at the time of Celia Fiennes's visit, was 'a very ragged place, many villages in England are better, the houses all thatched and stone walls but so decay'd that in many places ready to tumble down . . .'. John Speed's plan of 1610 shows only a small number of houses scattered about within the defences.

In contrast, the sixteenth and seventeenth centuries saw a great increase in the prosperity of a number of seaports, such as Dartmouth, and, indeed, the foundation of some new ports, which we shall examine below. Towards the end of the period the rapid rise of new industrial centres like Halifax, Sheffield, Manchester, Birmingham and Wolverhampton added a new dimension to the townscapes of Britain and foreshadowed a development which was to accelerate rapidly a century and a half later.

The social structure of Tudor and Stuart towns

The social structure of towns in the sixteenth and seventeenth centuries need not concern us except to note two aspects which were particularly influential on their physical appearance. One tendency, developing in late medieval times and reaching a peak in the sixteenth century, was for the prosperity and importance of a town to be inflated out of all proportion to its size by the contribution of one individual or family: Thomas Spring of Lavenham, William Stumpe of Malmesbury, Thomas Horton of Bradford-on-Avon, or the almost legendary John Smallwood, 'Jack of Newbury'. These men were clothiers, and their contribution to the townscape will be discussed further below. Even in major provincial capitals similar figures can be seen: William Crudge, Merchant of Exeter; Robert Jannys, grocer of Norwich; the Marlers, grocers in Coventry. It is a striking feature of most of these successful urban families of the early sixteenth century that they rarely lasted more than three generations, and made no attempt to retain urban property as a long-term investment (Hoskins, 1956). In a large town with a broad-based economy the removal of a wealthy merchant family might not have mattered greatly; but in a smaller town the effect might have been serious. Leland comments on the decay of Bath, which had been seriously affected by misfortune to its dominant clothing industry. After the 1570s the situation began to change, as population increased rapidly in the towns and there was more interest in urban property as an investment. In a number of towns there is clear evidence of merchants financing the building of new streets.

The second important tendency is the increasing segregation of the poor in certain districts of the town. Although as late as the sixteenth century there was still some mixing of social classes outside those few principal streets which had long been the preserve of the well-to-do, the general tendency was for the back lanes and side streets within the walls, and the suburbs where land was cheaper, to become increasingly the home of the labouring classes. In Warwick, for example, in the 1582 household lists there is a strong contrast between the prosperous rib of High Street and Jury Street running through the centre of the town and the poor suburbs of West Street and Saltisford. This pattern was not without its variations. In Leicester in the sixteenth century Hoskins (Hoskins, 1955b) has shown that the suburb outside the south gate was the poorest part of the town, and the north-eastern suburbs were also poor; but in complete contrast the south-eastern suburb was much wealthier, perhaps because of its position alongside the busy London road.

The town plan in the sixteenth and seventeenth centuries

At the beginning of the sixteenth century most towns outside London were still small, and contained considerable open space within their boundaries. This was true even of provincial capitals. In Exeter, the fifth city of England in 1523, nearly one third of its intra-mural area was still unbuilt, while Norwich, the largest provincial town of all, could still be described as a city interspersed with orchards.

The basic street plan of most towns was well established by the end of the medieval period, and expansion could be accommodated in several ways: subdivision of burgage plots, by infill of the open spaces within the town, colonization of abandoned castle and town-defence sites and monastic precincts thrown onto the market after the Dissolution (1535–9), and by extension along suburban streets. Radical alterations or innovations in the town plan are not evident on any scale until the last half of the seventeenth century, and then they are rare.

Streets and squares

It is difficult to assess how many completely new streets were added
to towns during the sixteenth and seventeenth centuries. Stow's
survey of London describes much building activity in the East End
by Elizabethan merchants and shipwrights, and the growth of London
can be followed in some detail from cartographic evidence (Stow,
1598). Street names sometimes provide clues. New Street in Plymouth was built by one of the town's principal merchants in the
sixteenth century, and as two other streets in the same town are also
named after contemporary wealthy merchants, it is likely that they
have a similar origin (Hoskins, 1956). In Glasgow there is a street
called Candleriggs, the second element of whose name clearly indicates
that it was laid out over the town fields. In the mid-seventeenth
century the magistrates forbade the trade of candle-making within
a hundred yards of any existing dwelling, and they gave the candle-
makers permission to build instead on a field just outside the medieval
town. This appears to be the only new street added to Glasgow's
medieval street pattern before the eighteenth century (Kellett, 1969).
Many new streets of this period followed a conservative pattern and
it may be very difficult to identify them without documentary evidence.
In Bicester modern development along the line of Sheep Street has
consistently failed to reveal medieval material, and J. C. Blomfield,
a local historian of the nineteenth century, says that the street was
laid out in the seventeenth century; but its layout, with long strip
properties on either side, is indistinguishable from that of a medieval
street. At Frome, a whole new area, Trinity, was built.

In 1630 a completely new concept in town planning was introduced
from the Continent. Inevitably this appeared first and was developed
most widely in London. After the Dissolution the first Earl of
Bedford had acquired a block of land on the site of the garden of
the convent of Westminster. The fourth Earl decided to develop
this as a high-class residential area, and for this purpose employed
the Court architect, Inigo Jones. Jones had visited Italy to study the
work of the sixteenth-century architect Andrea Palladio, and had
returned to introduce into England a style of Italian Renaissance
architecture which was totally different from anything else then being
built. He also introduced on the Earl of Bedford's estate of Covent
Garden a town-planning concept which was without precedent in
England at that time—the Italian idea of the piazza (Webber, 1969).
The central feature of the project was an open square to the north
of the garden of Bedford House. Terraces of uniform brick houses

with ground-floor loggias lined two sides while the remaining side was occupied by a new classical church flanked by two isolated houses.

At first Covent Garden fulfilled its intended function as an aristocratic residential area; but as the tide of fashion moved westwards its decline set in. Permission to hold a daily vegetable-market in the square was acquired as early as 1671. Bedford House was demolished in 1703 and replaced with poorer housing. It became a haunt of the theatrical community, and acquired considerable notoriety for its night life. The last part of Jones's terraces was demolished in 1890. Today all that remains to give an impression of the original plan is the church of St Paul, rebuilt to the same design in 1795, and the western corner of James Street, reconstructed on the original model.

Inigo Jones was involved in other town-planning projects in London, particularly with Great Queen Street, regarded as the first regular street in the capital with an integrated architectural design (1635–40). He was, however, greatly handicapped by the political and religious troubles of his time, and we have to wait some thirty years before his example was followed. For the remainder of the century London was the only city to display much evidence of the new town-planning ideas, as the West End was developed in a whole series of squares and subsidiary streets (Fig. 26). Bloomsbury Square, laid out in 1661 to the south of Lord Southampton's new mansion, was the first London square to be called by that name. St James's Square was developed on similar lines by Lord St Albans after 1665, and, like Covent Garden, was given its own church, St James, Piccadilly, designed by Sir Christopher Wren (1682–4). The plague of 1665 and the Great Fire in the following year accelerated the movement of wealthy families out of the city to the new western suburbs, and the combination of great landlord and speculative builder operating through the system of building leases created rapid development towards the end of the century. Soho Square, Red Lion Square, Old Bond Street, Downing Street, Essex Street, Buckingham Street, Villiers Street and Great Ormond Street were amongst the new creations of this period.

The most grandiose town-planning scheme of the seventeenth century in the end never achieved fruition. One of the factors in the westward movement of the aristocracy noted above was the Great Fire of London, which began in Pudding Lane on 2 September 1666 and raged on an unprecedented scale for three days, devastating 373 acres within the walls (about 80 per cent of the city), another 63 acres outside the walls, destroyed 13,200 houses, eighty-four churches, and many other important buildings.

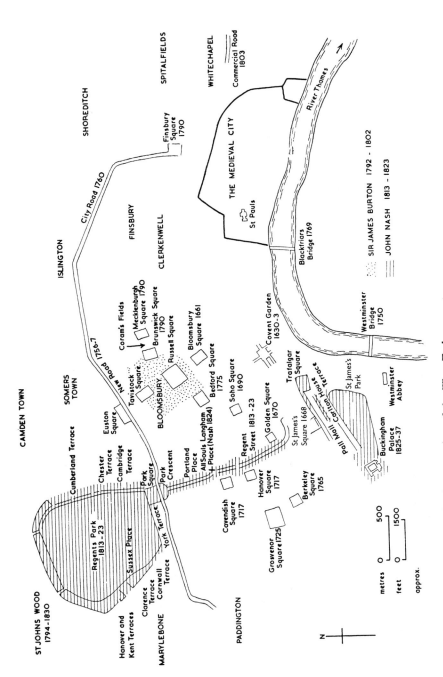

CAMDEN TOWN

ST JOHNS WOOD
1794-1830

Hanover and
Kent Terraces

Clarence
Terrace
Cornwall
Terrace
MARYLEBONE

PADDINGTON

Cumberland Terrace

Chester
Terrace
Cambridge
Terrace

Regents Park
1813-23

Sussex Place

York Terrace

Park
Square

Park
Crescent

Portland
Place

AllSouls Langham
+ Place(Nash 1824)

Cavendish
Square
1717

Regent
Street 1813-23

Grosvenor
Square 1725

Hanover
Square
1717

Berkeley
Square
1765

ISLINGTON

SOMERS
TOWN

New Road 1756-7

Euston
Square

Tavistock
Square

BLOOMSBURY

Russell Square

Bedford Square
1775

Soho Square
1690

Golden Square
1670

St James's
Square 1668

Pall Mall Carlton House Terrace

St James's
Park

Buckingham
Palace
1825-37

Coram's Fields

Mecklenburgh
Square 1790

Brunswick Square
1790

Bloomsbury
Square 1661

FINSBURY

CLERKENWELL

City Road 1760

Finsbury
Square
1790

SHOREDITCH

SPITALFIELDS

WHITECHAPEL

Commercial Road
1803

THE MEDIEVAL CITY

St Pauls

River Thames

Blackfriars
Bridge 1769

Covent Garden
1630-3

Trafalgar
Square

Westminster
Abbey

Westminster
Bridge
1750

SIR JAMES BURTON 1792 - 1802

JOHN NASH 1813 - 1823

metres 0   500

feet   0   1500

approx.

N

26 London: Some elements in the expansion of the West End.

Eight days after the fire had ceased a citizen in Blackfriars began
to rebuild on the site of his old home, and King Charles II immediately
forbade any further reconstruction until the opportunity to replan the
capital on modern lines had been considered.   Several alternative
designs were submitted for the replanning of London (Fig. 27).   Two
of the proposed schemes, those of Robert Hooke and Richard New-
court, were based on the grid, and only the presence of open squares

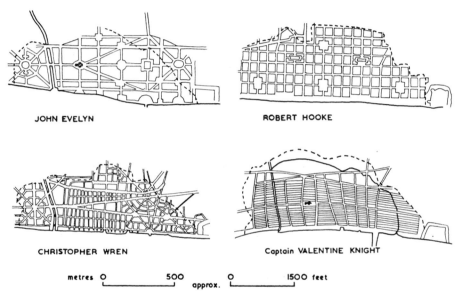

JOHN EVELYN   ROBERT HOOKE

CHRISTOPHER WREN   Captain VALENTINE KNIGHT

metres O   5OO   O   I5OO feet
                                    approx.

27 Schemes proposed for the replanning of London after the Great
Fire of 1666.

distinguishes them from an unusually ambitious medieval new-town
plan.   Three possibilities submitted by John Evelyn were more adven-
turous, including square, ovoid and diamond-shaped open spaces and
roads radiating from key points.   The first, and most revolutionary,
plan to be submitted came from Christopher Wren.   His scheme was
in a more developed Baroque style, paying considerable attention to
street vistas and intersections.   Many streets were aimed at churches
in such a way that the eye could rest on the focal point of the church
but could still anticipate further views to come beyond it.   There
were to be some half-a-dozen open spaces for purely aesthetic reasons,

including an open garden between St Paul's and the Thames. (Morris, 1972; Bell and Bell, 1969).

How far Wren intended his plan to be taken seriously and how much it was a piece of pure self-advertisement, is open to question. Certainly it had severe drawbacks, not the least of which was its failure to take into account the contours of the Walbrook valley, which would have disrupted some of the vistas which look so impressive on paper. In the event, none of the plans submitted was put into effect. The problems of replanning were so enormous, the pressure to rebuild so intense, that the authorities had to admit defeat, and allow the rebuilding of most properties on their old sites and street lines. Only two new streets, King Street and Queen Street, were created. Nonetheless regulations were brought in to control street widths, building types and materials, and if post-fire London was not very different from medieval London in plan, it was certainly vastly different in prospect.

Buildings

If the general distribution and internal plan of towns in the period was relatively static, the same cannot be said for buildings. The sixteenth and seventeenth centuries saw a tremendous amount of new construction, and a considerable legacy of the more impressive buildings has survived to the present day. From what remains, we can discern the divergence of two major architectural traditions. On the one hand we have the home-grown vernacular traditions the hallmark of which was the skiful use of local materials in a style which still owed much to late medieval Gothic. This reached its highest achievements in Elizabethan times, and is dominant up to about 1640. On the other hand we have the growing influence of imported, classical styles and of alien building materials, which have their first impact on buildings at the highest levels of society, but then slowly percolated down the social scale. Of particular significance is the increasing use of brick in towns. Brick began to reappear in Britain as early as the thirteenth century, and in late medieval times it was not uncommon in eastern England. More and more brickworks were established in different parts of the country, and by the late seventeenth century it seems to have been almost as common as timber in town building. Celia Fiennes clearly shows that brick was regarded as the hallmark of wealth and progress, while timber was characteristic of older and poorer properties. In Manchester in 1698 the houses were 'mostly of brick or stone' but 'the old houses are timber work'. There is a revealing contrast between the new port of Deal, which 'looks like a good thriveing place the building new and neate brickwork', and its neighbour, Sandwich, decayed through the silting of its harbour, 'a sad old town all timber building . . . run so to decay that except one or two good houses its just like to drop down the whole town'. Brick had come to stay, and has remained the dominant town-building material almost to the present.

1. DOMESTIC BUILDINGS

(a) *Vernacular town building:*

The 'Great Rebuilding' of the sixteenth and seventeenth centuries was first defined by Hoskins (Hoskins, 1953), and it is perhaps the most important single factor contributing to the distinctive individual character of towns today, above all to the small towns such as Lavenham, Burford, Weobley or Montacute, which have suffered less from subsequent periods of rebuilding. Even in a larger town like Worcester, greatly altered by Georgian, Victorian and modern redevelopment, good timber buildings of the sixteenth century survive in Friar Street and New Street, away from the main commercial axis.

The use of local building materials creates tremendous contrasts between individual towns of otherwise very similar character. Chipping Campden and Henley-in-Arden are both medieval new towns with a single main street, both about the same size and both retaining a high proportion of buildings of this period. They are less than twenty miles apart, but the contrast between them could hardly be greater. Campden is all yellow-grey Cotswold limestone and local brown stone slates, while Henley is predominantly timber-built, now usually painted black and white, with roofs of locally-produced red tile, which in some cases have replaced earlier thatch. Brick appeared much earlier in Henley, where there was no adequate building stone. In other parts of the country flint, chalk and a whole variety of sandstones, limestones and igneous rocks were used locally but failed to achieve much currency outside their own areas.

While stone was widely used throughout the country during the sixteenth and seventeenth centuries, timber building was even more widespread, and its techniques were of greater antiquity. The typical medieval construction of crucks and widely-spaced but massive timbers was giving way, between 1450 and 1650, to post-and-truss construction, with rectangular wall-frames, often made up of close-set vertical studding, supporting a proper roof-truss. Despite the superficial impression, this technique demanded less timber because many members were of much smaller scantling; it also had the advantage that more than one storey could be accommodated without difficulty. Frequently upper storeys projected out on overhangs, giving rise to such picturesque alleys as the Shambles in York or Cheap Street in Frome (Plate VIII). In the early seventeenth century this jettying was discontinued in towns, perhaps because of the fire risk, and the frame was built instead in a single piece. Again greater constructional experience allowed less timber to be used.

Apart from the chronological variations, there was also considerable regional difference in the treatment of timbering. In some areas the timbers were exposed, often richly carved, and the panels in the framing ornamented with lozenge, herringbone and fleur-de-lys patterns. This was a particular characteristic of the West Midlands and Welsh Border, and may be seen at the Feathers Inn, Ludlow (1603) or Leominster Market Hall (1633). In East Anglia the timbers were covered with plaster, which was itself decorated with moulded designs or *pargetting*, examples including the Ancient House at Clare and Sparrowe's House at Ipswich (c. 1670). In districts as far apart as Norfolk and Somerset the timbers were plastered and colour-washed, while in the South-East they were often covered with tile-hanging or weatherboarding (Clifton-Taylor, 1972).

Timber building reached its greatest architectural achievements less than a century before it finally went out of fashion. Wood was in increasingly short supply, and its demise in building was hastened by a series of disastrous fires, in Nantwich in 1583, Dorchester in 1613, London in 1666, Northampton in 1675 and Warwick in 1694. Subsequent rebuilding using combustible materials was usually expressly forbidden.

As with medieval houses, the vernacular buildings of the sixteenth and seventeenth centuries which have survived are not entirely representative. Documentary references give a broader picture. In London we are told that in the most important streets, 'the houses of the citizens . . . are very narrow in the front towards the street, but are built five or six roofs high, commonly of timber and clay with plaster'. The main streets of the provincial capitals may have experienced similar congestion, and the most extreme example of all was Edinburgh. It was so constricted by its site, its walls, and the narrow limits of its Royalty that, by 1752, its 'houses stand more crowded than in any other town in Europe, and are built to a height that is almost incredible'. Little physical evidence remains of such buildings; they have nearly all been swept away by slum clearance and redevelopment. In any case, they were probably always exceptional. In Leicester few houses of this date rose over two floors, and only a small minority had attics or a cock-loft on the third floor (Hoskins, 1955b). What the smaller town labourers' cottages were like is very difficult to ascertain; the poorer classes rarely left wills, having virtually nothing to leave, and their houses have not survived.

(b) Renaissance architecture:
The first impact of the Renaissance was on the country houses of the landed gentry. On the whole Elizabethan and Jacobean Renaissance styles are poorly represented in towns. Only when Inigo Jones became Surveyor-General of Works to the Crown in 1615 does any building in the new style begin, and even then it is rare outside London.

Jones's most influential building was the great Whitehall Palace, of which only the Banqueting Hall (1619) was ever built. Its plan was rectangular and compact. The ground floor has alternately triangular and segmental window pediments between Ionic pilasters; the upper storey has Corinthian pilasters with a carved frieze of masks and swags at the level of its capitals. Jones's lesser town houses are exemplified by Covent Garden: brick-built with stone dressings and tall, plain, dignified façades, introducing a fenestration pattern widely copied in Georgian building, with the tallest windows on the first floor and the smallest on the top floor. (West, 1963; Kidson, Murray and Thompson, 1965).

Inigo Jones's impact on domestic architecture, as on town planning, was enormous, but its effect was delayed until the last quarter of the seventeenth century. More settled social conditions and the increasing practice on the part of the landed gentry to keep a town house for the winter season in their nearest provincial capital were two of the factors involved. Also important was the opportunity for complete rebuilding presented in towns devastated by fire, which speeded the spread of Renaissance ideas down to the smaller domestic range. In London in 1666 the Commissioners for Rebuilding insisted on uniform street frontages without overhanging eaves. All houses were to be of brick or stone, and wall thickness and size of floor and roof timbers were rigidly controlled. In six of the principal thoroughfares all houses were to be no more or less than four storeys, in other 'streets of note' three storeys, and in back lanes two storeys only. (Reddaway, 1940). Little domestic building of this period has survived in London, but an impression of the effect may still be seen in Warwick, which underwent a similar experience when some 250 houses were destroyed in a fire in 1694. Again the opportunity was taken to widen the principal streets and to outlaw timber and thatch. All houses were to be of brick, stone and tile, and of two storeys with garret and cellar. Rooms were to be 10 feet from floor to ceiling, and walls 18 inches thick at the ground floor, 13 inches at first-floor level and eight inches at the garret; the ground floor was to be 14 inches above street level, with steps up. Three years after the fire Celia Fiennes found Warwick's 'streets very handsome and the buildings regular and fine', while Defoe declared that 'few towns in England present so fine an appearance' (Plate XI).

The domestic house style of the late seventeenth century is usually described as 'Queen Anne', although it was well established before her reign. It is characteristically rectangular in plan, occasionally with short wings. The plain symmetrical brick façade has prominent stone quoins and dressings, rectangular windows of the sash type imported from Holland in the 1680s, and doorways with triangular or rounded pediments or shell canopies. Roofs are steep-pitched and hipped, with projecting dormers above a cornice. Chimneys are large. Good examples include Fenton House, Hampstead (1693), Landor House, Warwick (1692) and Northgate House, Warwick (1698).

2. CIVIC BUILDING

One of the important effects of the Reformation was to divert benefactions away from the church and towards civic projects. Wealthy townspeople no longer poured their surplus wealth into the endowment and embellishment of chantry chapels, but turned instead to improving access to their town by building bridges and causeways or paving streets, and to increasing its commercial, educational and social facilities. Examples were already beginning to appear in the late fifteenth century with Maud Heath's Causeway, a stone-pitched path four and a half miles long built in 1474 to improve the passage over the marshy Avon valley to Chippenham market, or Hugh Clopton's handsome bridge at Stratford-on-Avon, built before 1490.

Schools and almshouses were popular objects of bequests throughout the period. Lawrence Sheriff, who made a fortune as a spicer in London, founded a school in his native Rugby in 1567; Peter Blundell, clothier of Tiverton, founded his school in 1599; Monmouth Grammar School was founded in 1614 at the bequest of William Jones, a native of the town who made his fortune as a merchant in Hamburg. Camden records that grammar schools had recently been founded in Oakham, Uppingham and Shrewsbury. Original buildings of some of the smaller schools of the period survive. One of the most attractive is the little timbered grammar school founded by Robert Smyth at Market Harborough in 1614. Queen Elizabeth's Grammar School, Ashbourne, endowed in 1586 by anonymous citizens of London who had Derbyshire origins, still stands by the church, a gabled sandstone building. At Stow-on-the-Wold a plaque on the former St Edward's School records its building in 1594 at the expense of Richard Shepman, merchant of London. The beautiful gabled almshouses built by Sir Baptist Hicks at Chipping Campden in 1612 still remain, and the same man built the little arcaded stone market hall fifteen years later.

The increasing population of towns in the seventeenth century demanded improved water supplies. In the Holborn district of London Lamb's Conduit Street recalls the benefaction of William Lambe, Master of the Clothworker's Company, in 1577. Sir Hugh Middleton, a London goldsmith, financed a more elaborate scheme in 1608, involving a great cistern at Camberwell, from which lead and elm pipes led water into the city. Hobson's Conduit in Market Hill, Cambridge (1614) and Otho Nicholson's Carfax Conduit in Oxford (1616) still exist, though neither is on its original site.

The later seventeenth century saw Renaissance design being introduced fairly extensively in grander town buildings. The two University towns were witnessing a great upsurge of building activity; the Sheldonian Theatre in Oxford, begun in 1664, was Christopher Wren's first building. Wren also built Tom Tower in the same city, and carried out work at Emmanuel, Pembroke and Trinity Colleges in Cambridge. The last quarter of the century saw considerable activity in building county, town and market halls: Abingdon (1677) was fittingly described by Celia Fiennes as the finest in England. On a more modest scale, Wallingford (1670), Buckingham (1680–9), Amersham (1682), Guildford (refronted 1683), Tamworth and Woodbridge (both c. 1700) provide a sample. The Custom Houses at Exeter and King's Lynn, both built in 1681, are also good examples.

3. ECCLESIASTICAL BUILDING

As far as church building is concerned the first thirty years of the sixteenth century still belong to the medieval period. The last fling of the Perpendicular Gothic is represented by the rebuilding of Cirencester church nave (1516–30), Newbury church (1500–32) (financed by Jack of Newbury, the clothier), or of St Andrew Undershaft in London (1520–32). Heedless of the coming débâcle the great monasteries were still erecting sumptuous structures such as Abbot Lichfield's magnificent bell-tower which still dominates Evesham.

The religious upheavals of the Reformation put a stop to church building for a century, and when it recommenced it was restricted to London, to the few new port and spa towns of the period, and to the replacement of medieval churches destroyed by accident. The first classical churches appear in London: St Katherine Cree (1628–31) and St Paul, Covent Garden (1631–3, rebuilt 1795). For the latter the Earl of Bedford instructed Inigo Jones that he would be content with something not much better than a barn as he did not wish to lay out unnecessary expense. Jones promised him 'the handsomest barn in London', and gave it a great Tuscan portico with free-standing columns, the first in northern Europe, modelled on sixteenth-century Italian examples. Unfortunately this could never be used as the entry from the piazza, as Archbishop Laud insisted on the altar being at the east end.

Only one town church was built during the Commonwealth, that at Berwick-on-Tweed (1650), although some alterations were made to existing churches elsewhere, such as the building of the tower at All Hallows by the Tower in London (1658).

The Restoration is marked by several new churches dedicated to King Charles the Martyr; among them are two serving new towns of the period, at Tunbridge Wells and Falmouth. That at Tunbridge Wells is purely classical in style, rectangular, of red brick, with an attractive wooden turret. Built in 1676, it was already too small in 1690 and had to be enlarged. Falmouth church is slightly earlier, being founded in 1665. It is an extraordinary blend of Gothic and classical styles, with nave windows of broadly perpendicular style, granite columns with plastered Ionic capitals and a medieval-type roof. Its oblong tower was added in 1684.

The most important group of seventeenth-century town churches are those of post-fire London. By 1670 the reconstruction of the city had progressed to the point where attention and capital could be diverted to the replacement of the churches. Christopher Wren was commissioned to build fifty-one new churches in place of the eighty-four destroyed. The first big group of post-Reformation churches, they are generally box-shaped to provide optimum preaching conditions, and had no need of transepts or chancel. Their plans are varied, being cleverly adapted to the confined and awkwardly-shaped sites which were available. Portland stone had just been introduced into London, and was the dominant building material employed. The exteriors are usually plain, the interiors well lit by big windows and decorated with white plaster and gold leaf. The details of the design were often left to the craftsmen of each parish, Wren providing only the general plan and, at a later stage, the tower. It is the elaborate steeples which remain Wren's most distinctive contribution to the London townscape, though they are now too often dwarfed by monolithic modern tower blocks. The steeple is a Gothic concept, but

Wren was already using classical forms in the inventive and original way which became the hallmark of the Baroque architects of the following century.

Fifteen of Wren's churches were destroyed by bombing in 1940–1; and between 1782 and 1939 no less than nineteen Wren churches were deliberately pulled down to pay for new suburban churches. Today only sixteen survive substantially as he built them. Among the most important are St Martin Ludgate, St Vedast Foster Lane, St Mary-at-Hill, and, restored after severe war damage, St Mary-le-Bow and St Bride, Fleet Street (Fig. 28). The most original of Wren's city churches is St Stephen Walbrook, which incorporated a dome, a completely revolutionary feature in an English church. This may be seen as a trial run for his crowning achievement, the new St Paul's Cathedral, begun in 1675 and completed in 1710 (Colvin, 1954).

Of the churches rebuilt late in the century in other fire-damaged towns, All Saints, Northampton, completed 1701, is a classical design owing its inspiration to Wren's St Mary-at-Hill; but St Mary's, Warwick (1698–1704) is almost a complete reversion to perpendicular Gothic (Plate XI).

The rising tide of Nonconformity resulted in the earliest wave of chapels which were to proliferate so strikingly in towns over the next 200 years. One of the best examples is the Old Baptist Chapel in Tewkesbury, hidden in a court at the back of a burgage alley off Church Street. This dates from 1626, and retains many of its seventeenth-century furnishings.

Town defences

By the beginning of the sixteenth century many town defences had already fallen into disuse and ruin, or were covered by buildings. More settled conditions had rendered defences redundant, while developments in artillery meant that medieval town walls no longer provided the protection they once afforded.

By far the best example of Tudor town defences in Britain is to be seen at the frontier town of Berwick-on-Tweed (Plate VII). Here the development of artillery defences from adaptations of medieval design is clearly demonstrated. Henry VIII added a large round gun-tower at the north-eastern corner of Edward I's original wall, and improved the defences of the castle. The next stage was the planning of a star-shaped citadel under Edward VI, straddling the southern end of the east wall. This was abandoned uncompleted in 1557 and replaced by a completely new system begun the following year. The

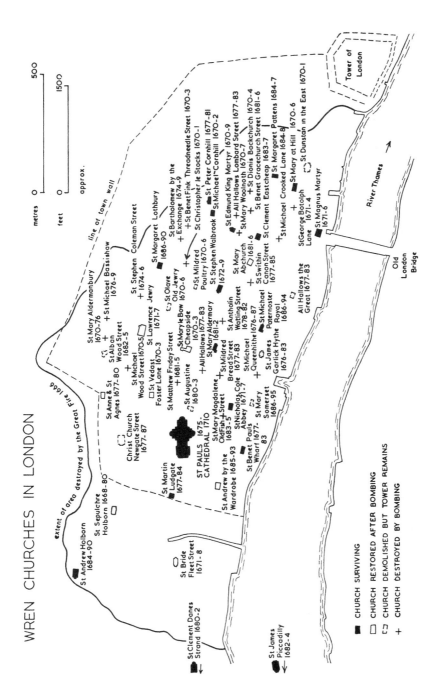

WREN CHURCHES IN LONDON

extent of area destroyed by the Great Fire 1666

line of town wall

metres 0 — 500
feet 0 — 1500
approx.

St Andrew Holborn 1684-90
St Sepulchre Holborn 1668-80
St Bride Fleet Street 1671-8
St Clement Danes Strand 1680-2
St James Piccadilly 1682-4

Christ Church Newgate Street 1677-87
St Anne & St Agnes 1677-80
St Michael Wood Street 1670-5
St Vedast, Foster Lane 1670-3
St Matthew Friday Street 1681-5
St Mary Aldermanbury 1670-76
St Alban Wood Street 1682-5
St Lawrence Jewry 1671-7
St Michael Bassishaw 1676-9
St Stephen Coleman Street 1674-6
St Margaret Lothbury 1686-90
St Martin Ludgate 1677-84
ST PAULS CATHEDRAL 1675, 1710
St Andrew by the Wardrobe 1685-93
St Augustine 1680-3
St Mary Magdalene Old Fish Street 1683-5
St Nicholas Cole Abbey 1671-7
St Benet Pauls Wharf 1677-83
St Mary le Bow Cheapside 1670-3
+ All Hallows 1677-83
St Mildred Bread Street
St Mary Aldermary 1681-2
St Antholin Watting Street 1678-82
St Michael Queenhithe 1676-87
St James Garlick Hythe 1676-83
St Mary Somerset 1686-95
St Michael Paternoster Royal 1686-94
St Olave Old Jewry 1670-6
St Mildred Poultry 1670-6
St Stephen Walbrook 1672-9
St Mary Abchurch 1681-6
St Swithin Canon Street 1677-85
All Hallows the Great 1677-83
St Bartholomew by the Exchange 1674-9
St Benet Fink Threadneedle Street 1670-3
St Christopher le Stocks 1670-1
St Peter Cornhill 1677-81
St Michael Cornhill 1670-2
St Edmund King Martyr 1670-9
All Hallows Lombard Street 1677-83
St Mary Woolnoth 1670-7
St Dionis Backchurch 1670-4
St Benet Gracechurch Street 1681-6
St Clement Eastcheap 1683-7
St Margaret Pattens 1684-7
St Michael Crooked Lane 1684-8
St Mary at Hill 1670-6
St George Botolph Lane 1671-4
St Magnus Martyr 1671-6
St Dunstan in the East 1670-1

Tower of London

River Thames

Old London Bridge

■ CHURCH SURVIVING
□ CHURCH RESTORED AFTER BOMBING
[CHURCH DEMOLISHED BUT TOWER REMAINS
+ CHURCH DESTROYED BY BOMBING

28 Wren churches in London.

loss of Calais and the very real threat of a Scottish invasion called for drastic measures, and the castle and the whole of the northern third of the town were abandoned to reduce the defensive circuit required. The extreme southern end of the medieval town was also to be excluded, but in fact this part of the plan was never carried out. Between 1558 and 1569 the existing northern and eastern sides of the new alignment were built but never fully completed; they included five great bastions with orillons which protected flanking gun emplacements covering the curtain wall between. The riverside defences still relied on the medieval wall, and this is the situation shown on John Speed's plan of 1610. Further improvements were carried out between 1639 and 1653, including the provision of earthwork parapets and cavaliers on top of the bastions (MacIvor, 1965).

No other sixteenth-century defences have survived in a condition approaching that of Berwick; at Southwold and Tilbury they have disappeared completely. Portsmouth was hastily refortified in 1539 due to the threat from France; work was substantially completed, but by 1541 the new defences had 'clene fallen down'. Some further work was carried out during the Armada scare. Harwich was also refortified in 1588, and no trace has survived. Great Yarmouth's medieval walls were reinforced with artillery defences at the same time: four great ravelins were added to seaward, three smaller bulwarks on the riverside, a star fort protected the bridgehead, and two outer bulwarks with a boom closed the estuary.

In Scotland there are remains of a town wall at Peebles built in 1570–4 and incorporating earlier gates. However, this is primitive in its form, bearing more resemblance to a medieval structure than to the elaborate defences of Berwick. A building contract for the West Port of St Andrew's is dated 1589; the gate itself was completely rebuilt in 1843.

The final phase of fortification in many English towns came during the Civil War (Fig. 29). Artillery fortifications were thrown up somewhat hastily around Colchester, Newcastle, Hartlepool, King's Lynn (Smith, 1970), and Hull. At Worcester new bastions were simply built onto the medieval wall, with a spur-work linking to a star fort outside the city, whose site survives in Fort Royal Park. At Chester, Oxford (Lattey, Parsons and Philip, 1936) and Reading (Slade, 1969) a completely new line was taken well outside the medieval perimeter. At Pontefract the Civil War defences chopped right across the long-disused Anglo-Norman defences. Very few towns have much to show of their Civil War fortifications: the best surviving example is Newark-on-Trent (R.C.H.M., 1964).

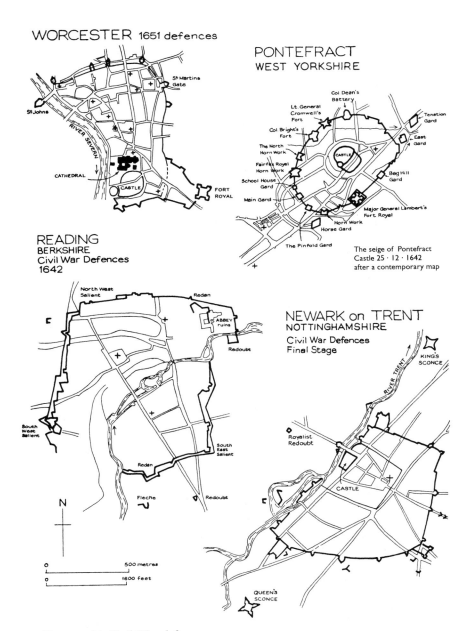

WORCESTER 1651 defences

St Martins Gate

St Johns

RIVER SEVERN

CATHEDRAL

CASTLE

FORT ROYAL

PONTEFRACT
WEST YORKSHIRE

Col. Dean's Battery

Lt. General Cromwell's Fort

Tenation Gard

Col. Bright's Fort

East Gard

The North Horn Work

Fairfax Royal Horn Work

CASTLE

School House Gard

Bag Hill Gard

Main Gard

Major General Lambert's Fort Royal

Horn Work
Horse Gard

The Pinfold Gard

The seige of Pontefract
Castle 25 · 12 · 1642
after a contemporary map

READING
BERKSHIRE
Civil War Defences
1642

North West Salient

Redan

ABBEY ruins

Redoubt

NEWARK on TRENT
NOTTINGHAMSHIRE
Civil War Defences
Final Stage

RIVER TRENT

KING'S SCONCE

South West Salient

Redan

South East Salient

Royalist Redoubt

CASTLE

Fleche

Redoubt

N

500 metres

1600 feet

QUEEN'S SCONCE

29 Towns with Civil War defences.

Civil War damage was often noted by later commentators. Celia Fiennes says of Colchester, 'formerly there was 16 Churches, tho' now much of it is ruinated', while Defoe recalls that 'It still mourns in the ruins of a civil war . . . the batter'd walls, the breaches in the turrets, and the ruin'd churches still remain. . . . The lines of contravallation, with the forts built by the besiegers . . . remain very visible in many places: but the chief of them are demolish'd'.

The industrial character of towns

Few towns had any particularly distinctive industrial character in the sixteenth century, although clothing, leather, metal-working, food and drink and building trades are widely encountered in varying proportions from town to town. Contemporary comments on the dirt and smoke of the few Midland towns engaged in salt production, such as Nantwich, Droitwich and Northwich, tend to emphasize just how unusual this was.

Many industries were still basically rural in character, but in some areas we can begin to trace the emergence of a quasi-urban landscape, with concentrated groups of craftsmen/farmers combining weaving or smithing with a smallholding. Large straggling villages and workshops were intermixed with small fields, paddocks, farmhouses and cottages. By the end of the seventeenth century new industrial agglomerations were beginning to emerge. Defoe's description of the area around Halifax, where the steep hillsides were thick with houses amid small enclosures, the women and children spinning and carding wool, the men already gravitating towards the first larger clothing manufactories, is well known. Within the parish, apart from the old church, there were already a dozen or so chapels-of-ease and about sixteen Nonconformist meeting-houses.

A combination of social, economic and technological factors was shifting the whole basis of the cloth trade away from the old urban clothing centres like Beverley, Bristol and Winchester. In the Cotswolds the old wool towns, places like Chipping Campden and Northleach, had already passed the peak of their prosperity, and a new clothing industry was becoming established along the swift-flowing streams of the south Cotswold scarp. The main centre was developing at Stroud, originally only a hamlet in Bisley, but already a separate parish by 1360. By the sixteenth century Stroudwater Scarlets were renowned all over the continent and the Stroud district was specifically exempted from an Act of 1555 which was fighting a rearguard action in trying to restrict cloth-making to the towns. A sixteenth- to seventeenth-century clothier's house, fulling-mill and weavers' cottages form a nucleus which can often still be identified at the core of the great eighteenth- to nineteenth-century mill towns which succeeded them.

In the West Midlands the smithy, rather than the weaving shop or mill, was the dominant industrial feature. In 1620 Dud Dudley tells us that 'within ten miles of Dudley Castle there be near 20,000 smiths of all sorts'. Recognizable local metal-working specialities were already developing: lock-making at Wolverhampton and Willenhall, nail-making at Dudley and Stourbridge. Court describes 'a countryside in course of becoming industrialized: more and more a strung-out web of iron-working villages, market towns next door to collieries, heaths and wastes gradually and very slowly being covered by the cottages of nailers and other persons carrying on industrial occupations in rural surroundings' (Court, 1938). Around the fringe of the Black Country even today in areas like Lower Gornal, traces of this incipient industrial townscape remain.

By the later seventeenth century towns were much more diversified in their economy, and Celia Fiennes offers many valuable observations. Cloth was still the country's main industry, but other textile trades were appearing: the manufacture of pillow-lace, for example, was noted at Honiton and Stony Stratford, where 'they sit and worke all along the streete as thick as can be'. Silk and paper mills had recently been built in Canterbury, and there were new glass works at Stourbridge and Castleford. At Pontefract 'the town is full of great Gardens walled in all round . . . on the edge of the hill so the Gardens runns down a great way, you descend into them by severall stepps; its a fruitfull place fine flowers and trees with all sorts of fruite, but that which is mostly intended is the increasing of Liquorish, which the gardens are all filled with, and any body that has but a little ground improves it for the produce of Licquorish, of which there is vast quantetyes . . .'.

New market towns

The early seventeenth century saw the beginnings of a big commercial expansion which was signalized in many areas by the establishment of new markets. Sometimes these were in old medieval towns whose markets had lapsed. In other cases some completely new market centres were initiated: Blackburn, Colne and Stevenage first acquired their markets in this period, as did the Cumbrian towns, Hawkshead, Ambleside and Shap (Millward, 1974, and Chalklin, 1974).

New ports

The stirrings of the seventeenth-century commercial revolution are reflected most clearly in the creation of several completely new port towns, of which the earliest was Falmouth. The Fal estuary had been described by Leland as 'a havyn very notable and famose . . . the most principale of al Britayne', and in 1548 Henry VIII had protected its entrance by the building of Pendennis and St Mawes Castles. The main medieval ports were further upstream at Truro and Penryn, and in 1600 there was only a single house, called Smithwick, on the site of the present town, in the parish of Budock. Then in 1613 Sir John Killigrew, a notorious privateer, established a small settlement near Smithwick which he called Pennycomequick (from Cornish *pen-y-cwm* = 'valley head' + Anglo-Saxon *wick* = village). Penryn, Truro and Helston unsuccessfully petitioned the Privy Council against their new rival, but Killigrew wrested the market right from Penryn and acquired the Custom House soon after. In 1660 Charles II ordained that 'Smithike alias Penny-come-quick' should thenceforth be called Falmouth, and a charter was granted the following year. Over the next thirty years the main street, Church Street, was developed. While little visible evidence of its origin can be seen here, a few seventeenth-century cottages still survive on the side lanes behind Market Street and down Fish Strand Hill and Quay Hill. The church, partly financed by Sir Peter Killigrew, was founded in 1665.

Whitehaven, like Falmouth, was developed by the local landowning family, the Lowthers, who had acquired the lands of the former monastery of St Bees early in the century. The estate included coal resources, and an old fishing hamlet. A market charter was acquired in 1660, but true urban growth did not begin until the 1680s when Sir John Lowther laid out a spacious rectangular grid of streets to the north-east of the existing tiny hamlet. The houses were to be three storeys high, not less than 28 feet from street level to eaves, the ground- and first-floor windows to be transomed, and the door-ways and windows to be of hewn stone. Ample provision was made for gardens. One block was left vacant for a new church, and in 1694 another site was given for a Presbyterian chapel. Most of the streets were relatively narrow, about ten yards, but the principal thoroughfare, Lowther Street, which ran through the town centre from the Lowther family residence to the waterfront, was laid out on the more generous width of 16 yards. The old chapel of White-haven was demolished to make way for Lowther Street, and its materials used in the building of a new school for the town.

As a coaling, shipbuilding and general carrier's port, Whitehaven was a rapid success. Its population was over 2,000 by 1690, and the grid of streets overlooking the harbour was fully occupied. Soon it was to rival Liverpool and Newcastle as a port. Its very success, however, destroyed its original gracious atmosphere; its gardens and open spaces were swamped over the next 200 years by a proliferation of crowded courts and alleys. Today the processes of slum clearance are making way for a new townscape of flats, but some elements of the original plan remain, including the street framework and the church, substantially of eighteenth-century date as it now stands (Bell and Bell, 1969; Millward, 1974).

Not all port foundations of the period were private ventures. Port Glasgow stands as a unique example of civic enterprise and initiative on the part of the magistrates of the parent city from which it took its name. In 1668 Provost John Anderson negotiated the purchase of a plot of land some twenty miles lower down the Clyde, and the first quays and warehouses were provided at the corporation's expense. All Glasgow merchants engaged in overseas trade were obliged to register their ships there. Its promise as a great seaport, however, was reduced by the improvements to navigation on the Clyde in the late eighteenth century which allowed large vessels to get right up to Glasgow itself (Kellett, 1969).

Deal may be quoted as an example of less deliberately planned growth. The medieval centre and old 'fisher village' mentioned by Leland was at Upper Deal, now, through the processes of coastal accretion, a mile inland. In the late seventeenth century there was considerable growth at Lower Deal, where three new main streets were built parallel with the shore. The principal landowner, the Archbishop of Canterbury, showed very little interest in its development, and the new streets were of variable width with the buildings very mixed in style and materials. The initiative to acquire a charter of incorporation and a market (realized in 1699) and even the move to build a chapel in the lower town came, not from the Archbishop, but from the community itself (Chalklin, 1974b).

Other ports were of military rather than commercial origin. Chatham dockyard was originally founded at the time of the Armada threat, and removed to its present site in 1622. Perhaps the best example, however, is Devonport, the *raison-d'être* of which was the long period of enmity with France between 1689 and 1815. Dartmouth and Falmouth were both considered as possible sites for a new strong naval base and dockyard which might counteract the threat from Brest and Rochefort across the Channel. Both were rejected in favour of a site near Plymouth, a stretch of empty flat ground adjacent to the deep water of the Hamoaze. Here the first dock was completed in 1695, and the following year the transference of naval ships began and the first houses were built outside the dockyard wall. Celia Fiennes found in 1698 'a great deale of buildings on the Dock, a very good house for the Masters and severall lesser ones and houses for their cordage and makeing ropes . . . it looks like a little town the buildings are so many, and all of marble with fine slate on rooffs . . .'. Its greatest growth came only in the later eighteenth century. Although it did not acquire its first Anglican church till 1771, by 1800 it was the biggest town in Devon and much more important than its ancient neighbour, Plymouth. It still retained at this time the somewhat prosaic name of Dock, and when in 1824 its inhabitants petitioned to change it to the more dignified Devonport the end of the war had put a stop to its mushroom growth. By 1914 it had been overhauled again by Plymouth. A slightly later development was at Portsea, where in the first decade of the eighteenth century the men employed in the naval dockyard of Portsmouth laid out a new suburb immediately north of the medieval town. By 1809 this area had acquired its own fortifications (Fig. 30).

Resorts

The only other significant new town developments of the seventeenth century foreshadowed the great expansion of fashionable wateringplaces in Georgian times. The curative properties of certain spring waters had long been recognized. At least two spas were of Roman origin. At Bath the town had acquired ownership of the springs from the abbey at the Dissolution and had attempted to promote their use by developing a parallel entertainment industry. This met with some success, as James I's queen visited the town in 1613. However, accommodation was limited to 'two or three sorry houses of entertainment', and when Beau Nash first came there in 1705 he found 'one of the poorest cities in England, its buildings extremely mean and the inhabitants rude and unpolite'. Bath's chief early rival was Buxton, also of Roman origin. A treatise on its waters was published in 1572, but again there was little significant resort development in the town. Llandrindod Wells has also been claimed as a Roman spa: Charles II was advised to take the waters there by his physician in 1670, but before 1700 it consisted of only scattered houses. Wells at Clifton and Malvern were also being exploited before the seventeenth century, but little significant development had yet taken place.

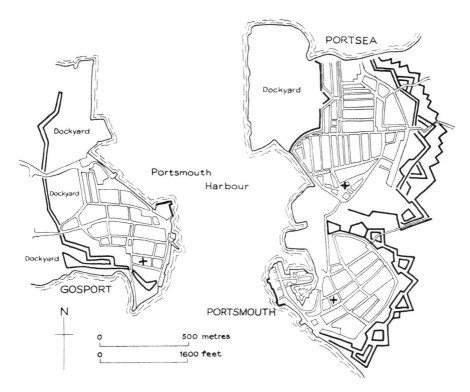

30   Post-medieval dockyard towns and their defences.

The gathering interest in the water cure is illustrated by the attempts to promote springs newly discovered during the sixteenth and seventeenth centuries. Some, such as Alford, Astrop, Starbeck, Shanklin, Malton or Bakewell, saw only limited and short-lived popularity. The success of others, such as Harrogate, Scarborough, Leamington and Matlock, was delayed for a century or more.

By far the most immediately successful discovery was made by Lord North in 1606. Returning to London from a visit to Kent, he paused to drink from a spring on the uninhabited common of Bishop's Down, some five miles south of the medieval town of Tonbridge. He noticed a yellowish scum similar to that he had seen at the renowned healing springs at Spa in the Ardennes, and took some of the water away for analysis. It was pronounced beneficial

133

and widely publicized. At first there was only a handful of cottages anywhere near the spring, and on the occasion of the first royal visit, by Henrietta Maria in 1629, the entire court had to camp on the common.

The development of the spa preceded the growth of the town which was to become Tunbridge Wells by some seventy years. The well was enclosed, and in 1638 a promenade known as the Walks, floored with mixed clay and sand, was laid out, with a double row of lime trees down the centre. Two groups of wooden cottages were begun in 1639, at Southborough and Rusthall, two miles north and one mile west respectively: these hamlets provided the chief accommodation into the 1670s. The freeholders of Bishop's Down Common had vested interests in the Rusthall and Southborough lodging-houses, and this delayed development around the well itself. The temporary booths along the Walks did not begin to be replaced by permanent shops and houses until the 1680s. Some attempt to plan this development is indicated by the banning of thatch, the insistence on slate and tile roofs and the restriction of building height to retain the open atmosphere. The shops were of a variety of design, both timber and brick. They were given an attractive link by a raised walk under a continuous arcade, carried on pillars and partly balconied. The influence of Covent Garden is clear. The lower terrace of the Walks, outside the covered arcade, was subsequently paved with the square pinkish-grey tiles from which the area takes its present name, The Pantiles (Plate XII). About a dozen of the original pantiles remain against the step to the upper terrace near the well-house; the next have since been replaced by red tiles and stone slabs. Amongst the goods for sale in the shops along The Pantiles, Celia Fiennes noted 'all sorts of curious wooden ware which this place is noted for', the Tunbridge Wells Ware first made in 1685.

The new community was served by a church built in 1676 just beyond the well; until 1887 it remained a chapel-of-ease to Tonbridge, and so has no graveyard. Nonconformity was also much in evidence: residential developments in the 1680s were taking place in two areas named Mount Ephraim and Mount Zion, bestowed by Puritan visitors reputedly because of a fancied resemblance to the site of Jerusalem. On Mount Ephraim Celia Fiennes noted 'a large Chapple, where the Presbyterians have preaching' (Bell and Bell, 1969; Chalklin, 1974b).

Tunbridge Wells in the late seventeenth century was the spa of the rich. A somewhat different development, catering mainly for the middle classes, followed on the discovery of medicinal springs a mile west of Epsom church in 1618. In Charles I's time Epsom salts were selling at 5s. an ounce, but its chief popularity was after the Restoration, when Charles II, Nell Gwynn, John Evelyn and Samuel Pepys were among its patrons. A bowling-green was opened in 1670, and five years later, the well was roofed over. Celia Fiennes was not impressed with it: 'the Well is large, without bason or pavement on the bottom, it is covered over with timber and is so darke you can scarce looke down into it . . . it look'd so dark and unpleasant, more like a dungeon, that I would not chuse to drinke it there.' Unlike Tunbridge, Epsom was already in decline as a spa by 1710, developing instead as a summer residence for London merchants, and finding alternative attractions, particularly horse-racing on Epsom Downs. Some scattered late seventeenth-century houses remain, but there is little to see of Epsom's former role as a spa. A fragment of raised pavement outside a shop in the High Street is the last remains of the Epsom Pantiles. A small modern housing estate called The Wells marks the site of the original well; a road in the estate is still called Spa Drive, and leads to the only pre-twentieth century building in the area, the Well House built as a residence in 1885.

There was also a number of lesser spas around London in the late seventeenth century, catering on the whole for the poorer classes: Streatham, Hampstead and Barnet Wells being among the more notable. About the only other discovery to give rise to significant urban growth in this period was in Scotland, at Moffat in Dumfriesshire. A sulphur spring was discovered in 1630 and chalybeate springs in 1633; it rapidly became as fashionable as the English spas, and Moffat acquired its burgh charter in 1648 (Fig. 33).

Conclusion

The sixteenth and seventeenth centuries are important as a period of transition. The small-scale medieval market town with its basis firmly in the local rural area was in the process of evolving into a very different community, with social and industrial functions on a much grander scale. The result was soon to be a divorce between the character of the town and that of its local surroundings, and a much greater uniformity in towns across the country, with alien styles of architecture and new notions of town planning gaining the ascendancy. During the transition, however, we see local building styles reaching their highest achievements and maximum regional diversity; and the remnants of this period are an invaluable contribution to the character of towns in the present century.

Chapter VII

Georgian and Regency Towns

One of the most striking features of towns in the eighteenth and early nineteenth centuries is their sheer increase in size. In London Defoe describes 'new squares and new streets rising up every day to such a prodigy of buildings, that nothing in the world does, or ever did, equal it, except old Rome in Trajan's day'. Spreading northwards, westwards and eastwards it engulfed villages like Islington, Mile End and Bethnal Green, while the construction of two new bridges over the Thames at Westminster (1750) and Blackfriars (1769) caused rapid expansion in Southwark, Lambeth and Newington. By 1830 the built-up area of London covered about thirty times the area of the medieval walled city. Birmingham, in medieval times a modest market town, was in 1830 ten times bigger. Manchester's increase in size was twelvefold over the same period. At Edinburgh the congestion of the walled medieval town had become so desperate that in the 1770s a complete new city was begun on the opposite bank of the North Loch. Glasgow similarly burst its medieval bounds in mid-century and by 1830 had undergone spectacular expansion. Even very minor urban centres showed some development during this period. Such growth was not experienced uniformly by all towns, and there are some striking changes in the urban hierarchy. London remained pre-eminent, but places like Norwich and Exeter had passed their zenith. They were overtaken during the century by a new generation of towns of very different character: Manchester, Birmingham and Liverpool, with Leeds and Sheffield not far behind. Lower down the scale, some of the old county towns, like Carlisle, Lancaster, Stafford and Warwick, began to see their local supremacy rivalled by rising new centres.

The industrial development of towns

The development of industry was a crucial factor in town growth, particularly in the later eighteenth century. The phenomenal rise of the cotton industry transformed the landscape of south-east Lancashire, with Manchester emerging as a new regional capital. Preston, Bolton, Rochdale, Bury and the other small market towns of the region expanded beyond recognition. Oldham, a small hamlet of a hundred houses in 1761, had a population of over 21,000 by 1800. In the West Riding the effect of the developing woollen textile industry on Halifax, Huddersfield and Bradford was almost equally dramatic. Here too a new regional capital emerged in Leeds, which had already outstripped its ancient rival, Wakefield, by 1700. Defoe notes the expanding cutlery trade of Sheffield, where the houses were 'dark and black, occasioned by the continued smoke of the forges, which are always at work'; similarly at Barnsley, 'eminent still for the working in iron and steel . . . [it] looks as black and smoaky as if they were all smiths that lived in it'. In the North Midlands bleak upland hamets such as Burslem and Hanley were beginning to expand on the basis of their pottery trade. In the East Midlands the old county towns of Leicester and Nottingham were developing rapidly as major centres of the hosiery industry. In the West Midlands the growing prosperity of Birmingham and the emerging Black Country was based largely on the hardware trades. In Wales, following the establishment of four big ironworks there, Merthyr Tydfil mushroomed from an isolated mountain village to the largest town in the Principality in the space of fifty years.

The biggest towns were marked by increasing localization of certain industries in specific districts. This was most marked in London where, around the fringe of the commercial centre in the City itself, there were concentrations of clock- and jewellery-makers in Shoreditch, Clerkenwell and Bishopsgate, of silk weavers in Spitalfields, and inevitably of boat-builders, rope-walks, anchor forges and the like in the riverside parishes. In Birmingham the expansion of the gun trade after about 1750 resulted in gunsmiths moving from Digbeth in the old town to a new quarter beyond Snow Hill and Steelhouse Lane, while a colony of jewellery workers, which still survives, was becoming established to the north of the Newhall Estate.

Outside these great industrial nuclei, towns served mainly as market centres for agricultural produce and manufactured goods. Defoe refers repeatedly to market towns around London supplying the capital with agricultural produce: Farnham, the greatest corn market of all, Chichester, Croydon, Chertsey, Marlow, Henley, Maldon and Woodbridge. Clothing was still the most widespread industry, flourishing particularly in the South-West, in Taunton, Frome, Devizes, Trowbridge and Bradford-on-Avon. The silk industry, introduced from the continent was present in Canterbury, Norwich, and elsewhere, and has left a legacy of mulberry trees in the towns concerned with it.

Seaports

The increasing commercial and industrial expansion of the later eighteenth century was reflected in the rapid expansion of many seaports and the creation of several completely new ones. Ports less fortunately placed often suffered from the competition. Defoe comments on Southampton's fishing activities 'but for all other trade it may be said of Southampton as of other towns, London has eaten it up'. The trade of Ipswich was similarly eclipsed. On a smaller scale, the new port of Falmouth was 'by much the richest, and best trading town in this county' by 1700 while the older port of Truro 'has been much fuller, both of houses and inhabitants, than it is now'. In Somerset, 'the town of Minehead is risen out of the decay of the towns of Porlock and Watchet' because of its more capacious harbour. The seaport of Ayr, once the fifth town of Scotland, was 'decaying and declining every day' and 'now like a place forsaken . . . nothing will save it from death, if trade does not revive'.

In contrast to this depressing picture, Bristol was now 'the greatest, the richest and the best port of trade in Great Britain, London only excepted', and Liverpool was, by 1680, already 'the next town to Bristol, and in a little time may probably exceed it, both in commerce and in numbers of people'. Defoe's prophecy was fulfilled, for twenty years later, it was 'one of the wonders of Britain . . . an opulent, flourishing and increasing trade . . . no town in England, London excepted . . . can equal Liverpool for the fineness of its streets and beauty of its building'. Later that century Newcastle, Hull and Sunderland and to a lesser extent the dockyard towns of Portsmouth/Portsea and Plymouth/Devonport were to experience similar spectacular expansion.

Of the completely new ports of the eighteenth century the most impressive took its name from its site on the superb natural harbour of Milford Haven in south-west Wales (Fig. 31). In 1793 Sir William Hamilton, owner of an estate on the north side of the inlet, obtained permission to make 'Quays, Docks and Piers and other erections'. He delegated the project to his nephew, Charles Greville, who engaged Louis Barallier of Toulon to plan the new town. A colony of Quaker whalers from Nantucket Island, Massachussets, led by Samuel Starbuck, was invited to settle the site. Street names like Starbuck Road, and Nantucket Avenue, commemorate the first settlers, while their meeting-house remains in Dartmouth Gardens. In 1797 a site for a naval dockyard was acquired on lease, and seven ships were built there over the next seventeen years. A daily service was established to Ireland, trading in coal, limestone and corn. A new church was begun in 1803, and a technical college projected.

After Greville's death in 1809, Milford's growth faltered. The first blow to the town's hopes came in 1810 when the introduction of gas lighting killed the demand for spermacetti whale oil. In 1814 the lease of the naval dockyard fell in, and when Greville's successor

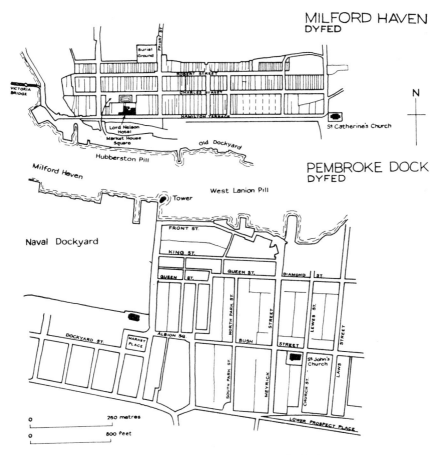

31 Eighteenth-century planned new towns on Milford Haven.

demanded a higher selling-price than had originally been agreed, the Navy promptly moved across the Haven to Pembroke Dock. Finally in 1836 the Irish packet service was removed. A period of stagnation set in, and Milford's revival had to await the coming of the railway (Rees, 1957).

The expiry of the Admiralty lease on Milford Haven dockyard and the decision to move to a new site caused a second new town to be established on the Haven, some two miles north-west of Pembroke (Fig. 31). A monument in Albion Square in Pembroke Dock commemorates its foundation: 'The town was built almost entirely by the working classes who, by their thrift and industry, erected during the century upwards of 2,000 houses. In 1814 the first houses were built on freehold land acquired by the Corporation.' The first two ships from the new dockyard were launched in 1816.

Another new seaport was Maryport, founded in 1749 by Humphrey Senhouse and named after his wife. Beginning as a coal port, within thirty years it had attracted an ironworks and three shipyards, but never became a serious rival to the earlier plantation of Whitehaven, twelve miles away (Millward, 1974). In the extreme South-West, a local trading company began to build quays near the mouth of the Hayle River in the 1740s. In 1757 a copper smelter was established nearby; copper slag, a by-product of the smelter, was cast into blocks which were given to employees prepared to build their own houses on land provided by the company. The settlement which grew up still bears the name Copperhouse. A new canal was cut to improve navigation to the Copperhouse quays. In 1779 a local blacksmith, John Harvey, established an iron foundry turning out pipes and engine parts, and built his own fleet of boats. In 1820 the Copper Company, whose copper-smelting business had failed, set up a rival iron-foundry. A steam packet service to Bristol began in 1831. The new town of Hayle shows no evidence of the careful planning which characterizes Milford Haven or Maryport. Its growth was never spectacular, even after the arrival of the railway, and today it is a curiously anomalous and somewhat forlorn little industrial outpost surrounded by caravan sites. The remains of Harvey's foundry, the packet quays and the Copperhouse Canal Dock are still visible, but the Steam Packet Hotel built in 1831 was demolished some years ago (Wigley, 1972). Another port dependent upon the copper trade was Amlwch founded in the 1770s to serve the mining and smelting of Anglesey copper. Its dependence on a single industry halted its expansion during the stagnation of the copper trade in the early nineteenth century. Helensburgh was founded in 1776 by Sir James Colquhoun to take advantage of trade on the Clyde estuary. Like Humphrey Senhouse, he named his town after his wife. Further down the Firth of Clyde Ardrossan was founded in 1806 for the Earl of Renfrew who hoped it might soon rival Port Glasgow; unfortunately money ran out before it was completed. The Welsh slate industry gave rise to two new towns both established by the same rich landowner, William Maddocks: the market town of Tremadoc, and its coastal partner Portmadoc, developed in the 1820s as a port (Bell and Bell, 1972). Along the north-east coast small fishing hamlets were beginning to develop as ports for the export of coal. Blyth began to expand in the early eighteenth century, but did not reach its peak for another 150 years. It was always exclusively a working port, and shared none of the residential refinements of North Shields, where, above the narrow strip of land along the Tyneside quays, some fine Regency squares were built for the wealthier ship-owners and master mariners. The earliest of the coal ports was Seaton Sluice, where the harbour was begun at the end of the seventeenth century. In the 1760s this was improved by a massive cut through the rock, and a member of the founding family, the Delavals, expressed the hope that 'we should soon see a large town start up'. This was not to be, and Seaton Sluice soon lost ground before the rise of Blyth (Newton, 1972).

Inland ports

The development of coastal ports was paralleled by the increasing importance of inland navigation. Most of the river ports of the Midlands, places like Bridgnorth, Bewdley and Tewkesbury, contain many Georgian buildings reflecting the prosperity due to increasing water traffic.

The late eighteenth century saw the appearance of a new form of inland transport and the coming of the canals had a considerable effect on many towns. Brindley's very first canal for the Duke of Bridgwater transformed the village of Worsley until by 1773 it had 'the appearance of a considerable Sea port town. His Grace has built some hundreds of houses and is every year adding considerably to their number'. Stone was given a new lease of life in the 1780s by the Trent & Mersey Canal: 'from a poor insignificant place is now grown neat and handsome in its buildings, and from its wharves and busy traffic wears the lively aspect of a little seaport.' In Birmingham the opening of the canal from the Wednesbury coal-mines in 1769 to the Paradise Street Basin, the subsequent linking of the Birmingham canal to the national network and the opening of the Newhall Wharves in

1772 created a new economic focus. During the 1770s there was great expansion in the north-west and west of the city, on the Newhall estate of the Colmore family and on land owned by Sir Thomas Gooch. Street names such as Navigation Street and Wharf Street on the Gooch estate bear witness to the role of the canal in stimulating this growth (Chalklin, 1974; Hadfield, 1966).

Several completely new towns were brought into existence by canals (Porteous, 1968). The earliest and best-known of these is Stourport (Plate XIV, Fig. 32). The Worcestershire historian Treadway Nash

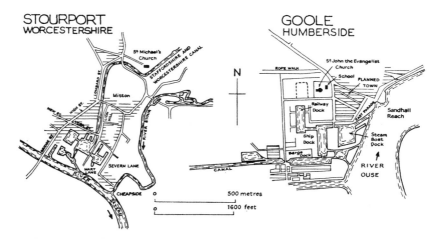

32 Canal port towns.

describes its origins: 'About 1766, where the river Stour empties itself into the Severn below Mitton, stood a little alehouse called Stour-mouth. Near this Brindley has caused a town to be erected, made a port and dockyards, built a new and elegant bridge, established markets, and made it the wonder not only of this county, but of the nation at large. In the year 1795 it consisted of 250 houses and about 1,300 inhabitants. Thus was the sandy barren common at Stourport converted, in the space of 30 years, into a flourishing, healthy and very prosperous village.' Stourport's *raison-d'être* was the opening, in 1771, of the Staffordshire and Worcestershire Canal. There is an oft-quoted statement that the canal was originally intended to join the Severn at the old river port of Bewdley, but that the proud inhabitants of that town told Brindley to take his 'stinking ditch' elsewhere. It has recently been shown that, far from rejecting the canal, Bewdley actually petitioned Parliament in 1766 asking for a canal connection to the Trent; and it is now clear that Brindley intended from the very outset to take the easiest contour route down the Stour valley to a terminus at Stourport. The opening of the Stourport basin was an immediate blow to Bewdley's trade, and in 1777 the possibility of a canal link between Bewdley and Stourport was explored. No more was heard of this, and as Stourport expanded Bewdley stagnated (Garrett, 1972).

Stourport's success was such that, in the early 1800s the basins had to be extended and barge-locks added to allow access by larger vessels. The original shanty town of the construction gangs had been replaced by neat red-brick terraces housing permanent employees, together with extensive warehouses, barge sheds and stabling. It is unlikely that Brindley himself had much to do with building the town. There is little evidence of organized planning by the canal company. For many years there was no town hall or church. Eventually a church was built in 1792, following a complaint from the inhabitants of the neighbouring hamlet of Lower Mitton that their existing chapel was too small to cater for Stourport's increasing population. This Georgian church and its Victorian successor were located some distance from the centre of the canal town, retaining their historic ties with Lower Mitton hamlet. It was left open for the Methodists to move into the centre of the town, their chapel in the High Street being built in 1787.

In its early years the delights of the surrounding country and the spectacle of boats in the basins and on the canal itself gave Stourport a subsidiary role as a 'resort of people of fashion'. A prosaic and purely functional warehouse was transformed into an attractive centre-piece by the addition of a white-painted wooden turret and weather-vane with a clock presented by the inhabitants of the town in 1812. (Hancock, 1951).

This recreational function is matched in other canal towns. At Runcorn the extension of the Duke of Bridgwater's Canal beyond Manchester to the Mersey created a new canal port town which was also, for a time, a favoured bathing-place. A similar process was seen at Ellesmere Port, where basins and warehouses were laid out by Thomas Telford in 1795 at the western terminus of a projected canal from the Mersey to Shrewsbury on the Severn.

The last of the canal towns was Goole (Fig. 32). This was from the outset more ambitious in scale and more strictly functional, without any of Stourport's fashionable overtones. The site, on drained marshland, was chosen in 1819 by the Aire and Calder Navigation Company as a new terminal for the export of south Yorkshire coal, replacing the old river ports of Airmyn and Selby. After several changes of plan Goole's Ship Dock and Barge Dock were completed in 1826 and the Ouse Steamship Dock in 1838. The influx of dock construction workers threatened to engulf the area in a shanty town, and the Company instructed its surveyor, George Leather, to produce a plan for a new town, and the first building to be completed was the Lowther Hotel, named after a chairman of the company. This austere rectangular block, at the harbour end of Aire Street, is the finest building in Goole. The company administered the town itself, and so no town hall was built. No entertainment facilities were provided, and it took two decades of petitioning before the company provided a church. The expansion of domestic building was rapid, and it was anticipated that 'the town, when completed, will, in point of elegance and uniformity, be the handsomest in the north of England.' By the present century the original nucleus of Goole had become extremely run down, and extensive slices of it were swept away by slum clearance in the 1960s (Porteous, 1969).

Spa towns

The eighteenth century saw the greatest popularity of the inland health resort, the place to which, in Cobbett's memorable phrase, 'East India plunderers, West India floggers, English tax-gorgers, together with gluttons, drunkards and debauchees of all descriptions, female as well as male, resort, at the suggestion of silently laughing quacks, in the hope of getting rid of the bodily consequences of their manifold sins and iniquities' (Fig. 33). It was the development of spas as fashionable residential centres in addition to their purely medicinal function which created their distinctive and impressive townscapes.

Foremost amongst the spa towns was Bath, which grew from a small walled town to a spacious city of some 32,000 inhabitants during the eighteenth century. Bath's opportunity came when the visit of Queen Anne in 1702 brought it into social prominence. In the next fifty years it was transformed by the activities of three men. Richard 'Beau' Nash was employed by the Corporation as Master of Ceremonies from 1705 to 1745; he was instrumental in attracting a new aristocratic colony to the town, and he can be credited with the virtual invention of the holiday industry. The second important figure was Ralph Allen, postmaster of Bath, who had made a fortune from his reorganization of the postal system, and had acquired the local quarries which provided the town with such magnificent building stone.

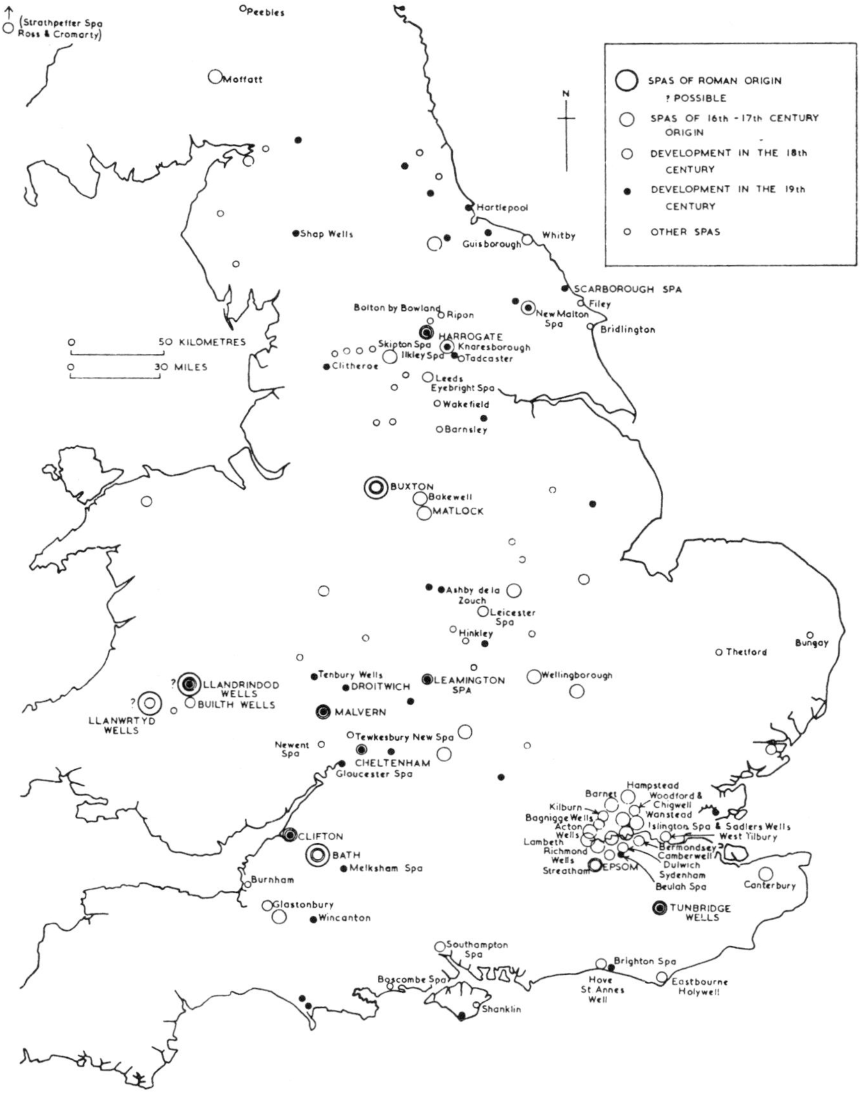
(Strathpeffer Spa Ross & Cromarty)
Peebles
Moffatt
SPAS OF ROMAN ORIGIN
? POSSIBLE
SPAS OF 16th - 17th CENTURY ORIGIN
DEVELOPMENT IN THE 18th CENTURY
DEVELOPMENT IN THE 19th CENTURY
OTHER SPAS
N
Hartlepool
Shap Wells
Guisborough
Whitby
SCARBOROUGH SPA
Filey
Bolton by Bowland
Ripon
New Malton Spa
Bridlington
HARROGATE
Skipton Spa
Knaresborough
Ilkley Spa
Tadcaster
Clitheroe
50 KILOMETRES
30 MILES
Leeds
Eyebright Spa
Wakefield
Barnsley
BUXTON
Bakewell
MATLOCK
Ashby de la Zouch
Leicester Spa
Hinkley
Thetford
Bungay
Tenbury Wells
DROITWICH
LEAMINGTON SPA
Wellingborough
LLANDRINDOD WELLS
BUILTH WELLS
LLANWRTYD WELLS
MALVERN
Newent Spa
Tewkesbury New Spa
CHELTENHAM
Gloucester Spa
Hampstead
Barnet
Woodford & Chigwell
Kilburn
Wanstead
Bagnigge Wells
Acton Wells
Islington Spa & Sadlers Wells
West Tilbury
Lambeth
Bermondsey
Richmond Wells
Camberwell
Dulwich
Streatham
EPSOM
Sydenham
Beulah Spa
Canterbury
CLIFTON
BATH
Melksham Spa
Burnham
Glastonbury
Wincanton
TUNBRIDGE WELLS
Southampton Spa
Brighton Spa
Boscombe Spa
Hove St Annes Well
Eastbourne Holywell
Shanklin

33 Spas in Britain.

Allen introduced to Bath the builder John Wood, to whom we owe the physical transformation of the city. Wood's initial contract was for Allen's own mansion, Prior Park, which overlooks the city from the south. He stayed on to design the first major residential expansion of the city northwards, work which was continued by his son, also named John. The growth of the city was even greater in the second half of the century, with new squares and crescents spreading northwards up the hill towards Lansdown, and eastwards across the Avon onto the Bathwick estate of the Pulteney family. In terms of architecture and planning, Bath is the most magnificent product of the eighteenth century (Plate xv) (Bell and Bell, 1969).

The first major rival to Bath was Cheltenham, a small market town of only local significance until 1716, when a flock of pigeons was noticed in a meadow just outside the town pecking at the salty crust around a spring. The owner of the meadow, recognizing its possibilities, railed it in and built a thatched shed over the spring. Several decades later the approach was improved, walks laid out, and a pump room and pavilion provided. Visitors began to arrive in some quantity, and by 1780, the single street was nearly a mile long and the new brick buildings included nearly thirty lodging-houses. It was still relatively insignificant compared with Bath, but in 1788 a visit by King George III and his family brought it instant popularity. There was a period of rapid expansion, aided and encouraged by the enclosure of the town's open fields and the discovery of further springs. The suburb of Montpellier began to expand south of the old town after 1809. The magnificent tree-lined Promenade was begun in 1818. A slightly later speculative estate called Pittville was begun in 1825 on the north side of the town by Joseph Pitt, the lay rector and Member of Parliament. Another big scheme was begun on the Lansdown estate at the same time, but the speculators had overreached themselves and with houses being completed at a rate of one a day, expansion had passed saturation point. There was a financial crisis, and neither Pittville nor the Lansdown scheme was completed as planned (Finberg, 1955).

Unlike Bath, little of the local stone was used, most of the building being in stucco-faced brick. Cheltenham's terraces and crescents lack the classic grandeur of their Bath prototypes, but their severity is softened by their setting in broad tree-lined streets. They are generally more tasteful than those of the third great spa town of the period, Leamington.

The first attempts to develop the mineral springs of the Warwickshire village of Leamington Priors were carried out by local and relatively humble people, and they made little impact on its appearance.

The discovery of further springs and a series of medical accolades towards the end of the century gave it renewed momentum, and when it attracted 'no fewer than three duchesses in one season' its future seemed assured. The first significant expansion was to the south of the old village, where Clemens Street was begun in 1806, opening the way for the development of Brunswick Street, Charlotte Street and the surrounding area. The speculation in this area was over by 1813 and the site of a projected 'Grand Spa' near Charlotte Street was soon condemned to oblivion by the appearance of the gas works. Attention turned instead to the north bank of the Leam, where a group of speculators 'tired of planning improvements in the old town, determined to found a new one'. The foundations of the first row of houses in the Parade, the central axis of the new town, were laid in 1808. The first really stylish hotel, the Bedford, was opened here in 1811. However, the search for further mineral springs in the new town area proved disappointing and the new Royal Pump Room, opened in 1814, was down at the bottom of the hill by the Leam. Ironically further wells had been discovered in the old village, where much piecemeal development was taking place.

After 1814 there was a pause in the rate of development. Then, in 1819, the Prince Regent visited Leamington, and a new phase of yet more spectacular expansion began, reaching a peak in the mid 1820s. Eventually, as at Cheltenham, the promoters overreached themselves. Only a fragment of the magnificent terraces intended to frame the square at the north end of the Parade was ever built. The north and south lodges were the only parts completed in the Crescent scheme west of Clarendon Place, the intervening space eventually being occupied by detached Victorian villas. A vast double circus of villas projected as the western terminus of the scheme was never begun, while an equally ambitious plan for the eastern side of the town was abandoned with only a few terraces built. The hopes of the Leamington developers receded as the nineteenth century progressed. When Queen Victoria granted the spa the privilege of placing 'Royal' in front of its name after her visit in 1838, this must be seen as a last desperate attempt to rescue Leamington's fading image, and not the zenith of its achievement (Chaplin, 1972, 1973, 1974).

Of the lesser spa towns which existed before the eighteenth century, Buxton, Bath's main early rival, increasingly failed to keep pace with it, despite the patronage of the Dukes of Devonshire. Epsom's wells were no longer fashionable, but the town had developed a different resort function based on horse-racing. Clifton had similarly declined as a spa, but in the late eighteenth century developed as a high-class residential suburb of Bristol, with many fine terraces of Bath stone produced by speculative builders in the 1780s. At Tunbridge Wells too the waters has lost their popularity, but the town had become a place of retirement for invalids. The residential expansion of Tunbridge was in a quite different style from that of Bath, it was rustic rather than palatial, pleasing from its rich variety of styles rather than impressive. Harrogate was fairly dormant as a spa throughout the century, and did not begin any significant residential expansion till the Regency. At Malvern the springs of Malvern Wells were the first focus of attention in the 1750s; but it was Great Malvern, two and a quarter miles away, which blossomed as the main residential area, particularly after 1800. The nucleus of Malvern's Regency development is still identifiable in the centre of its great Victorian expansion.

Several other towns developed as minor watering-places for the first time in Georgian times (Fig. 33). Llandrindod Wells enjoyed increasing patronage from outside visitors during the early eighteenth century, and after 1750 speculators began to provide additional accommodation. Its popularity declined later in the century, the main hotel being demolished in 1787 when the lease fell in. Builth Wells was also attracting visitors after c. 1740, but it remained a small market town, the little octagonal Pump Room of the Park Wells being about the only visible impact on its appearance. In 1805 the opening of a new coal-mine at Moira in Leicestershire led to the discovery of saline waters. A set of baths and a hotel were built by the colliery, but the environment was not conducive to a fashionable spa, and in 1822 the Marquis of Hastings financed the building of the Ivanhoe Baths in nearby Ashby-de-la-Zouch, followed in 1826 by the Hastings Hotel. The baths were supplied with water from Moira carried by tanks along the canal and then by trucks to a large reservoir above the baths. During the 1830s the building of a number of new terraces witnessed Ashby's modest success in attracting visitors but this did not last (Hoskins, 1957). At Scarborough the spa was given a new lease of life with the opening in 1827 of the Cliff Bridge, making access from the town easier. Hartlepool in 1816 was 'a watering place of considerable celebrity', boasting 'by far the best mineral water in the county'. By Granville's time, however, its development as a coal port had 'driven the fine company of bathers away', while the dock and railway construction obliterated the spring, 'clearing the coast, at the same time, of the last remnant of sickly dames and invalids'. Similar short-lived spas and their associated residential developments can still be identified at

Leicester (1780s), Gloucester (1814), Melksham (1815) and elsewhere. There were also many other minor spas of the period in rural situations which never gave rise to significant town growth, such as Llanwrtyd Wells, Gilsland Spa and Kirkbampton.

Seaside resorts

During the later part of the eighteenth century the fashion for continental travel opened up new vistas. Although new spas were still being created, there were signs that their popularity was dwindling. A new type of resort was coming into fashion, which has retained its popularity to the present day.

The link between the spas and the seaside resorts is Scarborough, which had begun to develop as a spa in the 1620s. Sea-bathing there had been advised as a cure for gout as early as 1667, and was already popular by the early eighteenth century. Despite its new role, Scarborough did not abandon its spa. When the spring was buried in a cliff fall in 1737 there was an immediate search to relocate it, and a further spa building had been erected slightly before Granville's visit.

Although Scarborough was perhaps the first resort to exploit its seaside position, the prototype which provided the inspiration for later seaside resorts was Brighton. This was a somewhat decayed fishing village, when Dr Richard Russell, author of the influential 'Dissertation concerning the Uses of Sea-Water in Diseases of the Glands' retired there to set up a surgery in 1754. The fact that Brighton was the nearest point to London on the south coast soon attracted fashionable society beginning to follow Russell's prescription. Brighton received its first royal visit, by the Duke of Gloucester, in 1765, and in 1784 the Prince Regent paid his first visit, returning almost every season for the next forty years. He liked Brighton so much that in 1786 he bought Grove House on the Steine, and began the series of alterations which were to transform it by 1820 to the Royal Pavilion we know today. Humphrey Repton and John Nash were both involved in the final extraordinary domed product in Moorish/Chinese style.

The Steine was originally an open common to the east of the Lanes of the medieval town where the fishermen pulled up their boats and dried their nets. This became the first centre of aristocratic settlement, the Duke of Marlborough building a house there in 1769. For most of the century the sea was still regarded with mistrust, despite medical injunctions to drink it and swim in it. In consequence the early developments on the Steine all faced resolutely away from the sea, and it was not until 1799 that the Royal Crescent on the East Cliff, the first group of houses actually to face the sea view, was begun. The second estate to face the sea, Regency Square on the West Cliff, was begun in 1818.

The patronage of the Prince Regent had brought Brighton to the forefront of fashionable popularity, and in the 1820s, after he became King George IV, the greatest phase of building activities began. In 1821 the Chain Pier (now destroyed) was built, the first pier of any importance anywhere along the south coast. In 1822 a new carriage drive along the front, subsequently called King's Drive, was begun and opened by the King. In 1823 the development of Brighton's most grandiose estate, Kemp Town, began. The proprietor, Thomas Read Kemp, was one of the lords of the manor. He had spent his way rapidly through his own considerable inherited fortune and that of two successive wealthy wives, and hit upon the idea of a major residential estate for rich families and their servants on a site about a mile east of the Royal Crescent as a means of salvaging his declining finances. Unfortunately the scheme was slow to attract its intended custom. Thirty years later many of the houses still remained empty (Fig. 34) (Gilbert, 1954; Dale, 1947).

An interesting development which illustrates the uncertainty whether the sea-bathing fashion would last was the creation of Brighton Spa in 1824. Brighton had no satisfactory mineral spring of its own, and this minor obstacle was overcome by importing water from Karlsbad

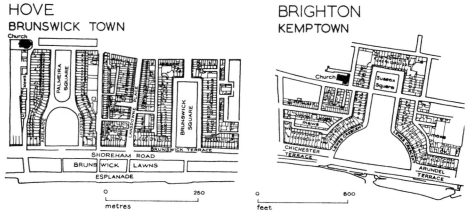

34 Superior planned developments in early nineteenth-century seaside resorts.

and other German spas. They were administered in an Ionic-style temple by one Dr Struve, a Dresden physician.

The next decayed medieval ports to aspire to resort status were the adjoining Dorset towns, Weymouth and Melcombe Regis, beginning in a small way in the 1750s. The Duke of Gloucester built a fine house just outside Melcombe Regis in 1780, and King George III became a regular visitor during the 1790s and 1800s while his son held rival court at Brighton. The first major development was the Grand Esplanade along the shore, begun in 1785, and described by Granville as one of the finest he had seen in England. Melcombe Regis quickly outgrew its medieval confines and has been described as architecturally richer than any resort other than Brighton. Weymouth, on a more constricted site, was less fashionable and had less opportunity for expansion, but nonetheless shared in the same general tide of prosperity (Taylor, 1970). Hastings received a new lease of life in 1794 when it was recommended as a health resort, and the stationing of a large force there under the Duke of Wellington during the Napoleonic War attracted many visitors. Tynemouth underwent a similar experience.

Other resorts sprang from lesser beginnings. Margate was a small agricultural village with a harbour of some importance for exporting Thanet grain to London before the 1720s. As early as 1736 a local carpenter, Thomas Barber, advertised an indoor bath fed by sea-water in which persons of either sex could bathe without exposing themselves to the open air. This was so popular that he was advertising a new, greatly enlarged bath the following year. Margate's relative accessibility from London by coach and sailing vessel made it one of the earliest seaside resorts to cater for the poorer classes. In 1804 *The Times* reported 'Though the town is so remarkably full, there are not here, at present, many persons of high rank and fashion' (Whyman, 1973). Torquay was an insignificant harbour in the parish of Torre Mohun, and its main development after 1810 was as a winter residence for invalids rather than a summer sea-bathing place. As such it succeeded to the mantle of a string of resorts stretching eastwards back to Weymouth and including Sidmouth, Exmouth, Dawlish and Teignmouth which had each in turn enjoyed brief heights of fashion.

The first seaside resort to appear without any earlier nucleus was Southend. As its name suggests, it was just the south end of Prittlewell parish till 1767 when a row of brick cottages was built for visitors from London. Other buildings sprang up around the spot, and in the 1790s the nucleus of a more organized speculative development, New Southend, was begun. Princess Caroline stayed there for three months in 1803, from which the Royal Terrace and Royal Hotel acquired their name. The first wooden pier was built in 1838, and, like Margate, it grew rapidly because of its proximity to London. It was separated from Prittlewell to become a distinct parish in 1842. Sandown on the Isle of Wight was a desolate uninhabited heath till 1788, when the first house was erected: a plaque on the corner of High Street and Wilkes Road commemorates the event and the site. Southport, the first major resort of the North-West, began with a driftwood hut built on an uninhabited beach in 1792 by a local inn-keeper. The first permanent villa followed five years later, while the next year the wooden hut was replaced by the first hotel. A second hotel followed in 1805, and two years later Wellington Terrace, the beginning of the main thoroughfare Lord Street, was built to house hotel staff and servants. Southport was unique amongst English resorts in its close association with a canal; most of its early visitors reached it by packet boat along the Leeds & Liverpool Canal to a quay some five miles inland. Its subsequent development as a town was closely controlled by the Bold estate, and its character remains unusually spacious and verdant. The last great Regency seaside resort was St Leonards, again established on an uninhabited stretch of coast, by Sir James and Decimus Burton, two of the key figures in the development of London. In contrast to the earlier resorts, St Leonards was laid out from the outset in such a way as to exploit the longest possible sea frontage, with a long string of detached villas and public buildings interspersed with gardens. It was not an immediate success. Sir James Burton died there in 1837 with much of his Bloomsbury fortune spent. Granville summed up its progress around the same time: 'Magnificent as it may appear on the sea-side, with its showy and lengthened frontage . . . St Leonards viewed from behind . . . presents nothing but a monotonous ladder of unfinished, ill-placed and ill-sheltered houses, of dingy material, and but imperfectly inhabited, enough to damp every cheerful expectation'.

St Leonard's was not alone in failing to achieve immediate success. Bognor got off to an equally uncertain start. Its promoter, Richard Hotham, a wealthy Southwark hatter, had, by 1813, built 'several rows of elegant brick structures, but so detached that the place is at least a mile in length, erected with the professed design of making Bognor the resort of a more select company than is to be found at other bathing places'. Unfortunately, the site was ill-chosen for a seaside resort, being almost half a mile inland. It was not until the 1820s, when building reached the sea front, that any significant expansion took place.

The social structure of Georgian and Regency towns

The segregation of rich and poor noted in the previous chapter increased in intensity in the eighteenth century. Right at the beginning of the period Defoe comments on the rich going to the spa of Tunbridge Wells, the middle classes to Epsom, while the common people went to Dulwich or Streatham Wells more for 'meer physick' than entertainment. Certain towns, such as Bury St Edmunds, Lewes, Winchester, Shrewsbury, Lichfield and Preston, he singles out as full of 'gentlemen of good families and fortune' or of 'good company'. The implied contrast with places with a higher industrial content is illustrated by his description of Exeter as unusual in being both full of trade and full of gentry. The same sort of social distinction was beginning to emerge in the new seaside towns towards the end of the century.

The segregation of different classes within individual towns is equally apparent. The tendency was emerging for high-class residential housing to settle on the healthier, windward south-western side of most large towns. The less fortunate working families stayed on in the older parts of the town, in increasing densities under deteriorating conditions, or were herded out to new industrial districts on the north or east side of town. Thus in London, the West End, conveniently placed for the City, the Court and the administrative centre of Westminster, became the spacious preserve of the aristocracy and wealthier middle classes, tolerating only such working-class pockets as were necessary for the supply of servants and tradesmen. In contrast, the East End districts, Stepney, Spitalfields, Whitechapel and Bethnal Green were densely built up and occupied by poorer folk from the outset. In Birmingham the leafy streets of Edgbaston in the south-west contrast with the grimy close-built terraces of Duddeston or Ashted on the opposite side of town. In Manchester the most prosperous manufacturers were moving out to build large residences in Chorlton-upon-Medlock or Hulme, leaving the working population herded in congested dwellings in the town centre. Most provincial towns of any standing were developing at least one residential district for the rising ranks of the moneyed upper and middle classes.

This tendency was so marked that many ambitious residential schemes appeared doomed to failure from the start, simply because of their east-side location. The Ashted district of Birmingham was originally advertised as 'very inviting to ladies and gentlemen wanting a pleasing retirement', but there was nothing very inviting about its subsequent development. In east Glasgow the attempts to establish property of high prestige and value in Charlotte Street (1779), Monteith Row and St Andrew's Square (1787) were successful for less than a generation before coming into the hands of small tradesmen and poorer families. Residential projects nearby for St James's Square and Graham Square were in consequence abandoned. The westward migration of the aristocracy was, moreover, a continuing process. Several of the new streets built in the third quarter of the eighteenth century in Glasgow were intended to be restricted to gentlemen's residences; but as they were in their turn replaced by superior later developments further west, banks, hotels and offices moved into the vacated premises. In London the decline of Covent Garden was noted in the previous chapter. Others of the inner western squares, such as Soho Square, once a highly favoured address, followed suit. Somers Town, a respectable suburb in 1800, was soon to degenerate into one of the most notorious of all London slums. In most large towns careful scrutiny of the faded inner suburbs which have not yet fallen to redevelopment will reveal traces of their former prosperity.

In some towns the gentry and prosperous traders and manufacturers were always in a small minority. There was less opportunity to lay out extensive high-quality estates, and we find instead small select squares or individual streets for the well-to-do amidst a sea of contemporary artisan housing. Their subsequent decline was again predictable. An example is Old Square in Birmingham. Here, just outside the northern limit of the medieval town, in about 1700, John Pemberton, a wealthy ironmonger, acquired the site of the medieval priory of St Thomas and laid out a large square garden surrounded by sixteen residences for prosperous merchants and manufacturers. The rapid expansion of the town soon engulfed Old Square in a mass of inferior development. It was an anachronism little more than a century after it was completed, and the construction of Corporation Street in the 1880s destroyed all but a vestige of it. Today only the name survives, applied to an embayment in the middle of a modern shopping complex.

That such segregation was becoming generally accepted is clearly shown by the care with which specific functions and occupations were located in complete 'new town' developments. At Blandford Forum the complete reconstruction of the town after it was levelled by fire in 1731 included the siting of houses for the professional and merchant classes on the outskirts, houses for shopkeepers and lesser merchants in the centre, and working-class estates between the two. At the new canal port of Goole the solid three-storey housing provided for the professional classes overlooked the river and harbour, in a position calculated to impress the new arrival. Humbler two-storey terraces lined the secondary commercial axis of Ouse Street, while the poorest accommodation of all was hidden away from the docks in the central and northern parts of the town.

Georgian and Regency town planning

The Georgian contribution to town planning is important both quantitatively and qualitatively. The rapid increase in urban population placed upon the landowner and builder an unprecedented demand for new streets and buildings, while the absorption of Rennaissance plan elements and their widespread application created some of the most impressive uniform townscapes ever seen in Britain.

The square was the most widely-used feature. In London most of the piecemeal developments of the West End during the eighteenth century focussed on new squares, supported in depth by a grid of lesser streets (Fig. 26).

When Defoe was writing there were twenty-seven squares in London and the number was still increasing. Some builders acquired immense wealth. James Burton, whom we have already met as the founder of St Leonards-on-Sea, began as a small builder in Southwark and made his fortune from the development of Bloomsbury.

The square, which had met with such success in London, was soon being copied in most expanding provincial towns. One of the finest examples is Queen Square in Bath, developed by John Wood I in 1728–36.

Once the principle of the terrace and square were fully established, the way was open for their modification into crescents, circuses, ovals and polygons. Again Bath provides the earliest and finest examples (Plate xv). John Wood I's Circus, begun in 1754, is a superb example of the Grand Style, consisting of three concave-fronted terraces, each of eleven houses, surrounding a central circular open space. John Wood II's Royal Crescent, begun eleven years later, is even more impressive, consisting of thirty houses linked in a semi-elliptical façade, looking out on an open swathe of sloping turf. These features were widely copied and imitated from the 1780s well into the following century. Bath itself contains many further examples. Rival spa towns also produced their quota: Buxton's Crescent of 1781 and Clifton's Royal York Crescent (1791) are amongst the finest. Other provincial towns produced simpler versions, such as Taunton's Crescent of 1807 (Plate xiii). Complete circuses are less common than crescents, an example of the former being Bedford Circus in Exeter, begun in 1773, not completed till 1826, and demolished following bomb damage in 1942 (Fig. 35).

Despite all the new plan elements coming into fashion, the basis for the bulk of Georgian town development, especially that of a less prestigious kind, was still the simple grid. Ashton-under-Lyne was systematically laid out in a rigid grid of wide streets by the Earls of Stamford after 1758, as it grew into a thriving cotton town. The ports of Maryport and Ardrossan were similarly planned. At Milford Haven Louis Barallier laid out three main streets parallel with the coast, intersected at right angles by shorter linking streets. Pembroke Dock was originally planned on a similar, if less ambitious layout (Fig. 31). Extensions to older industrial towns frequently took grid form. In Birmingham the Colmore family began the development of their Newhall Estate in the 1740s, laying out a new quarter to the north-west of the existing town on a rigid grid system. The central axis, Newhall Street, followed the alignment of the tree-lined avenue to the family home, New Hall, which was demolished in 1787. Other streets on the estate, Edmund, Lionel, George, Charlotte and Great Charles Streets, bear the names of individual members of the family. The only distinctive Georgian element in the plan was St Paul's Square, on a site given by the Colmores in 1768 for a new parish church. Estates in Manchester and Liverpool were also developed on grid systems with the occasional square. Yet another example is the area of Workington around Portland Square, laid out in 1775.

Grid planning was not peculiar to ports and industrial towns. An exceptionally spacious grid was laid out at Southport, based on the one and a half mile long spine of Lord Street and Albert Road. The width of Lord Street was fixed at 88 yards, and today this wide tree-lined avenue is still one of the finest shopping streets in Britain. The new town of Leamington north of the River Leam was also planned on a grid on either side of the central axis of the Parade.

One of the most impressive examples of Georgian town planning is the new town of Edinburgh. The congestion of the medieval town, with its tottering rookeries, narrow filthy lanes, cluttered market-place and complete lack of any civic facilities worth the name, was being roundly condemned in the 1750s. The North Loch, 'originally an ornament to the town', was so defiled with sewage and offal as to be 'a most insufferable nuisance'. The draining of the loch was begun in 1759, and the commencement of a bridge across it in 1763 opened the way for the development of the north shore. In 1766 the Council invited plans for a complete new town on the north bank and within

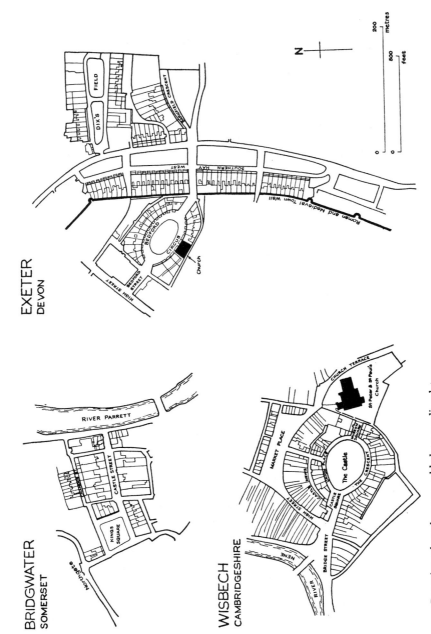

35 Georgian plan elements added to medieval towns.

four months the plan submitted by James Craig was chosen. This consisted of a simple grid, based on three parallel main streets. The streets bounding the scheme to north and south, Princes Street and Queen Street, were intended to be built up on their inner side only, preserving open vistas towards the medieval town and the Forth. The wide central avenue, George Street, was terminated in the west by St George's Square and in the east by St Andrew's Square, both intended to contain churches. The concept was somewhat prosaic, but its ponderous simplicity suited the site (Fig. 36). Unfortunately

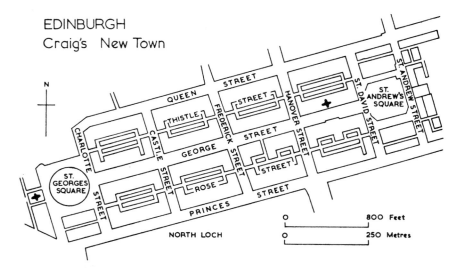

36 James Craig's new town scheme for Edinburgh, 1767.

difficulties were soon encountered. The Council was so eager to attract customers that, apart from insisting on pavements 10 feet wide and continuity of building line, it made no attempt during the first fifteen years to standardize buildings into a uniform elevation. Deviations from the original plan soon occurred. A private mansion had appeared by dubious means on the site intended for St Andrew's Church, while illicit buildings had encroached upon the southern side of Princes Street, blocking the open southward view. The embarassed council was sued as far as the House of Lords by a group of townspeople wishing to preserve the amenities of Princes Street, and was forced to buy back a site in George Street into which the church of St Andrew was eventually squeezed. Attempts were made to impose some architectural uniformity in the 1780s. Buildings on the three main streets were to be no higher than three storeys, on the two back streets two storeys; dormer windows were forbidden; stables and coach-houses were to be built only in the mews. These regulations were not entirely successful, and it was not until the 1790s, when the progress of building towards the western square threatened another fiasco, that the council abandoned their piecemeal policy. The western square, renamed Charlotte Square, was designed as an entity by Robert Adam, and remains one of the most impressive townscapes in Scotland (Bell and Bell, 1969; Lindsay, 1973). In Glasgow too we can see the guiding hand of James Craig, following the foundation of the Glasgow Building Company in 1786 and the great expansion to the north and west of the town.

Georgian town planning at its best is seen in the towns which had attracted a large well-to-do society. Land promoters had the opportunity to construct extensive estates of grand houses, wide streets, squares, crescents and other prestige developments on a scale which was impossible in towns with a less top-heavy social structure. One of the finest examples is Kemp Town in Brighton, begun in 1823. Here the central feature was Sussex Square, 100 yards from east to west and open to the sea on the south. This was flanked by the two arms of Lewes Crescent, funnelling the sea view to the maximum possible number of houses, and spanning in total some 840 feet, a quarter the width again of the Royal Crescent at Bath. Where the arms of the Crescent reached the front they were continued as Chichester and Arundel Terraces. Two additional flanking squares behind the sea-front terraces were planned, but never built (Fig. 34).

Just to the west of Brighton, in the parish of Hove, the less ambitious but more immediately successful scheme of Brunswick Town was promoted by the Rev. Thomas Scutt. The central feature was Brunswick Square, laid out in 1825, lying perpendicular to Brunswick Terrace on the front. On the north side of the square a gap was left between two groups of four houses in order to preserve the sea view from Wick House (now demolished), the residence of the Rev. Scutt. Behind the frontage were the attendant mews, back-street and market area. Brunswick Town was provided with its own community baths, public house and church (Fig. 34).

Although Bath contains many individual architectural masterpieces, most of the town was laid out on a piecemeal basis, and the only area to be planned as a coherent unit was the Pulteney's Bathwick estate east of the river. The building of Robert Adam's Florentine-style

Pulteney Bridge over the Avon in 1771 opened up the left bank for development at the time when the demand for residential accommodation in the town was at its peak. The main axis of the Bathwick estate was Great Pulteney Street, laid out in 1785 by Thomas Baldwin, the City Architect. 100 feet wide and 1,100 feet long, it is the finest street in Bath, leading to Sydney Garden, 'a wide and extensive hexagonal plantation . . . around which many handsome houses are suitably arranged'. Beyond the gardens a straight drive to Warminster was begun. Subsidiary streets and squares were laid out on either side (Plate xv).

A later spa estate was the Pittville suburb of Cheltenham, begun in 1825. The centrepiece was the Ionic pump room, modelled on the Temple of Ilissus at Athens and set in a contrived vista with lakes and stone bridges. Below this the residential estate was laid out on either side of a central garden rib, with handsome terraces, crescents, individual villas, and squares named after the Dukes of Clarence and Wellington.

The survival of the finest achievements of Georgian planning is apt to make us forget that much contemporary development was unregulated to the point of chaos. Defoe makes it clear that much of London's expansion was 'in a most straggling, confus'd manner, out of all shape, uncompact and unequal'. Despite the regulations after the Great Fire which had enforced the widening of streets, the end result had been an even greater density of building in the central areas as individual big houses were replaced by more concentrated infilling. At Swithen's Alleys, by the Royal Exchange, the site of a single merchant's house had been occupied by two dozen new houses. Rocque's London map of 1746 shows a chaotic jumble of courts and alleys in Clerkenwell, Moorgate, Shoreditch and Bishopsgate, while in Wapping, Shadwell and Rotherhithe a maze of docks, forges, foundries, breweries, tanyards and factories was interspersed with houses and taverns. Almost the whole of the north-eastern arc of London had been developed as artisan quarters, and there were hardly any of the elegant squares which characterized the West End.

In other towns uncontrolled piecemeal development by speculative builders was taking place in gardens, yards, burgage plots and surrounding closes, setting the scene for the evolution of the slum in the following century.

Town centre improvements and redevelopment

Apart from peripheral expansion, many towns were beginning to experience the first significant changes in their internal street plan.

The abandoned sites of medieval castles were becoming occupied by new streets and houses. At Wisbech, The Crescent, Castle Square, Museum Square and Market Street were laid out over the castle site between 1793 and 1816. Similarly at Bridgnorth, East and West Castle Streets were built and the former castle chapel rebuilt between 1786 and 1792 as a parish church for the new quarter of the town. Many other towns contain individual new streets in their central areas: Castle Street (1723) and King's Square (1800) in Bridgwater (Fig. 35), Exchange Street in Manchester (1776), Hammet Street in Taunton (1788), and Parliament Street in Hull (later 1790s). In Oxford a programme of improvement from 1770–2 included the demolition of the two surviving medieval gates; the opening up of Carfax, the central cross-roads, by the removal of the Conduit, butchers' shambles and various houses around the church; and the widening, paving and lighting of several other streets. One new street was constructed across the former castle precinct, betraying its late origin by its name New Road and by its straightness. Magdalen Bridge, the approach to the city from London, was completely rebuilt, and this is the only contemporary improvement which still visibly proclaims its eighteenth-century origin. In Exeter all the city gates were demolished between 1769 and 1819. New Bridge Street and a new bridge over the Exe were built in 1778, and various prestige developments on the edge of the medieval city, such as Southernhay, were begun (Fig. 35).

In the smaller towns it was rare for Georgian redevelopment to extend beyond a few streets, although individual buildings may have undergone considerable alteration and refronting. Exceptions are the towns devastated by fire. In the early years of the century Warwick was still being rebuilt after the fire of 1694 (Plate XI). Even more impressive is Blandford Forum in Dorset, a small timber-built market town which had suffered several fires since the sixteenth century. The worst conflagration of all came in 1731, when the town was almost completely levelled. The processes of reconstruction were controlled to a large extent by two local builders, the brothers John and William Bastard, whose aptitude for design enormously enhanced the results. In addition to domestic buildings their contribution included new hotels and civic buildings and a new parish church (Colvin, 1948; Plate X).

Towards the end of the eighteenth century the desire for improved internal communications resulted in some redevelopments on an unprecedented scale, a process which became more frequent in the following century and has reached its climax in our own time. One of the earliest advocates of comprehensive replanning instead of piecemeal alteration was John Fordyce, who urged the consideration of an overall plan for the Marylebone Park estate in London, which was to revert to the Crown in 1811; he also advocated the need for a great new street from Marylebone to Charing Cross. Fordyce died before his dreams were realized, but in 1811 proposals were adopted which had been prepared by John Nash, a favourite of the Prince Regent. Nash's plan involved the creation of a new route from the Prince Regent's residence at Carlton House northwards to join the New Road (built fifty years earlier to link Paddington with the City and now forming Marylebone, Euston, Pentonville and City Roads), just outside Regent's Park. The northern end of the route already existed. Portland Place had been built by the Adam Brothers in 1774, and was at the time the widest and finest street in London. Between Carlton House and Portland Place Nash's new road was carved through existing properties, particularly Edward and Swallow Streets which formed the boundary between the districts of Soho and May-fair. It did not follow the most direct route: two changes of direction were enforced by the presence of Foley House at the southern end of Portland Place, and by the insistence of the residents of Cavendish Square that the route should not pass too close to their properties. Far from detracting from the effect, these diversions were brilliantly achieved by means of sweeping curves, with an extended piazza on either side of the road. Despite the loss of all Nash's buildings, Regent Street retains something of its original character even to this day (Summerson, 1949) (Fig. 26).

Even greater changes were taking place in Newcastle-on-Tyne (Fig. 37), which was achieving its greatest prosperity during the early nineteenth century. Newcastle's big problem was the difficulty of access between the riverside and the higher town. At the same time considerable open spaces inherited from medieval monastic precincts remained within the walls, providing a magnificent opportunity for replanning. The first steps towards improving movement through the city centre had been made with the construction of Mosley Street in 1750. Then in the 1820s three key figures came together: John Clayton, the town clerk, John Dobson, architect, and Richard Grainger, builder. Their first achievements were the construction of Blackett Street across the former nunnery gardens from the site of the recently demolished medieval New Gate and, in 1826, Eldon Square. Bigger changes came after 1834, when Grainger acquired the Anderson Place area and produced a unified scheme for 'nine new streets . . . the new market, the new theatre, the new dispensary, music room, lecture room, two chapels, the incorporated companies hall,

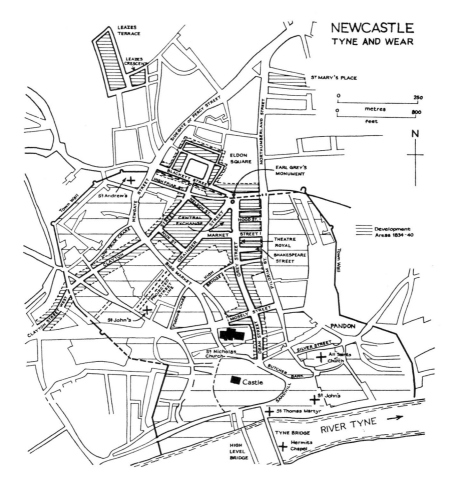

37 Newcastle-on-Tyne: Early nineteenth-century redevelopment within the medieval town.

two auction marts, ten inns, forty private houses and 325 houses with shops'. The masterpiece of the scheme was the magnificent curve of Grey Street, focussing on the new monument to Earl Grey erected in 1838. The two other main streets were Clayton and Grainger Streets. The whole of the grand design was virtually

163

completed as planned by 1840 (Newton, 1972; Wilkes and Dodds, 1964).

Villa suburbs

For most of the Georgian period planned town expansion had been characterized by grid streets and squares lined with terraced houses. A significant breakaway from this pattern came with the development of St John's Wood on the Eyre estate in London between 1794 and 1830. This was designed as a suburb from the outset, with detached and semi-detached villas in their own gardens. A larger scheme was planned by John Nash at Regents Park in 1811, with fifty detached villas scattered amongst the trees and a whole series of terraces surrounding the perimeter of the park. Not all the features of Nash's scheme were built as planned. The perimeter terraces were completed, but the number of villas inside the park was reduced to eight. The proposed canal through the middle was diverted round the edge. The double-circus and National Valhalla intended as the central feature was never built, and the Park Circus at the entry from Portland Place was reduced to a crescent.

This type of villa suburb was also developed in the main provincial towns. For example, on the favoured south-western side of Birmingham the lord of the manor of Edgbaston, Sir Henry Gough, resisted the temptation to speculate in high-density residential, commercial or industrial development, and encouraged instead the building of large detached stuccoed houses in their own grounds. Edgbaston remains the most distinctive of the middle ring of Birmingham suburbs.

A slightly different concept, in which crescents, terraces and detached villas were set amongst formal avenues and gardens, is exemplified by the uncompleted plan for the Lansdown estate in Cheltenham devised in 1825, described recently as 'the first English garden city' (Pevsner, Gloucs., 1970).

Buildings

Regional vernacular styles were in decline during the eighteenth century. Some buildings may still be seen which owe little to classical influences despite their Georgian origin. Frequently, however, we find earlier structures encased or refronted in the fashionable new style (Plate IX). The effect of individual buildings striving for symmetry and regularity, not always with much regard for their neighbours' efforts in the same direction, is still a dominant factor in many townscapes.

Although the intent to impress, through the use of clean lines and overall symmetry, runs right through the ideals of Georgian building, there is in fact considerable variation within the period.

I. DOMESTIC BUILDINGS

At the beginning of the century the 'Queen Anne' style was being widely used in urban domestic building. However, a different architectural phase was developing out of the work of Christopher Wren. His use of some of the elements of Classical Rennaissance architecture in a highly original way, sacrificing all rules and conventions to achieve grandiose and monumental effects, laid the foundation of the English Baroque style, popular up to the 1730s. This style is at its most exuberant in great country houses, but it also appears in a limited number of town houses. The greatest Baroque mansion of all, Blenheim Palace, is faintly echoed in the adjacent town of Woodstock by several houses, especially Hope House, built around 1720, and the Rectory. Not far away, in Stow-on-the-Wold, St Edward's House, overlooking the market-place, is perhaps the most attractive of all urban Baroque buildings. Its three-storey front is dignified by giant fluted pilasters with Corinthian capitals and by a blank round-arched curved recess immediately above the door.

On a smaller scale we may examine the work of the Bastards at Blandford Forum. Their most elaborate products were the new classical parish church and town hall, the latter with a ground-floor arcade leading into a stone-flagged loggia (Plate x). Their domestic buildings are no less carefully designed, being of a broadly uniform appearance, but given variety by their adaptation for different social classes. The largest houses had symmetrical elevations and ornate central doorways. The town-centre shops usually had their entrance to one side, while the working-class cottages were often built in pairs, with a shared entrance and common passage. Contrasting with a background of blue bricks, dark red bricks were used to outline window openings and quoins, and light red bricks to define window-heads (R.C.H.M., 1970).

In the 1730s there was a reaction against the florid quality of the Baroque and a return to the more correct classicism of Palladio which had enjoyed little favour since Inigo Jones's work nearly a century earlier. Again we find the first effects in country mansions. The reappearance of Palladian buildings in towns begins among the houses of the nobility, one of the earliest being the remodelling of Burlington

House in Piccadilly, parts of which survive in the Royal Academy. Soon, however, architects such as John Carr of York and the Woods of Bath were adapting the Palladian style in very successful designs of their own . At Bath John Wood I dominated his Queen Square of 1728–36 by giving the northern terrace a unified 'palace façade' using corner blocks and central porticos with pediments. The concave façades of the Circus, begun in 1754, were adorned with a different classical order on each storey, Doric on the ground floor, Ionic on the first and Corinthian on the second. Perhaps the highest achievement of all was John Wood II's Royal Crescent of 1765–75, where the façade was unified by giant Ionic columns into a palatial front. John Carr's rival Crescent at Buxton, which included hotels at either end and post office, promenade, assembly rooms and library in the middle, was of two storeys with a rusticated arcade along the ground floor and fluted Doric pilasters between all the first-floor windows.

The outstanding architectural figure from the 1760s onwards was Robert Adam, who is noted more for his very original interiors than for his exteriors, which were still in the Palladian tradition. The most ambitious Adam project was the great Adelphi scheme (now largely demolished), devised in 1768 to provide medium-sized houses for professional people over the Thamesside warehouses and vaults running up to the Strand. Home House in Portman Square, perhaps Adam's finest town house, built in 1773–7, survives, as does much of his work in Fitzroy Square, London and Charlotte Square, Edinburgh.

The pattern of the standard London terraced house was by now well established. Each house had a simple rectangular plan, with a narrow street frontage, rising up to four storeys. Contruction was in brick or, occasionally, stone, with thick dividing walls to reduce the fire risk and accommodate flues. The entrance was placed to one side, approached by steps, and leading into a hallway giving access to the internal staircase. The front doors were large and panelled, with semicircular webbed fanlights lighting the hall; sometimes a pediment or semicircular arch capped the doorway. The windows were carefully proportioned on the Italian Rennaissance model, the tallest being on the first floor, the smallest on the third, an intermediate height being employed on the ground and second floors. Sash windows were used, with thin wooden glazing bars and small panes of regular size. During the last quarter of the century chimneys became less prominent and roofs became lower in pitch, often being concealed by a parapet above the cornice. Welsh slate was widely used for roofing.

Similar terraced houses were built in most provincial towns, notably in York, Winchester, Wisbech and Ludlow.

By the end of the century the standards of taste and the rules of proportion laid down by the Palladian school had permeated down to the jobbing builder with the help of the pattern book. A good example of late Palladian building may be seen in the canal town of Stourport. Its houses built between 1770 and 1800 are all of dark red brick, with ochre-washed dressings, uniform fenestration and well-proportioned porticos. If the overall effect is somewhat austere and lacking the finer architectural graces of earlier decades, it still has a solid, well-built air of permanence which saves it from the monotony and meanness of much Victorian building (Plate XIV).

Around the turn of the century a recognizable new domestic style emerges, in which the various strands of Georgian classicism fused. Although strictly speaking the Regency lasted only from 1811 to 1820, architecturally this term is usually applied to the more extended period from c. 1800 to 1830. Two materials, stucco and ornamental iron-work, are particularly characteristic of Regency building. Stucco was a type of rendering used over brick as an inexpensive way of simulating stone. As a condition of their leases, Nash's Regents Park terraces had to have their stucco recoloured and rejointed every four years in imitation of Bath stone (Clifton-Taylor, 1972). Ornamental ironwork was widely used for balconies, verandas and railings, wrought iron being progressively replaced by the cheaper cast-iron. A recent pioneer study has attempted to date and subdivide the ornamental ironwork of Cheltenham (Chatwin, 1975). Regency domestic archi-tecture is seen at its best in the terraces and crescents of Nash's Regent's Park perimeter in London and in the resorts of Cheltenham, Brighton, Weymouth, Melcombe Regis and Leamington. Windows were tall and narrow, often with iron balconies, thin glazing bars and plain surrounds. Bow windows were introduced to give relief to flat façades, and were in their turn replaced by angular bays. Doorways were often round-headed. Roofs were low-pitched with Italianate projecting eaves; sometimes they were completely flat. Decoration was sparingly applied, and favoured the plainer classic orders, Doric and Ionic. Occasionally materials other than stucco were used: Beaumont Street, Oxford (1828-37), is of genuine ashlar, while in the long terraces of Southernhay, Barnfield Crescent and Dix's Field in Exeter the red brick was left unrendered. Detached villas were built in many residential suburbs, such as Edgbaston and the Worcester Road area of Malvern.

The attractive qualities of much of the surviving later Georgian housing is apt to make us forget the rapid deterioration in the standards of working-class accommodation which was taking place at the same time. During the first half of the century the provision of artisan housing had, on the whole, kept pace with demand without any drop in quality. Land was still relatively cheap and the price of materials and building trade wages relatively low. Industrial workers often occupied premises built originally for higher classes of society. In Spitalfields in London, for example, silk weavers had moved into Fournier Street soon after its construction in the 1720s. Although now very shabby and run-down, this street still bears evidence of its original residential pretensions, though rows of windows above the cornice betray the presence of attic workshops. In Birmingham the gun and jewellery trades were housed in solidly-built artisan districts of red-brick terraces. New economic opportunities and higher earnings provided many workers with the chance to improve their standards of domestic comfort. In some cases industrial companies provided housing of reasonable quality. At Belper, between 1792 and 1830, the Strutts built several hundred brick or gritstone cottages for their workers, which were regularly repaired and whitewashed internally by the company; many were provided with large gardens. However, during the second half of the century the shadow of overcrowding began to loom in towns like Liverpool, Leeds, Birmingham, Nottingham and Hull. The 1780s saw the biggest building boom of the century, but in many towns there was simply insufficient land available for expansion. Nottingham was hemmed in by a straightjacket of open fields which could not be built over without prior enclosure, a process which was delayed by certain burgesses and property-owners until 1845. The same problem caused severe overcrowding in other towns not often thought of in this context, such as Cambridge and Tewkesbury. In Leeds the landownership pattern was dominated by smallholders, so that only tiny plots of land tended to come onto the market at a time. Development was therefore piecemeal, with the maximum possible number of houses crammed onto each plot without reference to the street pattern of the neighbouring plot.

The response to the pressure for more housing within the existing limits of towns was met by the infill of any open spaces remaining in old inn-yards and gardens. In Nottingham the burgage plots on the north side of the Market Square were just wide enough for a line of lean-to houses, one room deep, backed up against the boundary wall of each plot. They were already being used for this purpose as early as the 1740s. Thus the tradition of back doors and windows was lost, the front and only entrance of each house facing inwards to the remnants of the yard which acted as a small court. Large numbers of these 'blind-backs' were run up in the last two decades of the century, when the domestic hosiery industry was undergoing a period of prosperity. Despite their ominous situation, the first generation of blind-backs did not represent a serious decline in industrial housing standards. They were often solidly built in brick, with three storeys, the top floor having long windows to light the working space. Sometimes there was a cock-loft above and a cellar below. Similar houses were being constructed in the yards behind the Headrow, Kirkgate and Briggate in Leeds in the 1780s, and in the central districts of Liverpool.

Once the blind-back principle was accepted, it was inevitable that the laying-out of new working-class estates would soon use blind-back terraces sharing a common rear wall. Thus the infamous back-to-back pattern was born. Back-to-back houses were being built in Leeds, Nottingham, Liverpool and Birmingham from the 1780s in some quantity, but because their first generation was fairly solidly built in brick and because the house-type had evolved insidiously from existing patterns of building, it aroused little contemporary comment. Some of the earliest back-to-backs in Leeds were erected, not by speculators, but by building societies such as the Crackenthorpe Gardens Building Club, which in 1787 built fifty-two back-to-backs in Union, Ebenezer, George, Nelson and Sidney Streets.

The outbreak of the Twenty Years War in 1793 saw a sharp rise in the cost of land, materials and wages. The size and structural quality of working-class housing was drastically reduced in order to keep rents within the reach of the occupants. Poor materials, skimped workmanship and the cramming of houses into the smallest possible space brought the cost down so effectively that in the 1820s and 1830s houses were being constructed in the courts of Birmingham for as little as £60 each. The speculator was quick to see the advantages of the back-to-back in minimizing building costs and making the most out of every odd patch of ground. There was little contemporary objection. The middle classes who controlled the vote did not live in the worst conditions and in most cases were hardly aware of what was happening. The degeneration of working-class living conditions in towns continued, reaching its nadir in the early years of Victoria's reign (Chapman, 1971) (Fig. 38).

2. CIVIC BUILDINGS

The town halls, market halls, assembly rooms and custom houses of Georgian date are an important contribution to the centre of many

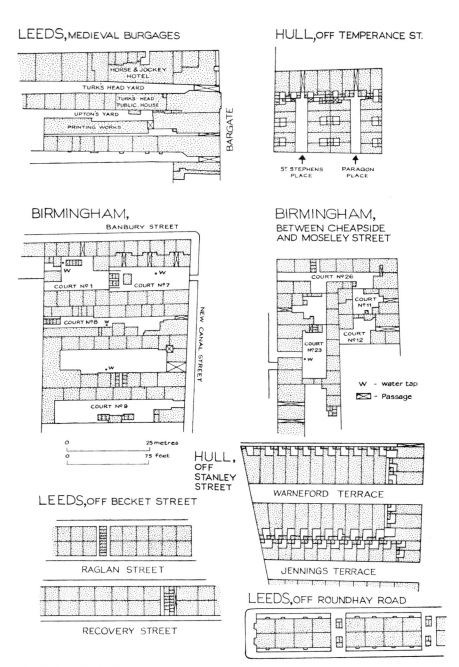

38 Back-to-back, blind-back and court housing.

towns, and display all the variations of style noted in domestic buildings. Probably the best Baroque example is Worcester Guildhall (1721–3), of brick with stone dressings, its windows segmental-headed with roll mouldings, its façade adorned with statues and niches and giant Corinthian pilasters supporting an elaborate pediment, its skyline broken with urns, statues and a cupola. More sober Palladian examples are plentiful, including work by most of the major architects of the period. The Assembly Rooms at York (1730–2) were designed by Lord Burlington, one of the most influential figures in the spread of the Palladian style; Liverpool Exchange (1749–54) was from designs of John Wood 1 of Bath; William Chambers, the chief proponent of the school in the third quarter of the century, began Somerset House in the Strand in 1776, intended for the use of various learned societies and part of the civil service. On a smaller scale is his Town Hall at Woodstock (1766). Robert Adam's work includes High Wycombe Market Hall (1761) and Bury St Edmunds Market Cross (1771). For the Regency style Godalming Market Hall (1814) is a good example, with stucco, open-arcaded ground floor and cupola.

Outside the capital the greatest concentration of Georgian monumental designs was in the two English university cities. In Oxford almost every college was involved in building during the century. Queen's College demolished its earlier buildings to create a new front on the High Street in 1734, with a screen and domed gatehouse in Baroque style. Nicholas Hawksmoor, a pupil of Wren, and one of the principal English Baroque architects, carried out work at All Souls' during 1709–50. In contrast Christ Church College was building its Peckwater Quadrangle in a very refined classical style at the unusually early date of 1705–14. Oxford University itself made some major contributions to the townscape, including Hawksmoor's Old Clarendon Building, designed for the University Press (1711–25) and the Radcliffe Camera, a rotunda standing in an open piazza created by the clearance of a block of tenements and gardens in 1737–49.

The later part of the period was marked by an increasing number of hospitals, such as the Radcliffe Infirmary, Oxford (1759–70), the Royal Salop Infirmary, Shrewsbury (1826–30) and the Royal Berkshire Hospital, Reading (1837–9) in a variety of Greek styles. Prisons, gaols and lockups also appear in some quantity, an example being Shrewsbury Gaol (1787–93), cruciform in plan with a central octagonal chapel. The best group of buildings of this type is at York, where Carr's Assize Courts (1777) and prison (1780) flank Vanbrugh's

Debtor's Prison (1705). These contributions to the townscape reflect in different ways an evolving concern with social welfare and order.

3. ECCLESIASTICAL BUILDINGS

The rapid expansion of many towns in the eighteenth century placed a considerable strain on the existing parochial system and created a demand for many new churches. In Manchester, for example, six new Anglican churches were consecrated between 1756 and 1794. The explosion of Cheltenham as a Regency spa was marked by the building of four new Anglican churches in twenty years.

The most representative group of Baroque-style churches from the first thirty years of the century is in London. In 1711 Parliament authorized the building of fifty new churches to serve the expanding suburbs. In the event only a dozen were actually built under the Act. Half of these built were by Hawksmoor, the best examples of his work being St Mary Woolnoth, Lombard Street (1716–27) and Christ Church, Spitalfields (1723–9). Other architects using the Baroque style in London included Thomas Archer, who built St John's, Smith Square (1714–28), and James Gibbs, whose church of St Mary-le-Strand (1714–17) was originally intended to carry a tall column with a statue of Queen Anne on top (a more orthodox steeple replaced this after the Queen's death). Outside London Baroque churches are less frequently encountered. A good provincial example is St Philip's, the first post-medieval church in Birmingham, built by Thomas Archer (1711–25).

Gibbs managed to come to terms with the changing tastes at the time of the Hanoverian succession, and we find him building a number of Palladian churches in London such as St Peter's, Vere Street (1723–4) and St Martin-in-the-Fields (1722–6). The latter is perhaps his best-known work, but even here he pained the purists, combining the west portico with a steeple which would not have appeared on any genuine classical building. A provincial example of Gibbs's work is All Saints, Derby (1723–5).

Between the 1730s and 1770s there was a steady increase in the provision of churches in the extending London suburbs. In a number of provincial cities, such as Worcester, medieval churches were being replaced in Georgian style. After c. 1770 the first examples of the Gothic Revival style which was to dominate Victorian church building appear: St Mary, Tetbury (1771); St Nicholas, Warwick (1779–80); and St Alkmund, Shewsbury (1793–5), which is particularly interesting in having cast-iron window tracery, a product of its proximity to the heart of the Industrial Revolution. A few late

Georgian churches break away completely from traditional shapes. All Saints, Newcastle (1796) is elliptical in plan. St Chad's, Shrewsbury (1790–2) has a circulaf nave with a gallery supported on cast-iron columns.

Regency churches are varied in character, and less distinctive than Regency housing. Some of the most interesting examples are those incorporated into a complete townscape scheme. John Nash carefully placed All Souls, Langham Place (1824), with its circular spire and Ionic portico, at one of the dramatic bends in Regent Street. The centre-piece of the new square at the north end of the Parade in Leamington was a chapel in Anglo-Norman style (1825), recently demolished. St Andrew's, Hove (1826), part of the Brunswick Town development, was the first church in England to be built in Italianate style.

Despite the number of new churches built, the Church of England was increasingly failing to keep up with its responsibilities in the rapidly expanding towns of the early nineteenth century. The growing hold of nonconformity in towns may readily be recognized by the enormous number of dissenting chapels built at this date. The established Church finally stirred itself, and in 1818 the Church Building Act was passed, sometimes called the Million Act because it voted a grant of £1 million to be spent under the supervision of Commissioners on the building of churches. A further grant of half a million pounds followed. In all some 214 Commissioners' churches were built, their greatest concentration being in the London suburbs and the industrial towns of the Midlands, Lancashire and Yorkshire. At first the Commissioners gave no guidance on style, and some of their earlier products were Greek Revival. The best of all is St Pancras in London (1819–22), of Portland stone, with an Ionic portico derived from the Erechtheum in Athens and a steeple adapted from the Tower of the Winds. This was expensive, however, and soon the Commissioners recommended a Gothic Revival style which could be built cheaply in brick and faced in stone. These churches usually consist of a large, capacious rectangular block, with the altar at the end of a shallow chancel, a high pulpit on one side and reading desk on the other, galleries round three walls, an organ in the west gallery, and two tiers of windows. Few have survived without modification, their frugal character failing to appeal to Victorian taste (Clarke, 1938).

4. INDUSTRIAL BUILDINGS

An important landmark of the Industrial Revolution was the building of Lombe's Silk Mill in Derby in 1718–22. Employing some 300 men and standing six storeys high, it may be regarded as the first factory in England. The scale of industrial enterprise underwent a significant boost in the 1760s, when the Darbys began the expansion of the Coalbrookdale Ironworks, Matthew Boulton opened the great Soho Foundry on the outskirts of Birmingham, and Josaiah Wedgewood founded his Etruria Pottery at Burslem.

The eighteenth century has left a rich harvest of industrial buildings in towns, to which it is impossible to do justice here. The transformation of the Lancashire towns by the cotton mills of the 1780s is still very evident in the present landscape. The woollen mills of Yorkshire, Gloucestershire and Wiltshire are equally striking. William Bass founded the new brewery at Burton-on-Trent in 1777, beginning the transformation of that town to England's foremost brewing centre; other eighteenth-century breweries remain at Chiswell Street in London, Baldock, Tadcaster, Wisbech and Margate.

The development of factory buildings on a scale different from anything which had gone before demanded totally new techniques, and these became available in the last decade of the eighteenth century. In 1796 the first iron-framed building, a flax mill, was erected just outside Shrewsbury. It still stands, though it is no longer used for its original purpose. The small industrial towns of Shropshire, Ironbridge, Coalbrookdale and their neighbours still display a wealth of uses for cast-iron in buildings. Iron-framing was soon widely adopted as a construction technique, for example at Salford Twist Mill (1799–1804) and Houldsworth's Cotton Mill, Glasgow (1804–5) (Hay, 1974). In some buildings iron beams were protected by earthenware pots to increase their fire resistance, Strutt's cotton mill at Belper being one example.

The increasing importance of water transport, both maritime and inland, was reflected by a number of important dock constructions. The most significant growth was at Liverpool, where the first dock replaced the Pool, from which the town took its name, in 1715. Four more followed before the end of the century. Portsmouth dockyard still has a good range of mid-eighteenth-century storehouses, while warehouses at St Katherine's Dock, London, built in 1824, combine cast-iron stanchions with traditional load-carrying walls. Of canal dock buildings the most impressive were perhaps the magnificent set of warehouses, now demolished, built by Thomas Telford at Ellesmere Port after 1795, in which boats could be loaded and discharged under cover.

Conclusions

The eighteenth century was a period of major urban progress in Britain, during which towns grew enormously in size and developed distinctive plan elements and building types which created an ever widening gulf between the town and the rural village. The greatly increased significance of industry was a critical factor in the development of some major new urban centres, while the increasing prominence given to recreation was also important. New industrial and resort towns had overtaken many of the older medieval market centres, but administrative status, ecclesiastical provision and parliamentary representation were slow to adapt to the changing situation. The sort of anomaly which resulted may be illustrated by Defoe's description of Edward iii's Queenborough, now 'a miserable, dirty, decay'd, poor, pitiful fishing town', a 'town memorable for nothing' whose 'chief business . . . as I could understand, consists in alehouses and oyster-catchers'. This place was 'vested with corporation priviledges, has a mayor, aldermen etc. . . . But that which is still worse . . . is, that this town sends two burgesses to Parliament, as many as the borough of Southwark, or the city of Westminster'. Compared with this, Manchester was 'neither a wall'd town, city or corporation; they send no members to Parliament'; it was 'the greatest meer village in England'.

Chapter VIII

Victorian Towns

The nineteenth century saw the most dramatic increase in town dwelling that Britain has ever seen. In 1780 only London and Edinburgh had a population of over 50,000, but by 1900 this figure was exceeded by over eighty towns in Britain. All the major provincial towns underwent spectacular expansion; Birmingham's population increased more than tenfold, that of Manchester and Leeds by almost the same amount. Many completely new towns appeared.

Railways and railway towns

One of the major new factors was the railway system. Its effect on towns was enormous. At first it tended to be destructive. By the time the railways appeared most towns were fairly densely built up, and the engineering works necessary to bring the line into central areas could be achieved only by extensive demolition. In Birmingham in the 1850s the approaches to New Street Station swept away the notorious slums of King Street, Peck Lane and the Froggery. Twenty years later in London almost the whole of Somers Town, a densely-populated working-class district, was cleared to make way for railway construction north of St Pancras.

Once this phase was over, however, railways were vastly more effective than canals had been in promoting urban growth. Their demands stimulated coal, iron, steel, engineering, docks, shipbuilding, food production and every kind of manufacturing, service and distributive trade. The arrival of the railway meant rapid expansion; to be bypassed meant stagnation. The fate of Stamford, where Lord Exeter succeeded in excluding the main London–York line, has been contrasted with that of Peterborough, which lay on the alternative route (Hoskins, 1955a). Peterborough's massive expansion was parallelled in Rugby, Doncaster, York, Darlington and Carlisle.

Perhaps the most striking effect of the railways was the creation of several new towns (Fig. 39). Those most distinctively railway-orientated are the towns which grew up around locomotive, carriage and waggon works: New Wolverton after 1838, Crewe after 1842, Swindon after 1843, and Eastleigh after the 1850s. The vast scale of the workshops themselves, and the provision of churches, institutes, hotels and housing by the various companies concerned, are reminders even today of the domination of the railways in those towns.

Several towns first established by the railways owed their greatest expansion to secondary industrial growth. Middlesbrough was a hamlet of four farmhouses in 1801. In 1828 it was chosen by the Stockton & Darlington Railway Company to become the site of their new coal port, replacing Stockton further up the Tees. By 1846 it was 'a handsome, well-built commodious town'. The enormous expansion of the iron trade after the 1850s swamped the original railway town, which degenerated into a slum as a thriving new town centre developed to the south (Fig. 39). Widnes owed its origin to the railway from St Helens to Runcorn Gap, opened in 1833, but it was the establishment of the alkali industry there in 1847 which caused its major expansion. The last of the railway towns, Barrow-in-Furness, was the creation of the Furness Railway Company in 1856. The establishment of new ironworks in 1859, docks in 1867, and flax and jute mills in 1869, gave rise to high hopes for its future. The building of the vast Gothic town hall and the consecration of four new churches in a single day in 1878 marked the apex of a period of optimism which was never realized. A combination of Barrow's remote position and sheer misfortune, such as the collapse of its jute industry after the mill was burned out in 1892, put an end to its ambitions (Bell and Bell, 1969; Millward, 1955).

Several new ports, such as Seaham Harbour, Neyland and Heysham, were closely associated with rail termini, as was the development of many new seaside resorts.

Seaside resorts

Compared with towns of industrial character, the growth of holiday resorts in the nineteenth century is often underestimated, but between 1800 and 1850 they had a greater growth rate than any other single group of towns. Some new seaside towns were already evolving before the coming of the railway. The development of Walton-on-the-Naze was begun in 1825, and in the 1830s there were signs that its promoters were hoping to extend it on a grand scale. New Brighton,

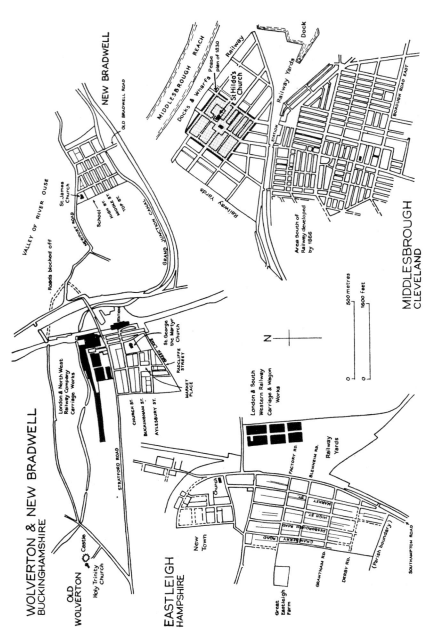

WOLVERTON & NEW BRADWELL
BUCKINGHAMSHIRE

OLD
WOLVERTON
Holy Trinity
Church
Castle

Valley of River Ouse

NEW BRADWELL

Roads blocked off

St James Church

School St
HIGH ST
MIDDLE ST
TOP ST

OLD BRADWELL ROAD

GRAND JUNCTION CANAL

NEWPORT ROAD

London & North West Railway Company Carriage Works

STATION

STRATFORD ROAD

CHURCH ST
BUCKINGHAM ST
AYLESBURY ST

St George the Martyr Church

RADCLIFFE STREET

GREEN LANE

MARKET PLACE

EASTLEIGH
HAMPSHIRE

London & South Western Railway Carriage & Wagon Works

FACTORY RD
BLENHEIM RD

Railway Yards

Church

New Town

Great Eastleigh Farm

CRAY FERRY ROAD
GRANTHAM RD
DERBY RD

DESBOROUGH ROAD

MARKET
HIGH ST

ST

(Parish boundary)

SOUTHAMPTON ROAD

N

500 metres
1600 Feet

MIDDLESBROUGH REACH

Docks & Wharfs Pease plan of 1830

Railway

St Hilda's Church

Dock

STATION

Railway Yards

Railway Yards

Area South of Railway developed by 1866

BOROUGH ROAD EAST

MIDDLESBROUGH
CLEVELAND

39 Railway towns of the nineteenth century.

Broadstairs, Weston-super-Mare, Fleetwood, Crosby and Ryde all underwent development in the 1830s. In 1855 a Mr Batley erected four houses on the low cliffs north of Harwich, and people had been so amazed that anyone should be misguided enough to build in such a desolate spot that it became known as Batley's Folly. However the owner of the estate stretching inland saw its potential and constructed a railway to it over his own land. The new resort, Felixstowe, underwent its greatest expansion after the visit of the Empress of Germany in 1891.

Brighton, which had been one of the first places to develop as a seaside resort, was also one of the first to profit from the railway. The line from London, which arrived in 1841, considerably increased its accessibility, and there was much piecemeal expansion with new schools, churches, hotels, piers, concert halls and theatres. Lytham, an insignificant port on the Ribble estuary, was transformed after the arrival of the railway from Preston in 1846. For thirty years it enjoyed success as a resort; then began to languish as mudbanks accumulated in the estuary. Its place was taken by St Anne's two miles further north, where the mud gave way to clean sand. In 1875 the site of St Anne's contained hardly a single cottage. Its spectacular growth as a carefully-planned middle-class resort reached its peak in Edwardian times. The railway arrived at Southport in 1848, and its new accessibility to Merseyside and central Lancashire led to its development as a dormitory suburb and centre for day trips rather than a resort for long-stay visitors. Further north, on the shores of Morecambe Bay, the village of Poulton underwent modest development as a fashionable resort before 1850; with the extension of the railway a hinterland in the woollen towns of the West Riding opened up. As it grew in size it changed its name to Morecambe, its character altered, and it abandoned its prospects as a resort of fashion (Millward, 1955). Southend's character similarly changed after the construction of a rail link in 1854 brought it within reach of London's East End. Most dramatic of all was the expansion of Bournemouth, following the arrival of the railway from the Midlands in 1870. In twenty years it nearly quadrupled in size, and in the present century has become the largest non-industrial conurbation in Britain.

In north Wales the construction of the Holyhead Railway along the north coast in 1848 sparked off the first new town to be created by the railways as a resort. This was Colwyn Bay. The station near the pier entrance on the promenade and the track separating the town from its sea front, clearly indicate its origin. A similar relationship between railway and promenade exists at Cleethorpes, a tiny fishing hamlet developed as a major resort by the Manchester, Sheffield & Lincolnshire Railway, which reached it in 1863. Thirty miles down the coast another new seaside town was laid out by the Great Northern Railway at Skegness between 1873 and 1881. Clacton was another mushroom growth of the 1870s, the mother village of Great Clacton being a mile inland, and the site of the resort in 1850 being occupied by a single house.

The impact of the railway was not always immediate; it still depended on the willingness and ability of landowners to take advantage of the opportunities presented. Eastbourne had enjoyed some success as a resort in the late eighteenth century, but had begun to fade, and the arrival of the railway in 1849 did not immediately revive it. Only after 1858, when the major estate there was inherited by the seventh Duke of Devonshire, did it begin its rapid rise to fame. The Duke laid out the sea front with spacious carriageways, lawns, flower-beds and terraced parades, and developed an informal network of wide avenues and open spaces. Many of the street names, Cavendish, Compton, Hartington, Burlington and Devonshire, reflect the family connections and estates of the Duke. The result is a fine example of 'garden city' planning. The magnificent beaches of Blackpool were brought within reach of industrial Lancashire by railway connections as early as 1846, but by 1890 it was still only half the size of Southport. The 1871 Bank Holiday Act and the institution of the annual 'wakes week' holiday in the coal-field provided it with its big opportunity. It took full advantage of this by acquiring, in 1879, the right to spend part of its municipal revenues on a vigorous publicity campaign. It quickly expanded in the 1890s as a resort catering almost entirely for the working population of the big industrial towns.

Spas

The new accessibility of seaside resorts to an ever-increasing market hastened the decline of the fashionable inland spa. The most successful of the new nineteenth-century spas were those which concentrated on the strictly functional aspects of healing. The social trappings of assembly rooms, theatres and promenades were less in evidence. Despite this, some of the Victorian spas have a very distinctive character of their own. Visitors to Droitwich from Leland onwards had been unanimous in condemning it as a dirty and unattractive town. The healing properties of its brine wells were first recognized in the 1830s, when the Old Royal Brine Baths were opened. The transformation of the town was the work of John Corbett in the 1880s. He laid out what was virtually a new town, with baths and hotels on the higher ground south of the medieval nucleus. The hallmark of Corbett's work in Droitwich is red-brick buildings, with half-timbered upper storeys. Woodhall Spa is another nineteenth-century new town, initiated by the building of a bath-house by Thomas Hotchkin in 1830. It is attractively laid out, and still retains much of the wooded aspect of the site. Harrogate was achieving its greatest popularity by the 1890s.

One of the main medical advances of the period was the somewhat drastic cold-water cure known as hydropathy invented by Dr Preissnitz at Gräfenburg in Silesia. This treatment was first introduced to Britain in 1842 at Great Malvern by Dr John Wilson. Over the ensuing twenty years, aided by the arrival of the railway, Malvern was transformed. The Preissnitz Hotel still stands as a reminder of the cure. Another spa which owes its origin to the hydropathic cure is Matlock Bank; development here was begun by John Smedley after 1853.

The waning of the spa fashion is, however, reflected by the number of failures. At Tenbury Mr S. Holmes Godson began an attempt to exploit a mineral spring discovered in 1839 by adding 'Wells' to the name of the town, building a pump room, baths and reading room, and laying out walks. The spa's contribution to Tenbury's growth was negligible, and the only reminder today is the somewhat incongruous Chinese/Gothic pagoda built over the well in 1862. At Bishopton, just outside Stratford-on-Avon, attempts were made to promote a new villa town under the name of Victoria Spa in 1837. A rustic Gothic spa-house and baths were built, roads and drives laid out, and a new church built in anticipation of a congregation. The project failed completely, and only the spa buildings and a few forlorn Tudor and Gothic villas in the fields remain.

Mining towns

It was, however, the continuing expansion of industry which was the dominant factor in town growth in the nineteenth century. Primary extractive industry stimulated the growth of many new towns, especially on the coal-fields. The highly individual landscape of the South Wales coal-field is largely a product of the later nineteenth century. Terraces of houses line the valley sides in step formation, providing some classic examples of urban form adapted to severe topographical constraints (Jones, 1969). Coalville, the third largest town in Leicestershire, betrays its origins in its name; it was a product of mushroom growth in the 1840s. Away from the coal-fields, Scunthorpe was a product of ironstone working after 1858, Redruth and Camborne grew up in association with tin-mining, and St Austell owes its origins to the china-clay industry. Some of these towns still have the air of overgrown mining camps, a havoc of uncontrolled development; such urban characteristics as they possess came later.

Military towns

In 1854 the Government purchased some 4,000 acres of waste land and heath around the village of Aldershot. A series of wooden huts was built there to house soldiers returning from the Crimean War. By 1930 it had grown to be the biggest military garrison in the British Empire, a municipal borough in its own right, with a civilian population appoaching 40,000. The military presence elsewhere, on Salisbury Plain and in the Catterick vicinity, adds a distinctive element to the towns in those areas.

Victorian town planning

In many Victorian townscapes the dominant impression is not so much of planning as the lack of it. This is particularly the case with industrial towns, where factory sites were located on coal-fields or on canal sides where coal could be imported cheaply. Housing was sited near the factory, often on low-lying land not previously occupied because of its liability to flooding. Coal-using industries such as the forges of Sheffield, the pot-kilns of Burslem, and the multifarious metal trades of the Black Country, coated their entire surroundings with grime. Tipheaps towered over disconnected blocks of terraced housing, workshops and factories. Subsidence left murky flashes, and crooked buildings corseted in iron strapping. Canals and railways threaded themselves through the maze, sometimes in deep cuttings or tunnels, sometimes on high embankments, aqueducts or viaducts. Worst of all were the places where glass, copper, lead and chemical works produced great quantities of poisonous waste: St Helens, Widnes, the Lothians, the Lower Swansea Valley, North Makerfield and the so-called Wigan Alps, where the atmosphere was poisoned, the streams fouled, and the vegetation blighted.

However, not all development associated with industry was so chaotic. Throughout the eighteenth century we find a steady, if unspectacular, trickle of planned factory villages: Winlaton, Cromford, Mellor, Belper. In some cases these were simply blocks of battery housing, providing maximum accommodation at the lowest possible price.   During the nineteenth century, however, the new class of non-conformist factory masters, who were concerned with the physical and moral condition of their labour force, as well as with profits, produced a number of distinctive philanthropic foundations. Among the first settlements of this type was New Lanark, where in 1784 David Dale had established a cotton manufactory and provided low-rent housing and dormitories for a labour force imported from the work-houses of Edinburgh and from the Highlands.   After 1800 Dale's son-in-law, Robert Owen, began a programme of building which included an Institute for the Formation of Character, a school, co-operative grocery store, bakery, slaughter-house, vegetable-market and communal wash-house, all out of company profits, together with further improved housing.   The site was constricted in a deep valley, and somewhat strung out.   Its focus was the open space at the mill gate between the counting-house and shop.   It was plain, even stark in appearance, and while of great significance as a social experiment, it was a failure as a town.   Its population is now a fifth of what it was at its height.

A much greater commercial success was Saltaire near Shipley, founded in 1849 by Titus Salt, a Congregationalist mill-owner in Bradford.   Bradford was described by one commentator in 1845 as the filthiest town he had ever visited, and Salt decided to leave it for a more attractive environment, concentrating his business in a single giant mill, and laying out a model town for his employees.   He asked his architects for a plan on a rigid grid system, including a $9\frac{1}{2}$-acre mill, twenty-two streets, 805 houses, forty-five almshouses, five chapels of different denominations, a Sunday School, public baths and wash-house, assembly hall, hospital and school, all in neo-Venetian Gothic style. The mill opened in 1853, and almost all the houses were complete within a decade.   The houses avoided monotony by slight variations in detail, and by gradations in accommodation for families of different size.   Some of the streets focussed on a vista of a chapel or the mill; and a park was provided for sport, recreation and floral displays (Bell and Bell, 1969).

Following in the wake of Saltaire many more factory towns and villages were planned, and a few built—Copley (1847–9), Ironville (1850), Bromborough-on-the-Wirral (1853) and Akroydon (1861)— but most of these were of a fairly minor nature.   It was not until the end of the century that there was any further significant development in factory estate planning, and when it did occur it was appreciably different in character.   New Lanark and Saltaire in their different ways aimed at the creation of a community which was essentially urban. Bournville and its fellows, while providing many urban amenities, sought a semi-rural atmosphere, and are suburban in concept.

The plan elements used in early Victorian towns were, to a large extent, based on the Georgian tradition of terraces, squares and crescents. The London districts of Belgravia, Pimlico, Bayswater and Notting Hill were laid out in terraces of white stucco in the 1840s and 1850s, followed by Camberwell in the 1860s (Dyos, 1961). Hesketh Crescent in Torquay (1849), Palmeira Square, Hove (c. 1850), Warrior Square, Hastings (1854–64), Sunderland Esplanade (1855–60) and Great Western Terrace, Glasgow (1870) are all examples of Georgian continuity.

The simple grid continued to be the most widely-used street plan, both in new towns and in extensions to earlier settlements. It was employed in various forms in several of the new railway towns. The earliest, Middlesbrough, as laid out in the 1830s, consisted of a square of 32 acres, based on five lateral and three transverse streets (Fig. 39). The main streets were to be 56 feet wide, the subsidiaries 36 feet. Within this framework there were to be 125 plots, each of 200 feet by 60 feet. At the intersection of the four main streets in the town centre a square was laid out, containing a graceful town hall with a clock-tower. Immediately to the north-east another square was reserved as a burial ground, and the new church of St Hilda was completed there in 1840. The subsequent degeneration of this area has led to its wholesale clearance in the present century, although the church and the old town hall survive, marooned incongruously amidst blocks of modern flats. The centre of Middlesbrough shifted southwards to the far side of the railway in the 1850s, when the development of the local iron industry gave the town a new lease of life. A second grid of streets was laid out around the north end of Linthorpe Road, where a new town hall was built in 1889. As Middlesbrough prospered, the grid was progressively extended southwards, its *insulae* becoming larger, more spacious, and socially more superior. The railway towns of New Wolverton, New Bradwell and Eastleigh were also laid out on a simple grid basis (Fig. 39). Barrow-in-Furness is somewhat akin to Middlesbrough in that, despite its railway origins, its greatest growth was due to the iron and steel industry. The first terrace built in 1846 by the Furness Railway Company, Nos 1–10 Salthouse Road, still remains. The discovery of new deposits of iron ore near Barrow in 1850 prompted the railway company to buy further land for development, and James Ramsden, Locomotive Superintendent with the company, and a founder of the Barrow Building Society, drew up a design for a new town. Ramsden's plan, produced in 1856, was on a grandiose scale. It consisted of two main parallel roads some 50–60 feet wide, Duke Street and Hindpool Road, crossed at right angles by eight side roads which were only slightly narrower. Three of the *insulae* thus formed were to be occupied by squares, churches, chapels or public buildings, and a fourth was to be a market-place. The concentrated concern with grand vistas and imposing façades was off-set by little attention to housing or social services. The company failed to keep a close enough grasp on controls, and speculators soon filled in the original planned town and hemmed in its periphery with squalid streets, causing the dissipation of the original scheme (Bell and Bell, 1969; Millward, 1955).

The grid was also the theme of many of the new seaside resorts. Blackpool's great expansion in the second half of the century was mainly through the activities of speculators buying successive blocks of land and laying out a series of grids of tightly-packed terraced housing. Skegness was laid out between 1873 and 1881 on a some-what more generous grid plan, with a central circus containing its church. The Upperton district of Eastbourne was developed in the 1870s with a new church in a central square. On a grander scale was Llandudno, where the Hon. E. M. L. Mostyn drew up a plan for a new town on his estate after 1849. Town commissioners were appointed to carry out the development by a private Act in 1854. There were stringent regulations covering house sizes and street and pavement widths, and it is clear that the commissioners were anxious to avoid the degeneration which had overtaken Barrow-in-Furness and the medi-ocrity which threatened Blackpool: 'No court or courts of houses will be permitted to be erected for habitation, no cellar shall be let as a distinct and separate habitation.' Within a grid of streets the different sized plots were determinedly organized in such a way that the best was made of the promenade on the front, with the shopping centre just behind it and residential development all around. There is sufficient open space to give it something of the air of a garden suburb, but it remains without any question a town (Bell and Bell, 1969).

The semi-Arcadian leanings of Llandudno were realized in full in several further resorts, chief of which are Bournemouth and New Brighton. Here the ideal of self-contained detached villas in their own grounds so dominated the early development that the town centre had more the appearance of a suburb. At Bournemouth the first house had been built in 1811 by Lewis Tregonwell, Deputy Lieutenant of Dorset; this is now incorporated into the Royal Exeter Hotel. Tregonwell also built an inn and few cottages for servants, friends and relatives. After Tregonwell's death in 1834 a 'marine Village' of detached villas was planned by the architect Benjamin Ferrey on land belonging to Sir George Tapps-Gervis on the east side of the Bourne valley opposite Tregonwell's colony. The first block, West-over Villas, was commenced in 1836. Granville was enthusiastic about the site as a winter health resort, but warned against the dangers of speculators building long straight lines of streets and terraces facing the sea. Its chief advantage, he pointed out, was its informal wooded nature due to Tregonwell's plantation of the sandhills west of the Bourne with 'trees of the Pine tribe, whereby the district has been converted, in the course of time, into a sort of tiny Black Forest'. After the death of Sir George in 1842 the Trustees of his estate employed Decimus Burton, whose report on the site echoed Granville's views: 'The wooded valley through which the Bourne runs to the sea is and must always constitute the principal object in the landscape . . . as a general principle in designing a building plan for Bournemouth, formality should be carefully avoided'. Great attention continued to be paid to making individual houses picturesque and attractive, and in maintaining the wooded nature of the landscape; but this had the effect of creating a somewhat unsatisfactory, formless, sprawling town, which in 1851, before the coming of the railway, still had only 695 inhabitants.

New Brighton, established on the desolate sandhills and heaths of the Wirral, was the creation of James Atherton, a Liverpool merchant who had made his fortune by speculative building in Everton. Its name bears tribute to Brighton's pre-eminence as a fashionable seaside resort, but its character was more akin to that of Bournemouth. Atherton's prospectus, issued in 1832, proclaimed that 'nothing will be left undone to make it a most attractive and fashionable watering-place'. It was to contain a church, market-place, shops, baths, reading room, billiard room, post office and other amenities, and all villas would be positioned 'on such sites that one shall not intercept the view of another'. The demand from Liverpool's wealthier classes soon caused the place to fill up with villas of cottage, Gothic and Lombardic style. Those on the higher sand ridges inland had the greatest aspirations to architectural dignity, and did come to resemble some of the better buildings of Brighton itself. It remained essentially a group of scattered villas into the 1880s, when the further development of baths, hotels and entertainment facilities began its transformation into a full-scale holiday town.

A few of the new resort towns were developing in areas of some topographic difficulty, which is reflected in their plan. Ventnor grew rapidly in the 1830s 'in the very worst style imaginable' through the practice of small lessees running up 'cheap small houses for the sake of immediate gain'. Its growth was constricted by its steeply sloping site, and the result has been a series of parallel streets on terraces running up to 500 feet above sea level, connected by a few narrow, steep and tortuous lanes and many long flights of steps. The sinuous street pattern developed in parts of Torquay is also attributable to the difficulties of the broken relief of the site.

Any geometric town plan other than some sort of grid is rare. The most interesting exception is Fleetwood, yet another planned new resort on the Lancashire coast. Its founder was a local landowner, Sir Peter Hesketh-Fleetwood. He hired the services of the ubiquitous Decimus Burton in 1836 to plan a fashionable resort in the genre of St Leonard's-on-Sea. Burton devised an unusul radial plan, with wide streets focussing on a high dune, the Mount, which was laid out as a central semicircular space. Several of Burton's surviving buildings, the North Euston Hotel, Custom House, Queen's Terrace and light-houses, elegant in the late Regency style, show what Fleetwood might have become. Unfortunately Sir Peter's finances were not up to the strain of promoting the new town. In 1840–1 he was forced to sell some of his land, which included, ironically, the future sites of Blackpool and Southport. He finally had to abandon the scheme with his finances in ruins in 1842. The town came into the hands of mort-gagees, who speedily dismissed Burton, and the original design broke down in spasmodic piecemeal development (Millward, 1955).

Town centre improvements and redevelopment

During the second half of the nineteenth century many industrial cities developed a strong civic pride. Sometimes this was manifested by a new town hall, art gallery or university. Sometimes great new streets were cut through the congested central areas to create a more spacious environment on a grander scale. In London several new bridges were built over the Thames, and their approaches often involved completely new streets. Queen Victoria Street, Holborn, Clerkenwell Road, Bethnal Green Road, Commercial Street, New Cannon Street and Shaftesbury Avenue were among the new roads blasted through older properties during the period. The construction of Farringdon Street was achieved by the demolition of crowded slums, displacing some 40,000 people in the process, while 5,000 were made homeless by the building of New Oxford Street. The improvement of the water-front was another feature of nineteenth-century London, the Victoria

Embankment being built over drained mudflats by the Metropolitan Board of Works in 1864–70. The need to improve internal communications within the city was promoting major new road schemes into the present century, such as Kingsway and Aldwych, built in 1905.

In Birmingham the main central redevelopment scheme was Joseph Chamberlain's Corporation Street. In 1875 a survey of the area west of the High Street reported on a maze of narrow streets, insanitary courts and dilapidated back-to-back housing, and it was decided to raze the lot and drive through a grand new triumphal avenue. Corporation Street was begun in 1878 and completed in 1882. Today still one of the chief shopping streets of the city, it has retained little of its original character, except at its northern end. The magnificent Tudor/Jacobean red-brick and terracotta Law Courts of 1887–91 is the main surviving contemporary building (Plate xvi).

On a smaller scale many other towns contain evidence of similar improvements in the nineteenth century. The congested and decaying market infill at Croydon was redeveloped in the 1890s (Cox, 1973). Prince of Wales Road in Norwich (Fig. 2), Parliament Street in York (Fig. 1) and Corporation Street in Taunton (Fig. 17) were other products of the same period. The siting of new railway stations often required a new approach road, such as Station Road in Cambridge (1845).

Suburban planning

The outward growth of towns in the nineteenth century was normally by piecemeal development, the construction of new roads and houses being determined by the nature and sequence of plots coming onto the market for building. The shape of the former fields can often still be traced in the layout of the new streets.

Occasionally middle-class suburbs of more unified planned character are encountered. The wish of the newly-rich family to escape from the crowded town centre, the polluted water supply and the proximity of the proletariat provided the demand for superior villa housing in satellite communities. On occasions the assay at exclusiveness went to extremes. On Edward Vigers's new villa suburb at Haling Park in Croydon the entrance to the estate was blocked by gates tended by green-liveried gatekeepers who were charged with the function of keeping out undesirable persons.

The form of this type of planned suburb in early Victorian times is exemplified by Decimus Burton's Calverley Park estate at Tunbridge Wells, begun in 1827 but not completed till 1852. Here a variety of detached villas in their own grounds and Regency-type terraces are distributed in a setting of roads flanked by low stone walls and neatly-trimmed hedges. Another good example is Park Town, the first significant development of North Oxford, established on open land originally intended for a workhouse, half a mile beyond the city's contemporary built-up limits. Here in 1853–5 a private trust built a mixture of Cheltenham-derived crescents and large Italianate villas with an elliptical central garden with flowering shrubs and trees.

Not all contemporary attempts to found Arcadian villa suburbs were as successful. East of Coventry a grid of wide streets was laid out at Hillfields in the 1830s, and a new church and a few villas built. Within a decade of its foundation, the ten-yard frontage of each proposed villa plot was being taken up by two or three terraced houses, and, instead of the intended middle-class occupants, the estate had become largely populated with silk weavers. Another new villa town was promoted on the south-western side of Aston Park just outside Birmingham in the late 1830s, and there the large plots intended for single detached houses were soon being crammed with back-to-backs. In both cases the inability of the developers to hold out until sufficient purchasers of the right type appeared shattered the hopes of providing an Arcadian retreat from the horrors of the city centre. The rapid expansion of Birmingham and Coventry soon engulfed both estates in the very development from which they were intended to provide an escape (Chaplin, 1972).

In mid-Victorian times the increasing spread of middle-class suburbs was beginning to break away from the formality of the grid, crescent and circus. Large detached houses with their own big gardens were preferred to any sort of terrace, which was seen as a life-style defiled through its adoption by the working classes. Streets were wide, curving, and lined with blossoming trees. At Great Malvern the arrival of the railway in the 1860s was followed by the development of land between the earlier town and the station, with great Gothic villas in gardens surrounded by high stone walls. The roads were laid out in sweeping curves, their gradients as gentle as possible in order to accommodate horse-drawn carriages. The development of the horse tram was often an important factor in opening up such developments as the wealthy Stoneygate suburb of Leicester in the 1870s. Perhaps the best mid-Victorian suburb of all is in north Oxford, which expanded rapidly in the 1860s following the decision to allow university dons to marry. In the space of thirty years a suburb more than double the area of medieval Oxford, containing both detached villas and model artisan housing, was developed by three local architects, William Wilkinson, Harry Wilkinson Moore and Clapton Crabb Rolfe (Saint, 1970).

A particularly influential development of the late 1870s was the Bedford Park estate at Chiswick. Intended for people of moderate income, it consisted of some 350 semi-detached red-brick houses in 'Queen Anne' style designed by Norman Shaw and E. W. Godwin. Its road plan was completely informal, and its building lines were varied in order to ensure the preservation of as many mature trees as possible. It had its own church, inn, club and shops.

The Bedford Park pattern was developed further at Bournville, four miles south-west of Birmingham. A fourteen-acre site there was bought in 1878 by the Quaker George Cadbury in order to move his cocoa business out of congested central Birmingham. A new factory was built, and twenty-four semi-detached houses, only one of which survives, were designed by George Gadd for essential workers. Once the company's success on its new site was assured, Cadbury began to develop his lifelong interest in social amelioration. In 1893 he bought a further 120 acres, and began to build more houses in blocks of two, three and four, varying from tunnel-back derivatives to cottage styles. The blocks were spaced 20 feet apart on the road frontage, and had large back gardens. Pavements were wide, with plenty of open spaces. Existing trees were preserved and new ones planted. Principal thoroughfares were winding and informal, with many cul-de-sac closes. The centre of the estate was a triangular 'village green', with an informal grouping of small-scale brick and half-timbered shops. The street names—Linden, Sycamore, Beech, Acacia, Hazel, Laburnum Maple, and Elm Roads—set the precedent for generations of later suburbs.

The estate has expanded considerably in the present century, and has become more varied in character; but although the housing density has increased slightly, the original vision has not altered greatly. Bournville marks the attainment of middle-class living standards by the working man. That it does not strike us as a particularly unusual landscape today is a tribute to its very success. It must be seen against the background, not of the innumerable garden suburbs which copied it, but rather against the long, monotonous terraces of neighbouring Selly Oak, which represented the standard contemporary accommodation of the working class.

Nine years after the Cadburys moved to Bournville, W. H. Lever moved his soapworks away from their cramped quarters at Warrington to an open site three miles south of Birkenhead. The site was a difficult one, low-lying and broken by ravines; but the presence of a reasonable anchorage on the Mersey outside the area of Liverpool harbour dues made it worthwhile filling the ravines and levelling the slopes to build a new factory suburb, called Port Sunlight. The plan is more formal than Bournville's, but is in no sense a return to the grid. It focussed on the factory entance, where Greendale Road, a French-style boulevard, curves round alongside a bowling-green and the main banks, shops, post office and library. Other public buildings, the Lady Lever Art Gallery, Christ Church, the technical institute, cottage hospital, schools and gymnasium, are scattered around the development. There are extensive public gardens, including some of a formal nature with avenues and terraces. The housing is extremely varied, drawing its inspiration from Cheshire vernacular, Dutch colonial, Gothic and other styles. The first group of twenty-eight cottages was begun in 1888 at a density of seven to the acre, in blocks of three to seven. No two blocks were identical. Internally the houses were of two types, one slightly superior at a higher rent. Formal front gardens were tended by the company in order to preserve a uniform appearance, and ample allotment space was provided (Bell and Bell, 1969).

A less well-known example is Vickerstown on Walney Island, begun after 1896, when the Vickers firm bought the shipyard of Barrow-in-Furness. The company established a 'marine garden city' with neat rows of cottages along gently curving streets, with a hotel and public house. It was from the outset a residential suburb of Barrow, a position reinforced by the opening of the bridge connecting the Isle of Walney with the mainland in 1908 (Millward, 1955).

Such developments foreshadow the Garden Cities of Letchworth, Hampstead and Welwyn, and point forward to the inter-war suburbs copied in almost every town in Britain.

Buildings

The building trade in Victorian times was faced with demands on an unprecedented scale. Its whole character began to change, as the local small craftsman and jobbing builder, reliant on their own good reputation, were no longer able to compete for the mass market with the large contractor. Many of the buildings required were virtually new types of structure: railway stations, workhouses, schools, public libraries, museums, art galleries, offices and waterworks.

As the scale and nature of the demand changed, so did the resources available to the builder and architect. New materials, iron, steel, plate glass and concrete, were widely used by 1900. The quicker, cheaper bulk transport offered by the railways finally disrupted the boundaries of local building materials. Welsh slate, knapped flint, all types of stone, terracotta and ornamental polished granites and marbles could be carried to any part of Britain and used in any imaginable combination. The removal of the brick tax in 1850 and the mechanization of the industry made it possible and worthwhile to produce enormous quantities of bricks which were almost identical in size, colour and texture. All parts of the country were swamped with bilious yellow brick from the South-East, bright red brick from the Midlands, pasty pink brick from Bedfordshire and dismal blue brick from Staffordshire, Lancashire and Durham. Small local brickworks operating by traditional methods failed to compete, and one by one ceased business. Similarly other local building materials were ousted. The Swithland slates of Leicestershire were no longer worked after 1887, and the last Stonesfield slate-mine in Oxfordshire closed in 1909.

Alongside new materials came new techniques of construction, based on mass production and prefabrication. The British Museum and Houses of Parliament, built by traditional methods, both took a quarter of a century to complete. The Crystal Palace, which rivalled them in scale, took just nine months (Kidson, Murray and Thompson, 1965).

Stylistically the Victorian period is confused. The main theme is revivalism, but the wider experience of foreign travel had introduced a bewildering variety of designs on which to draw. Gothic, Classical, Romanesque, Moorish, Byzantine, Egyptian and Chinese styles were all absorbed into the Victorian repertoire. Most architects and their patrons had little or no formal architectural training, and the results are sometimes unfortunate, with the simplest building becoming overloaded with a cumbersome mass of misunderstood and ill-used detail. It is difficult to trace any widely applicable sequence of stylistic development, partly because certain styles were always preferred for certain types of building, and partly because the pace of change was such that anachronistic buildings were being designed in quantity at every stage. However, to some extent, the Early Victorian period can be seen as one of sober historicism, with faithful copies of Greek, Romanesque, Tudor, Elizabethan, Italianate and English Gothic styles in plain stone or stucco. From about 1850 to 1880 a revolt against sterile academic revivalism results in the High Victorian phase, developing Italian, French and German Gothic prototypes into a highly original style, using bright colours, contrasting materials and intricate, broken silhouettes. In the late Victorian period there is a return to more uniform colours and textures, smoother outlines and more delicate, if fussier, ornament.

The most significant difference between Victorian town building and that of earlier periods is that a much more representative range of it has survived, from the greatest municipal extravaganzas down to the poorest working-class housing—although one must increasingly look hard to find the latter. However, the survival of Victorian building in such quantity makes it still one of the commonest settings for urban life.

I. DOMESTIC BUILDINGS

The story of Victorian domestic building is dominated by mass industrial housing. Only recently has this begun to receive the detailed study it deserves, yet the amount of material available for study is daunting, and it is difficult to make many valid generalizations. There was enormous variation from town to town in the style and standard of working-class housing. The congestion of Nottingham's slums contrasts with the monotonous but relatively spacious terraces of Leicester. Liverpool had its distinctive cellar dwellings, Hull its cul-de-sac courts, Glasgow its tenement blocks. Back-to-backs were abundant in Manchester, Liverpool, Leeds, Bradford, Nottingham, the Potteries, the Black Country and Birmingham (Fig. 38); but they were almost unknown in even the poorest parts of London, and were also absent from many northern towns.

During the nineteenth century many industrial towns increased their population as much as tenfold. A high proportion of the immigrants were already impoverished: destitute agricultural labourers, fleeing from rural poverty in the hope of factory employment; Highlanders dispossessed by the Clearances pouring into Glasgow; Irish driven across the Channel to Liverpool by the potato famines after 1845. With rare exceptions neither town councils nor employers saw the provision of accommodation as any part of their duties. As a result working-class housing became largely the preserve of the speculator and jerry builder, concerned with maximizing their own profits by cramming as many cheaply-built houses as possible onto each plot of land. The new urban immigrants could afford rents for nothing better.

The deteriorating structural quality of housing was soon apparent. A report on Manchester in the 1840s described back-to-backs with no foundations and walls only 4½ inches thick. This was exacerbated by the siting of much of the development on land previously unoccupied because it was liable to flooding or subsidence. In Middlesbrough in St Hilda's Ward almost all the drains were above basement level, and several of the lower streets were often flooded. In Goole street levels had been raised by dumping, but the houses were built on the original marshy ground level, creating a peculiar dank, low-ceilinged 'half-cellar' below the street frontage, accessible only from the rear. This was often let as a separate dwelling. Much of the development in the East End of London was on reclaimed marshland, and it was beset with drainage difficulties from the outset.

Overcrowding was always a major problem. It was reported in 1845 that 'nowhere else shall we find so large a mass of inhabitants crowded into courts, alleys and lanes as in Nottingham, and those, too, of the worst possible construction. Here they are so clustered upon each other; court within court, yard within yard, and lane within lane, in a manner to defy description . . . . 'Some parts of Nottingham [are] so very bad as hardly to be surpassed in misery by anything to be found within the entire range of our manufacturing cities'. In parts of Nottingham there were nearly a hundred houses to the acre, each house occupied by four or five persons. In Liverpool in 1840 some 86,000 people were living in 2,400 closed courts, and more than 30,000 were living in cellars. In Leeds, as late as the 1850s, back-to-backs were being built with a ground floor 5 yards square or less, with a single bedroom above.

Provision of water supply was frequently hopelessly inadequate. In Liverpool the fifty-two inhabitants of Banastre Street had one tap between them, while 800 people in Chartres Street had twenty-four taps. Each tap worked for a little over an hour, three times a week, and it was necessary to rise at 4.0 a.m. and queue for hours to ensure a quota. Ten Liverpool courts supposed to be on tap had had no water for three years. The sanitary condition of such areas was equally appalling. In Manchester in the 1840s courts of twenty or more houses had one common privy at the end. A court in Hull in 1850 had ten privies for 175 inhabitants. In London and York open sewers drained directly into the river which was also used for washing and drinking water. Elsewhere lavatories drained into leaking cess-pits adjacent to the communal wells. Privies in Birmingham were 'without doors and overflowing with filth'. When emptied, their contents could only be dumped in the street, because there was nowhere else available. In Liverpool for a time there was a regulation actually forbidding the connection of water-closets with the sewers, which were too slow to carry away the waste.

Yet another problem was the lack of ventilation. By its nature the back-to-back house admitted air and light on one side only, the other three sides abutting directly onto neighbours. Worse still, the cellar dwellings of Liverpool were enclosed on all four sides, with ventilation completely excluded. As pressure on space increased the courts, which had originally been open-ended, thereby allowing at least some through draught, were often closed at either end by additional houses. In Nottingham more than a hundred of these were, in 1832, built directly over the common privies. The only access to the interior of the court was then by a tunnel, which might be as long as 30 feet and as narrow as 30 inches.

The extreme restriction on light, the absence of through ventilation, the hopelessly inadequate communal sanitation and water supply, and the gross overcrowding made the back-to-back courts a breeding-ground for disease. The sudden appearance of the Indian disease, cholera, in four outbreaks between 1831 and 1866, killed some 200,000 people. Typhus, tuberculosis and smallpox also caused many deaths. The ravages of these diseases, although their causes were imperfectly understood, did much to awaken public opinion to the need to improve the standard of housing.

As early a 1841 a 'Bill for Regulating Buildings in Large Towns', which included clauses outlawing back-to-backs and insisting on a clear space of 20 feet between opposing rear walls, was promoted. but it was dropped after opposition. However, local authorities wer soon seeking their own Improvement Acts: Leeds and Liverpool in 1842, Birkenhead in 1843, London and Manchester in 1844, Nottingham, St Helen's and Wallasey in 1845, Newcastle, Burnley and Southport in 1846. The Kingston-upon-Hull Improvement Act of 1854 prohibited tunnel entrances to courts and insisted on a minimum width of 20 feet throughout for all new courts; all houses were to have a back-yard, though rear access was not compulsory, all house walls were to be 9 inches thick, and all courts were to be properly drained. Bradford in 1860 acquired a by-law insisting on open space at the rear and side of each house, so that only two back-to-back pairs could be built in a block. Some authorities acquired powers to control the use of existing buildings. In 1866 Glasgow Corporation introduced a system whereby houses of less than 2,000 cubic feet were to have a metal ticket fixed over their door detailing the number of occupants permitted by law, at a rate of 300 cubic feet for every person over eight years old. Frequent inspections were held in an attempt to apprehend the friends, relatives and lodgers who would otherwise be jammed into cupboards and under beds.

Although the local improvement schemes were rarely revolutionary, they probably achieved more than Chadwick's better-known 1848 Health of Towns Act. While the 1848 Act offered extensive powers to improve water supply and sewage disposal, it proved ineffective because it was not compulsory. It was not until Disraeli's Public Health Act of 1875 that standards of adequate construction, ventilation, sanitation and access could be enforced. The back-to-back was slowly eliminated. Even so, it took a long time to go. In Leeds, where the tradition seemed strongest, a by-law of 1866 restricted housing of this type to maximum blocks of eight, four to front and four to rear; but as late as 1905 they never comprised less than 50 per cent of all houses completed in any one year. The Housing, Town Planning, etc. Act of 1909 finally prohibited them, but the Leeds builders, after petitioning against the ban, found a loophole in the Act, and the last block of back-to-backs was finally completed in 1937 (Beresford, 1971).

The moral depravity associated with inadequate housing conditions caught the imagination of some Victorian reformers more than the physical wretchedness of their inhabitants. A survey of Liverpool in 1839 revealed that nearly 10 per cent of all the houses in the city were involved in vice or crime of some sort. Whatever their motives, various philanthropists were soon turning their attention to designing new types of working-class housing. The example came from the top, in the person of Prince Albert himself, who became patron of the Society for Improving the Conditions of the Labouring Classes, founded in 1844. The Society built a model dwelling block for the 1851 Great Exhibition, which now stands on the edge of Kennington Park. A semi-detached two-storey block, it accommodated four families, giving each a living-room, one medium and two small bedrooms, a scullery, lavatory and lobby. Soon various charitable and philanthropic societies were experimenting with larger blocks of flats. Foremost amongst them was the Trust founded in 1862 by George E. Peabody, an American banker and merchant. The first block of Peabody Buildings, opened in 1864, consisted of two red-brick five-storey ranges at the junction of Commercial Street and Folgate Street in Spitalfields. Within each range, two- and three-roomed flats lined either side of a central corridor. Lavatories were grouped in pairs on either side of the staircase, one between two families. Variations on this pattern were repeated extensively in Westminster, East Finsbury and the East End, always well built, with paved interior courtyards. A late example, built in 1901, stands in Rosendale Road, Norwood. Although their occupation density was high, Peabody Buildings guaranteed at least a minimum of air, light and sanitation. They were widely imitated outside London. In Nottingham about ninety dwellings in blocks and single houses were built near St Ann's Well Road by a private philanthropic company after 1852. The City of

Exeter Improved Industrial Dwellings Company, founded in 1873, opened Follett Buildings, its first four-storey tenement block, the following year, and Kendall's Dwellings, Blackboy Road, two parallel three-storey terraces, in 1876.

In some cases industrial concerns provided housing for their employees. Amongst the earliest to do this had been the Aire & Calder Canal Company, which built some of the first terraces at Goole before handing over to private speculators. A distinctive feature of the company town at Goole was the rounded chamfered corners at building-line junctions, providing adequate turning space for heavily-loaded drays in the constricted dock approaches and imparting a sense of architectural unity to the design. The railway companies were quick to follow suit. At Crewe the Grand Junction company provided not only water, gas, roads, sewerage, refuse collection, education and police, but also built four distinct types of dwelling, ranging from detached villas for the superior officers to small four-roomed cottages for the labourers. All had gardens. The architecture was unimaginative, but the wide streets, gardens, and general efforts to maintain cleanliness, gave Crewe the boast that, unlike Chester and Nantwich, it had no slums. Housing on a meaner scale was built by other railway companies at Swindon and Wolverton. Many other towns have small estates built by railway companies, such as at Corkerhill and Springburn in Glasgow. The Birkenhead Dock Company built the first blocks of working-class flats in Britain in 1845. The involvement of companies in housing ultimately saw the breakthrough to the garden suburb concept represented by Bournville.

In addition to companies and philanthropic or charitable concerns, local authorities and a wide variety of artisan building societies were also involved in house building. However, the greatest contribution was still coming from the speculator. Forced by legislation to turn away from the back-to-back, the speculative builder evolved a new type of housing, the 'by-law terrace', which met the standard enforced by contemporary regulations with minimum expenditure. Long, straight, parallel streets, 24 or more feet wide, were lined with terraced red-brick houses with slate roofs, at a density of about forty to the acre. The street frontage was minimal, in order to economize on the provision of services, but the depth could be three times the width. In the smallest examples the front door opened directly from the pavement to the living-room, also used as the kitchen, and there was one room upstairs. Others were built well above the bare minimum standard, with small front gardens, front doors opening to a narrow hall, and a stairway leading from the hall to two small first-floor rooms

(Plate xvii). The front parlour might have a bay window, and a coal-cellar below. To the rear a kitchen and scullery might be accommodated, with a lavatory and coal-shed beyond, entered from the yard. There was considerable regional variation in by-law housing. In Hull, one of the few towns where it has been examined in detail (Forster, 1972), more than half the houses built stood in parallel rows of between six and a dozen, facing each other across open-ended cul-de-sac courts, laid out at right angles to the main thoroughfares. In the West Midlands, in contrast, long terraces of 'tunnel-back' form are more common, with a narrow entry every two or three houses giving access through the depth of the terrace to shared rear courtyards. Aesthetically, by-law housing is not very attractive, and street after street of long identical terraces creates a monotonous townscape. On the other hand they were usually soundly built and were a great deal better than the back-to-backs.

The improvement of working-class accommodation was a long struggle, as local authorities, philanthropists and reformers strove to set and maintain adequate standards in the face of indifference, if not outright opposition, on the part of builders and landowners. In comparison with the magnitude of the problem, the contribution of the reformers was marginal. Before 1885, improved dwelling companies housed only 4 per cent of London's population. Glasgow Corporation, although one of the most active local authorities, provided accommodation for 1 per cent of its inhabitants in 1914. So often, well-meant improvements recoiled on the very people they were intended to help. Liverpool's Health Committee was prompt in waging war on the cellar dwelling, and by 1851 some 10,000 cellars had been cleared and filled with sand. The effect was simply to shift the problem to marginally better housing, which deteriorated yet more rapidly through the new stresses of overcrowding placed upon it. In London, Birmingham and elsewhere, the building of new railway termini and civic improvement schemes added to the problem by making thousands homeless. Those evicted from the slums, unable to move far afield from their work and unable to afford the rents of the model dwellings, could only take refuge in the neighbouring courts and alleys until the next round of slum clearance. As the worst of the sanitary horrors were slowly remedied, overcrowding in the inner suburbs of many cities was actually getting worse in the 1870s.

An attempted solution in London was the passing of the Cheap Trains Act 1883. This introduced inexpensive travel for workmen, making it possible for them to move out to the cheaper land beyond the built-up perimeter and commute without prohibitive charges. The

Great Eastern Railway Company was the first to provide a comprehensive service, and the first big working-class suburbs spread around the north and east of the city, from Willesden through Tottenham, Walthamstow and Leyton to West Ham.   Much of the building was by private speculators, and the standard was not always high, as it was easier to escape the eye of the sanitary official at this distance from the town.   Nonetheless the scheme met with considerable success.   The London County Council soon began to develop its own great suburban housing estates, the first four being at Norbury, White Hart Lane, Totterdown Fields and Old Oak (Wohl, 1971).   Similar developments began in other cities.

The study of industrial housing is still in its infancy.   A vast amount of local study remains to be carried out, not only in the great industrial cities of the Midlands and the North, but even in small country towns.   Few towns are without nineteenth-century artisan housing, but its recording is becoming increasingly urgent as entire streets are falling to the bulldozer (Plate xviii).   A similar need exists with the middle-class housing of the garden suburbs and the huge villas of the wealthier inhabitants.

2.   CIVIC BUILDINGS

The public buildings of the nineteenth century are among the most successful of their age.   No expense was spared in the effort to make them a fitting advertisement for civic self-confidence and pride.

In the first half of the century neo-Classical styles were preferred for civic and business premises.   At first the pure Greek revival style carried over from the Regency was dominant, exemplified by the British Museum in London, the National Gallery of Scotland in Edinburgh and the Portico Library in Manchester.   This was overtaken by richer Renaissance classical styles, such as Birmingham Town Hall (1834), the Fitzwilliam Museum at Cambridge (1837–47), the Ashmolean Museum in Oxford (1839–45) and Leeds Town Hall (1855–9).   The Gothic revival was creeping into public buildings by mid-century, a fine example being the delicate Perpendicular detail applied by Pugin to Barry's classical Houses of Parliament.

The third quarter of the century was particularly important for the transformation of many town centres by great public buildings.   The Gothic revival was now dominant, with elaborate and ornate essays such as Manchester's Town Hall (1869–77), and smaller town halls at Preston, Congleton, Chester and Wokingham.   Italian Renaissance detail was used in Halifax Town Hall (1860–2), which has an extraordinary massive tower rising to a jagged spike.   The Wedgwood

Memorial Institute in Burslem (1863–9) is in Venetian Gothic. In Bradford, following the building of the Wool Exchange (1864–7) and Town Hall (1869–73) in Florentine style, practically the whole of the centre was rebuilt over the next dozen years (Doe, 1974).

If town halls, libraries, and museums of the nineteenth century are sometimes overwhelmingly ornate and showy, the hospitals, work-houses and prisons are depressingly severe. Mean in style, they are often vast in size. The Poor Law Amendment Act of 1835 resulted in the building of new Union Workhouses on the margins of many towns. Usually three storeys high, with a communal dining-room and chapel, accommodating several hundred people, many were built on a hexagonal plan with wings radiating from a central point. Others were rectangular with two courtyards. Between 1844 and 1860 the Lunacy Commissioners built a conspicuous series of mental hospitals. The 1852 Interment Act give rise to numerous new cemeteries on the edge of towns.

Somewhere between the affluence of the town hall and the astringency of the workhouse came the school. After the 1830s, grants were available to elementary church schools, which were frequently built in a subdued Gothic style, but building failed to keep pace with need. The Education Act (1870) set up School Boards to remedy the deficiency wherever necessary; the Board Schools tend to be in Queen Anne style rather than Gothic. From the 1870s there was also a revival in the demand for grammar schools, and some of the first girls' grammar schools were opened in Oxford, Leeds and Nottingham.

Brief mention should also be made of the multitude of minor public monuments, statues, clock-towers and drinking fountains, which are often an underrated contribution to the townscape.

3. ECCLESIASTICAL BUILDINGS

The Victorian period saw a great number of churches built in the new industrial and resort towns and in the expanding suburbs. Before the 1860s the greatest concentration of effort was poured into 'mission' churches in the poor inner suburbs, while subsequently most church building occurred in the outer suburbs. Many medieval churches also received attention, which varied from minor repairs to complete rebuilding.

In the 1840s a few churches were still being built in neo-Norman or Lombardic styles. By the middle of the century, however, Gothic had come to be regarded as the only acceptable style for churches, all other styles being rejected as foreign. One of the most influential protagonists for the Gothic was A. W. N. Pugin, whose best churches are perhaps the Catholic cathedral of St Chad (1839–56) in Birmingham, and St Augustine's, Ramsgate (1846). Another important contemporary church architect was Sir George Gilbert Scott, the bulk of whose output, like St Giles', Camberwell (1844) and St George's, Doncaster (1854), accurately copied the Decorated Gothic style. Gothic was increasingly being adopted in nonconformist chapels.

The dominant figure of the High Victorian period was William Butterfield whose first church, All Saints, Marylebone (1850–9) marks a significant break in tradition. Victorian Gothic ceased to copy slavishly the medieval precedents, and developed into a highly original style in its own right making full use of new materials like cast-iron and polychrome brickwork. Butterfield's best work may be seen at St Matthias', Stoke Newington (1851), St Alban's, Holborn (1859–63), Keble College, Oxford (1873) and Rugby School Chapel (1875). A contemporary was G. E. Street, whose churches include St Peter's, Bournemouth (1855–79), St James', New Bradwell (1858), SS Philip and James, North Oxford (1860–6) and St John's, Torquay (1861–71). They were well proportioned and characteristically massive, but less ornate than Butterfield's. The break with the strict copying of the English medieval tradition by Butterfield, Street and their imitators, opened the way for continental influences to reappear. Arthur Blomfield's St Barnabas', Oxford (1868) is notable not only for its novel Italian Romanesque style but also because it was one of the first buildings to use concrete in its construction.

After about 1870 the Victorian energy for church building was beginning to wane. The churches which were built were less strident but more varied in style. The last great Victorian church architect to develop a distinctive style of his own was J. L. Pearson. His early work in the north of England was orthodox, but at St Peter's, Vauxhall, in London (1862–4) he broke away from tradition, using yellow stock brick in a French Gothic church. The hallmark of Pearson's later work is a derived form of Early English, using brick for walls and vaulting, stone for ribs, columns, arches and window tracery. Examples include St Augustine's, Kilburn (1871–98), St Michael's, Croydon (1880–5), St Stephen's, Bournemouth (1881–1908), St Barnabas's, Hove (1882) and Truro Cathedral (1880–1910). Blomfield built many other town churches and was particularly active in altering the Commissioners' churches of the early nineteenth century. On the whole, however, the products of the 1880s and 1890s are unremarkable (Clarke, 1938).

4. INDUSTRIAL BUILDINGS

If the builders of churches and town halls were, almost without exception, looking backwards for their inspiration, the engineers were quick to meet the challenge of society's new demands by developing new techniques and materials. One of the most significant developments was the increasing use of prefabricated cast-iron. This made it possible to create a wide roof-span which could carry a glass roof. An early example is the Palm House at Kew Gardens (1844–8). The early works were surpassed in scale by the most influential building of all, Paxton's ill-fated Crystal Palace, built for the Great Exhibition of 1851. The technique was widely copied, in the University Museum, Oxford (1855–60), Smithfield Market, London (1868), Bethnal Green Museum (1872) and the Borough Market, Halifax (1892). On a smaller scale cast-iron and glass were used in a wide range of seaside piers, park bandstands, pavilions and public conveniences. Towards the end of the century steel was making its appearance in buildings. The first fully steel-framed example in Britain is probably a furniture warehouse built in West Hartlepool in 1896. Railway stations were among the most widespread buildings to fulfill a completely new function. These are often a curious mixture of old and new technology. The façade, which frequently included office and hotel accommodation, reflected the best of traditional architecture. Classical façades were widely used, the best surviving example being Curzon Street Station, Birmingham (1838), original terminus of the London & Birmingham Railway and counterpart of the more famous, but now vanished, Doric Arch at Euston. Occasionally Gothic styles were used. At Bristol Temple Meads Brunel provided a magnificent stone Tudor Gothic front (1839–40), while even more spectacular was Gilbert Scott's St Pancras (1868–76), a wild example of High Victorian Gothic, liberally embellished with chimneys, crocketed towers and crenellations. However, the train-sheds behind the façades were a challenge which could be met only by new techniques. The earliest station vaults were of timber, and that at Bristol Temple Meads survives. The earliest iron-arched sheds, with a triple vault supported on two rows of iron pillars, are at Newcastle Central (1846–55). Other fine examples are at Kings Cross (1853), Paddington (1854), Manchester Central (1876–80) and York (1877).

Despite the many new building techniques, the greatest proportion of Victorian industrial buildings, the mills, breweries, maltings, warehouses and so on, still followed in an evolving tradition, based on the eighteenth-century style, with a dignified simplicity derived from their sense of scale and proportion (Plate XIX).

Conclusion

Many of the dramatic changes which were occurring in Victorian towns have their origins in the preceding century. It was the coming of the railways which, directly or indirectly, was responsible for the increased rapidity and scale of the changes. Not only were townscapes being transformed more profoundly than ever before, they were also attaining greater internal variety. Polarization had taken place between the industrial slums and the comfortable middle-class suburbs.

The efforts to overcome the worst excesses of the slum builder led inexorably towards increasing legislative control over planning and development, and it is against this background that we look forward now to towns in the present century.

Chapter IX

Towns in the Twentieth Century

By 1900 most towns were made up of several quite distinct landscapes. The congested central areas contained the principal civic buildings, office blocks, banks and stores. Many town-centre buildings were inherited from the previous century, and the new Edwardian contributions were not significantly different in appearance. Steel-framed construction was increasingly used, but façades still displayed a variety of opulent Gothic, Baroque or Rennaissance styles.

Immediately around the commercial centre there tended to be a mixed zone, including squalid industrial premises, slums, and run-down relics of superior Georgian residential areas. Beyond this a zone of by-law housing with occasional nineteenth-century factories provided workers with accommodation within easy reach of their place of work. Beyond this zone would be the middle-class suburbs, with housing at much lower densities. Much larger areas of agricultural land have been swallowed up to provide housing in the present century. In most towns this simple model would be complicated by azonal factors. Circumstances of landownership would tend to preserve enclaves of open land within the urban perimeter and development at any period has taken place most rapidly along the principal arteries radiating from the town centre, leaving the intervening wedges to be built up later. Physical factors can be recognized in the concentrations of industry on flat valley floors, while more broken hilly ground was preferred for residential development.

Most Edwardian building development was by private enterprise. Seaside resorts provide some particularly good examples. Among them was Frinton-on-Sea, founded in 1903 by Sir Richard Cooper. Its low cliffs were sloped, drained and turfed, a concrete sea wall and promenade was built, and tree-lined avenues, villas and superior hotels were developed for a mile along the coast.

The philanthropic movements against the industrial squalor of the nineteenth century were continued by the work of Ebenezer Howard, who first coined the phrase 'garden city' for his new urban settlement model (Howard, 1902). Drawing on the experience of earlier reformers, he produced a design which rationalized the planning of the town's internal functions. Public buildings and entertainment facilities were concentrated in the centre with shops adjacent. Factories and railways were on the perimeter. Between the centre and the industrial fringe were the houses, in broadly traditional style, with gables and small windows, each set in their own garden plot of 20 feet by 130 feet. Within the housing zone was a ring-park containing the schools and churches. Planned before the private car or bus became a significant factor in urban life, Howard's model town was strictly limited in size, so that all houses could remain within walking distance of the working, shopping and recreational facilities. Howard's ideas were put into practice, first at Letchworth (1903) and then at Welwyn Garden City (1920). A similar scheme was developed at Hampstead Garden Suburb after 1907.

The spate of Victorian legislation arising out of the increasing concern for the health and housing standards of the masses was continued by the 1909 Housing, Town Planning, etc. Act (Ashworth, 1954). This empowered local authorities to prepare their own town-planning schemes, with the object of regulating land use in order to ensure proper sanitary conditions, amenity and convenience. It granted no powers to deal with existing urban problems, but did exert a significant control over new suburban development schemes. The first plan authorized by the Act was Birmingham City Council's Quinton, Harborne and Edgbaston Scheme of 1913, which had a maximum density of twenty houses per acre, and included parks, open spaces and broad highways.

After a temporary halt during the First World War, the 1919 Housing Act introduced state subsidies for housing. The ensuing twenty years witnessed the construction of some four million new dwellings. The effect was to create a great sprawl of dormitory suburbs, particularly in the South-East and Midlands, which remained relatively unaffected by the slump. During the 1930s over 60,000 acres of farmland a year were taken for building. The powers for planning control were still relatively ineffective and house building was not integrated with town planning. The development of public transport had made it possible for many people to live at a greater distance from their place of work, while the low price of land permitted densities of twelve houses per acre or less. The Victorian tradition of segregating social groups was reinforced. Council estates contained the working classes, paying rent to local authorities, while private estates contained the middle classes, paying off mortgages to building societies.

Municipal estates were sometimes vast in extent. London County Council's Becontree estate had a population greater than that of York. They were usually planned on diluted garden city lines, the road system adopting intricate geometric patterns and sweeping curves, as in Birmingham Corporation's Kingstanding and Weoley Castle estates: the final rejection of the grid after two thousand years of town planning (Plate xx). Houses were of brick, sometimes rendered, plain in design, and totally identical.

The inter-war period saw the heyday of the private speculator. The street plan favoured by the speculative builder was usually simpler than that of the corporation estate. Ribbon development, which minimized the expenditure on roads and sewerage, was rife until the 1925 Restriction of Ribbon Development Act attempted to curb it. Tasteless semi-detached houses with mock half-timbering tacked onto gables were reproduced in uniform style all over Britain. The developer was under no obligation to provide any sort of social amenities, or to reserve space for shops, schools or public buildings.

A classic case of the evils of unbridled speculative development is the south coast resort of Peacehaven, founded in 1924. Its plan is about as unimaginative as possible, a rigid grid of long rectangular *insulae* extending for over one and a half miles along the coast and paying no heed whatsoever to the considerable natural potential of the site. No restriction was placed upon the type of dwelling erected, nor on the interval between the purchase of a plot and completion of the building. The promenade was left as a rough grassy strip along the edge of the cliff. No mains drainage was provided and for many years the streets were not properly made up, giving it the air of a shanty town. Only very recently have plans been made to provide it with a recognizable town centre (Brandon, 1974).

Up to the outbreak of the 1939–45 war the principal change in most towns was the enormous extension of their outer suburbs. The widespread bomb damage in London, Coventry, Plymouth, Hull, Exeter, Southampton, and several other cities turned attention back to the town centre. So complete was the devastation that the opportunity presented itself for wholesale redesign. Even in towns like Exeter, Plymouth and Southampton, where the basic medieval street pattern was retained, the new centres which arose out of the ashes were very different in appearance. The architect was no longer obliged to hide a modern reinforced-concrete or steel-framed building behind a traditional façade, but was allowed new emphasis on functionalism and integrity. Instead of applying false ornament, the character of new buildings was emphasized by the contrasting colours and textures of concrete, asbestos, aluminium, cedar cladding, plate glass and plastics. Soaring land values increased the tendency to build upwards instead of outwards. The most advanced of the post-war city centres was Coventry. Here, for the first time, pedestrians were partly segregated from the increasing volume of motor traffic.

The increasing scarcity and high values of land for building led to a corresponding change in the character of post-war suburbs. In place of detached and semi-detached houses with big gardens, extensive open spaces and broad verges, there was a return to higher densities. Terraced housing returned to favour, and there was widespread adoption of multi-storey flat blocks—the logical successors of nineteenth-century by-law housing and Peabody Buildings.

While the greatest amount of post-war development has taken place around pre-existing centres, the 1946 New Towns Act designated fourteen sites for development as new towns. Eight of these— Crawley, Bracknell, Hemel Hempstead, Welwyn, Stevenage, Harlow, Hatfield and Basildon—formed a ring around London. Two, East Kilbride and Glenrothes, were in Scotland, two more, Peterlee and Newton Aycliffe, in the North-East, one, Corby, in the East Midlands, and one, Cwmbran, in Monmouthshire. The planning of these towns reflected many of Howard's ideas, in so far as they were self-contained units of limited size, with separate residential, commercial, civic and industrial zones, surrounded by a green belt. The residential districts were planned in 'neighbourhood units', with their own schools, shops and playing fields. The first generation of housing was still un-imaginative in design; but significant advances were made in planning for motor traffic, with attempts to segregate through traffic, local traffic and pedestrians.

During the 1950s Government policy favoured the expansion of existing towns by local authorities rather than the creation of further new towns. The 1952 Town Development Act planted London overspill at Bletchley, Haverhill, Swindon, Kings Lynn and Basing-stoke. However, the lessons learned from the first dozen post-war new towns were incorporated in many of the new designs. Some of the most advanced concepts of town planning in the 1950s were embodied in London County Council's scheme for Hook, Hampshire, which, in the event, never got off the drawing-board. They were adopted, however, in Cumbernauld, the only new town of the decade, established in 1956. Estates were laid out on the Radburn principle, with vehicular and pedestrian traffic completely segregated. The housing density was greater than that of the earlier new towns, and more imaginatively designed. A large and complex multi-level town centre concentrated the principal shops, civic offices and entertainments in one precinct. The 1960s saw the establishment of a further eleven new towns: Livingstone and Irvine in Scotland, Washington in Durham, Skelmersdale, Warrington and Runcorn in the North-West, Telford and Redditch in the West Midlands, and Peterborough, Northampton and Milton Keynes in the East Midlands (Burke, 1971).

In the new towns planners have had a free hand in designing an urban environment of the twentieth century, unhindered by the constraints of an inherited urban framework. Inevitably, however, the principles applied to new towns have also had an effect on older towns. The 1947 Town & Country Planning Act endowed the authorities with powers over land use and development which far exceeded all previous controls. The planning of the urban landscape became an obligatory function of local authorities. Since then, the attempts to reconcile a vast increase in road traffic with a Saxon or medieval street pattern have frequently resulted in the encirclement of the latter with a motorway-standard road network, including complex clover-leaf and spaghetti-type junctions. The commercial pressures on valuable town-centre land have led to the amalgamation of plots into larger units, the greater height of buildings on each plot, and the greater depth of piling, cellarage and underground car parking.

It has become increasingly clear in recent years that the demands of modern commerce and the domination of motor transport are in basic conflict with the retention of historic townscapes (Buchanan, 1963). We shall see in the final chapter how it has become necessary to introduce conservation legislation in order to restrain the chain-reaction of wholesale redevelopment. The application of such legislation, fostered by increasing public awareness of the vulnerability of the urban environment, has already made a significant impact on the treatment of some town centres.

Chapter X

The Future of Towns

So far we have been concerned with the development of the urban landscape over the ages and the physical contributions made by successive generations of planners and builders according to the needs and constraints of their time (Fig. 40).

The cynic will be asking whether it matters anyway. Is historical information of any value at all in the modern world, with its manifold problems and seemingly different priorities? Need we worry about the archaeology of towns, the origins of their street plan, the age of their buildings? Should governments, local authorities, and educational institutions be spending money on the furtherance of our understanding of how towns have developed in the past?

Even in crude monetary terms it can be argued that a knowledge of the history and topography of towns pays dividends. Tourism is a boom industry. Most visitors go to York or Chester or Caernarvon to see castles, town walls, churches and old buildings, not shopping precincts, ring roads and car parks. Relatively little investment is needed when the attractions are already there. The recent proliferation of popular topographical handbooks and guides bears witness to the basic thirst for knowledge on the part of visitors to historic towns, and their desire to understand what they see.

Another practical application lies in the planning and management of the environment of the town dweller himself. There is more to life than economics. Some of the serious social problems which can arise when commercial pressures override all else are too well known to need discussion here. The varied townscape produced by centuries of growth is preferable to the uniformity of a one-period environment (Plate xx). The human scale of a quiet sixteenth-, seventeenth- or eighteenth- century street (Plate VIII) is a physical relief to the individual dwarfed by high-rise flats and offices, marooned in vast housing estates and constantly deafened by the roar of traffic. However, the responsibility for conserving the historic factors which contribute to

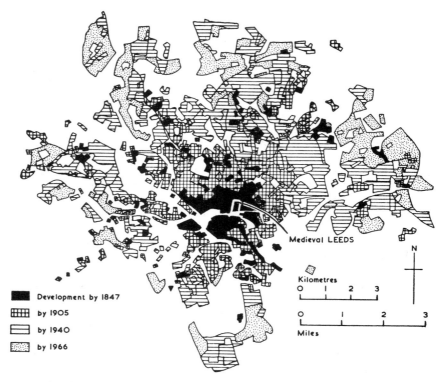

Development by 1847
by 1905
by 1940
by 1966

Medieval LEEDS

N

Kilometres
0   1   2   3

0   1   2   3
Miles

40   Leeds, the expansion of the town.

a town's individual personality cannot be undertaken unless those significant historic elements are first identified and understood.

Finally, of course, such information is of value in its own right. The increase of knowledge needs no justification or excuse. For a society to survive it must be aware of its heritage. The decisions of the future are built upon the experience of the past. A society without a past is like a man without a memory, and is prone to the same confusions. Some writers have argued that, for sanity's sake, we must know *how* we have arrived at the state in which we now find ourselves, and that one good test of the level of civilization reached by a society is how much it spends on non-profit-motivated research.

How have the various disciplines interested in towns responded to their rapid transformation in the present time? Historians and geographers have, perhaps, been least affected by the situation. Documents are rarely subjected to the 'last-chance' opportunity which is so often the fate of physical evidence, while for geographers the dynamics of the changes now taking place have tended, on the whole, to be of greater interest than the evidence which is thereby destroyed. Urban archaeology, on the other hand, has grown up with the 'rescue' problem, and it is here that the response has been most dramatic.

New ring roads and central redevelopments not only affect the appearance of towns more basically, they are also far more destructive of archaeological evidence than anything which has gone before. Prior to the nineteenth century most new buildings in towns were simply constructed over the foundations of their predecessors, and even the biggest Victorian cellars caused only localized damage. The deep piling and foundations required for modern high-rise buildings, together with the maze of underpasses, subways and service trenches which characterize modern development, are a far more serious threat. It has been estimated that, of 906 historic towns in Britain for which information is available, 583 are affected by redevelopment (Fig. 41). Of these, 231 have already undergone or are threatened with major destructive development, while another 352 have smaller development projects. In only 161 towns was there any sort of archaeological response to the threat, and in only twenty-one cases were there any satisfactory arrangements for excavation and publication of threatened sites (Heighway, 1972). 20 per cent of all historic towns remaining for study will probably have been largely destroyed archaeologically by 1991. The details of some towns are frightening. Within the City of London, of some 677 acres of land, 212 acres were redeveloped between 1945 and 1972, while a further 236 acres were covered by road surfaces. At the present rate of progress, almost all of what remains of London's archaeology can be expected to be destroyed within the next fifteen or twenty years (Biddle and Hudson, 1973). In Gloucester some 10 acres, nearly a quarter of the Roman *colonia*, was destroyed between 1960 and 1971 (Heighway, 1974). About the same area within the medieval walls of Hereford was threatened by redevelopment in 1974 (Shoesmith, 1974). In Cambridge in 1972 redevelopment had already destroyed, or was destroying, nearly a third of the area within the city boundary.

Although the cost of excavating an urban site is a mere fraction of the cost of the development which makes it necessary, urban archaeology is expensive in relation to the sums of money available for excavation each year. The depth of archaeological deposits in a

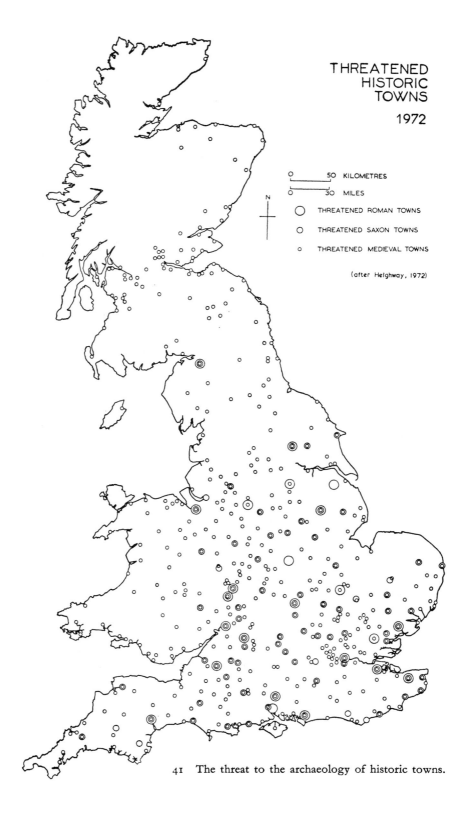

THREATENED
HISTORIC
TOWNS

1972

50 KILOMETRES

30 MILES

THREATENED ROMAN TOWNS

THREATENED SAXON TOWNS

THREATENED MEDIEVAL TOWNS

(after Heighway, 1972)

41 The threat to the archaeology of historic towns.

town can exceed 25 feet, and is commonly of the order of 12 feet. It is therefore impossible to excavate fully every site which becomes available. One might question whether the attempt should even be made. Every site is unique in a sense, but after a certain number of medieval tenements, or Saxon defences, or Roman *fora*, have been examined in detail, the law of diminishing returns may begin to take effect, and we may find ourselves simply adding fresh examples to what we already know. In addition, there are arguments for concentrating resources on large-scale extensive operations in a small number of towns, rather than dissipating effort in a larger number of smaller sites. On the other hand, any policy which involves writing off the archaeology of a considerable number of towns is obviously a calculated gamble; it runs grave dangers because, beyond a certain limit, no one can forecast what excavation may reveal.

The dilemma which archaeologists have faced in towns has caused them to re-examine their professional responsibility. In the past their public image has been dilettante, if not reactionary. The fear that they will stop or delay construction work is still widely held by developers and councils. Archaeologists have only themselves to blame for this: until quite recently their public relations and concern for the other side's point of view has been conspicuously lacking. Over the last few years, however, there has been a considerable improvement in understanding and co-operation between archaeologist and developer. Significant advances have been made towards creating a climate of opinion in which archaeological investigation is seen to be as relevant as any of the other activities on a development site. Excavators have had to become accustomed to planning their work to fit in with the schedule of developers and contractors, and, wherever possible, to be off the site before construction work begins. There are now cases where prior archaeological investigation of a site has actually been to the contractor's advantage, because solid masonry or soft sediments, missed by the engineer's boreholes, were identified and defined.

One of the products of the archaeologists' increased professionalism has been the 'Implications Report', a survey produced to define and publicize the archaeological implications of urban development. The first such study was produced for Oxford in 1967 (Benson and Cook, 1967), while the most comprehensive to date covers London (Biddle and Hudson, 1973). Upwards of a dozen individual towns have now been covered by Implications Surveys, while several county-wide surveys, each examining a number of towns, are currently in progress. The content of such surveys has become fairly standardized. A summary of the 'conventional' history of the town is followed by an appraisal of how the archaeological work carried out to date has changed this picture. This is usually followed by an analysis of past and forseeable future developments which have destroyed, or are likely to affect, archaeological deposits. The final section usually consists of a series of recommendations on future action, normally including the appointment of a full-time archaeologist and back-up team for a specific period, together with facilities for conservation and display of finds and publication of results. Considerable use is normally made of the visual impact of plans (Fig. 42), often in a 'before' and 'after' sequence.

Partly as a result of such surveys, an increasing number of towns now have some permanent arrangement for rescue archaeology. Although the situation has improved a great deal, there is still no room for complacency. Most towns are still without such arrangements. Even where the resources exist, there is still no way in which the recalcitrant council or developer can be required even to permit access, let alone thorough examination by archaeologists, no matter how critical the site. Even where thorough investigation does take place before destruction, excavation is sometimes a poor second-best to preservation. The safeguards for archaeology in Britain are considerably inferior to those in most European countries.

The crisis in urban archaeology applies equally to structures above ground. Yet, despite the infinitely greater visual appeal of buildings and the fact that far more buildings than archaeological sites receive the protection of the law, considerably less progress has been achieved. In Gloucester 603 buildings were listed as being of Architectural or Historic Interest under the 1947 Town & Country Planning Act. Only 459 remained in 1971. In Tewkesbury, a small town justly proud of its heritage of historic buildings, forty-five statutorily protected buildings were demolished between 1947 and 1971 (Miles and Fowler, 1972). In Andover, of fifty-nine Listed Buildings surviving in 1968 only twenty-nine were neither demolished nor threatened five years later (Champion, 1973). Only eleven towns in Britain had any satisfactory ongoing arrangement for recording buildings in 1972 (Heighway, 1972). Despite the legislation concerning historic buildings, there has been little effort in most towns to make an adequate record of even Listed Buildings threatened with demolition, despite the efforts of the hard-worked Royal Commission investigators. Where lip-service is paid to recording, it is usually limited to a few photographs, which, while better than nothing, are no substitute for accurately-drawn plans, elevations and sections.

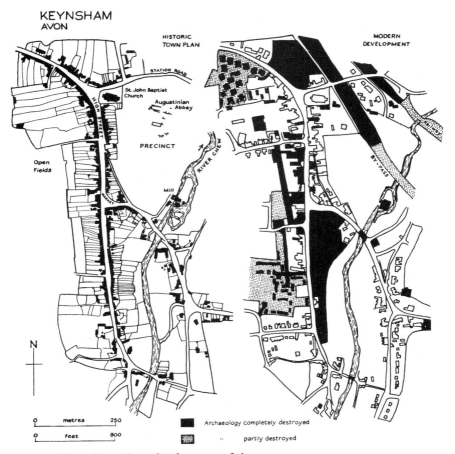

KEYNSHAM
AVON

HISTORIC
TOWN PLAN

MODERN
DEVELOPMENT

STATION ROAD

St. John Baptist
Church

Augustinian
Abbey

PRECINCT

Open
Fields

RIVER CHEW

HIGH STREET

Mill

BY-PASS

N

| | metres | 250 | | Archaeology completely destroyed |
| 0 | feet | 800 | | .. | partly destroyed |

42 Keynsham: the redevelopment of the town, 1974.

Even in towns where some sort of recording has taken place, attention has usually been concentrated on Listed Buildings. The Statutory Lists have normally been compiled from external evidence only. An inestimable number of unrecognized medieval, sixteenth- and seventeenth-century buildings survive in towns concealed behind eighteenth- and nineteenth-century façades (Plate ix). Many extremely important buildings have thereby escaped listing altogether. More- over, what of the innumerable buildings which have no aesthetic attraction, but are nonetheless far more representative of certain periods of urban life? Little thought was given in slum clearance programmes to the need for a record of what was swept away; yet a back-to-back court in Birmingham or Nottingham is as relevant a part of human history as Westminster Abbey or the Houses of Parliament.

In some ways there is no real need for interests concerned with archaeology and buildings to be in conflict with essential urban redevelopments. Given proper organization and resources, which can be achieved at a fraction of the cost of a new car park or shopping centre, the buildings can all be properly drawn and photographed before demolition and the ground then excavated and all archaeological features fully recorded before the contractor begins his work on the site. The result will be a rich and varied picture of many centuries of life on that patch of ground. However, while the specialist will have his technical report, all the general public will ever see will be a few objects on display in the local museum, a succession of slides in a public lecture, and, if they are lucky, the ghost of a medieval friary or town gate marked out in granite setts on the asphalt or commemorated by a blue plaque halfway up a supermarket wall.

Is this what society really wants? Few town councils would allow a public bonfire of their medieval charters, rentals and court rolls, even if they had all been copied out in typescript beforehand. The architectural and archaeological fabric of the town gives a far more complete and representative picture of its life in the past and has greater appeal to the man in the street, yet it is daily eroded in the name of progress.

No one can stop the clock, and it is inevitable, right and proper that towns will change in appearance this century just as they have in every preceding century. It is not so much the occurrence of change which calls for concern, as its scale, and sometimes, its motives. The historic core of any city is an irreplaceable resource. Should it be lightly sacrificed to make way for a new shopping centre, many of whose shops will remain untenanted for years because no one can afford the high rents needed to pay for the building? Are we right to spend stupendous sums of money in devastating town centres and inner suburbs for ring roads and urban motorways whose useful life is unlikely to exceed fifty years?

One possible alternative, assuming that our present life-style will continue to demand vast supermarkets and prestige office blocks all instantly accessible by motor, is to create a modern centre adjacent to, but physically separate from, the historic core. There is no immutable law of nature which says that a glass and concrete precinct must occupy the same site as a medieval market-place. Indeed, there are plenty of good historic precedents for shifting the centre of a town when a change of scale or function makes the old centre inappropriate. The alterations to the plans of Anglo-Saxon Hereford and Nottingham, medieval Rhuddlan and Pontefract, Regency Leamington and Victorian Middlesbrough, are all, in their totally different ways, examples of the same principle. Most towns have their semi-derelict areas in the inner suburbs or space on their margins where a new civic and commercial complex could be accommodated with provision for car parking and fast road access, with a minimum of disturbance to the town's historic fabric. The historic centre could then remain intact and revert to the function of being a pleasant area to live in.

In many cases it is already too late. Newcastle, Croydon, Bristol, Birmingham and some others have been firmly committed to progress, and their centres look like anywhere from Tel Aviv to San Francisco. Commercial prosperity has been achieved at the cost of total loss of individuality, character and interest.

Where a town centre does survive with its historic features substantially intact, considerable powers are now available for its protection. A re-examination of its buildings will undoubtedly reveal many more worthy of being listed as 'of architectural or historic interest' under the town-planning acts. Sites in towns can be scheduled under the Ancient Monuments Acts (1913–74), although at present scheduling is usually applied on a piecemeal and quite inadequate basis—a building here, a stretch of wall there, a castle mound elsewhere. While there may be practical difficulties in scheduling larger areas in towns, these are not insuperable. Perhaps the legislation offering the most hope of a more comprehensive view is the Civic Amenities Act (1967), which instituted the designation of Conservation Areas in an attempt to protect the character of areas rather than the structure of individual buildings. While these tend inevitably to be centred around building groups, the Act and accompanying circulars do urge that due attention be paid to ancient street patterns and archaeological features. Ways and means of enhancement and improvement should be an intrinsic part of conservation area policy.

While the protection of historic town centres gives the greatest cause for concern, another aspect of the demented scale of modern development is the suburban sprawl over former countryside. With an increasing population it is inevitable that towns would grow considerably beyond their medieval, Georgian and Victorian bounds.

217

Unfortunately, in the righteous reaction against the slums of the nineteenth century, the garden suburb notion has got completely out of hand. It has defeated its own objects by its endless repetition. The suburb dweller has the benefits of neither country nor town, but is in a sort of intervening limbo. Much of the benefit he would have gained by shorter working hours and higher wages is negated by higher rents, mortgages, rates and fares and a much longer journey to work. The slavish adherence to building, public health, fire and traffic regulations has produced a negative townscape, in which the dominant elements are buildings every bit as monotonous as by-law housing and more objectionable because they cover a much wider area. Vast areas are covered by verges, other quite unusable empty spaces, and sweeping roads with graded curves wide enough to accommodate juggernaut lorries on their way to the docks, but not necessary for local traffic. One alternative answer, the tower-block flat, has equally obvious evils—many of the problems of the back-to-back without its sense of community.

Conclusion

What we have attempted to show in this book is that towns are more than just places where people go for shopping, entertainment and employment. They are more than just streets and buildings. They are intricate compositions made up from the interrelationship of many features, natural and man-made, ancient and modern. Hill slopes, valleys, rivers, buried archaeological deposits, streets, lanes, open spaces, property boundaries and many different types of buildings are all elements of the townscape. The present uses to which those elements are put are the most ephemeral of all the factors contributing to the town's appearance, although at present they may be the most strident. The cumulative patterns which the different elements create are what gives each town its peculiar character, its flavour as a unique place on the earth's surface, different from all others. To those with eyes to see, the topographical record is an all-important document to the past development of a town. The curious open space before the entrance to the main parish church, the sharp right-angled bends in the roads of the town centre, the continuous break of slope which can be traced .through rows of back gardens, the flaking stucco and grimy classical details of the seedy inner suburbs, the ugly Victorian church and town hall, all have their story to tell.

Towns cannot be classified simply as 'historic' or 'not historic'. Places like Bath, York and Chester may have aesthetically the finest buildings; but Grimsby, Workington and Wednesbury are just as worthy of historic study. Dudley, in the Black Country, contains exactly the same historic elements as Dunster, which is visited by thousands every year (Fig. 43). A superficial glance at Doncaster

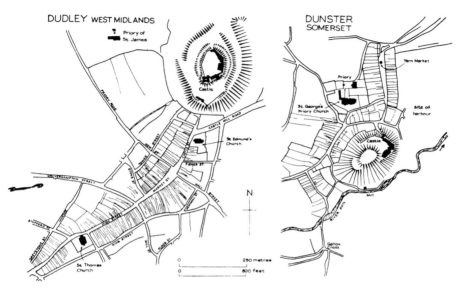

43 Industrial town and tourist centre: there is no essential difference in their historical topography.

would not immediately suggest the presence of two Roman forts and a *vicus*, a Saxon *burh*, a Norman castle, medieval town defences and two medieval friaries (Buckland and Dolby, 1972). Nor would the antiquarian seeker after fine perpendicular churches immediately think of looking in Wolverhampton or Rotherham; yet if he did so he would find examples to rival anything in the Cotswolds or East Anglia.

Most towns are a product of many centuries of development and evolution. Their aspirations and vicissitudes can still be traced in their present varied topography; but their fabric is now threatened on a scale unprecedented in previous centuries. A heavy responsibility devolves on planners and planning committees. They must be concerned with more than the economic pros and cons of a new shopping precinct or office block, the practicalities of getting more vehicles more quickly to or through the centre. The question increasingly to be asked is whether the place is still likely to be worth living in when the development project is complete.

In making a plea for rehabilitation rather than comprehensive redevelopment of towns, we both believe that the retention of historic features goes far beyond any mere academic or antiquarian interest. Only with a sympathetic environment, full of reminders of its past development, on a scale related to human form and movement, will towns continue to be of any value to people as places to work, shop, relax and carry on the business of living. An adequate appreciation of their landscape history and a secure future for the fragile and vulnerable remains of their past is vital to our sane existence.

Postscript

Since this book was written over twenty years ago, many important contributions have been made to the study of urban topography. Only a few brief pointers towards some of the recent literature can be included here.

The biggest yield of new information has come from archaeology. In 1976 we were just beginning to see the first fruits of new initiatives towards large-scale urban rescue excavations, and the results of much of that heroic effort have now become available. The potential and methods of urban archaeology have been discussed by Martin Carver (1987) and Patrick Ottaway (1992). The Council for British Archaeology published a summary of archaeological research undertaken between 1976 and 1981 (Schofield & Palliser, 1981), followed by a futher collection of essays which includes both period surveys and surveys of specific topics such as town defences, urban castles, public buildings, domestic buildings, religious houses, parish churches and waterfronts (Schofield & Leech, eds, 1987). Waterfront archaeology, with its special potential for the recovery of organic materials and for the understanding of a range of trades, has emerged as a major topic in its own right, and has been the subject of a separate volume (Good, Jones & Ponsford, eds, 1991)

Authoritative but accessible summaries of archaeological work are available for an increasing number of individual towns, including London (Schofield & Dyson, eds, 1980) and York (Daniells, Hall & York, 1978). The third volume of the British Atlas of Historic Towns, devoted entirely to London, first appeared in 1989 and has since been reissued (Lobel, 1991). Since 1975 the Royal Commission on Historical Monuments (England) have issued further volumes on York, Stamford, Salisbury, Beverley and Northampton (R.C.H.M.E., 1975, 1977, 1980, 1981, 1982, 1985, 1993).

As a companion to John Wacher's 1974 volume on the towns of Roman Britain (which was itself updated by a revised edition in 1995), the smaller Roman towns have been explored by Barry Burnham & John Wacher (1990), and a general synthesis on Roman towns has been provided by Guy de la Bédoyère (1992). The continuity of early industrial activity has been demonstrated at Droitwich (Woodiwiss, ed., 1992).

Much more has been learned of the mid-Saxon proto-urban trading places sometimes called *wics*, both collectively (Hodges, 1982) and individually (e.g. Morton, ed., 1992). John Blair (1988) has argued persuasively that more recognition should be given to minsters as generators of urban growth. An overview of Anglo-Saxon towns in the south has been provided by Jeremy Haslam (ed., 1984), while the *burhs* of Wessex have been discussed further by David Hill & Alexander Rumble (1996). The concept of 'primary towns' put forward by Alan Everitt (1974), nodal points served by routes which encouraged both the early development and the persistence of economic, administrative and even religious functions through successive ages has been influential, balancing Maurice Beresford's definition of medieval new towns, which itself remains of fundamental importance.

Medieval towns in England were examined by Colin Platt (1976) in a volume which admirably combines the evidence of archaeology and written sources. Medieval towns in Wales have been covered by Ian Soulsby (1983). John Schofield & Alan Vince (1994) update the evidence for a range of medieval urban themes, including topography, crafts and industries, trades and commerce, religious houses and environmental evidence. The role of the church in shaping the origins and development of the medieval town is discussed in a series of essays edited by Terry Slater and Gervase Rosser (1998). The techniques of town plan analysis pioneered by Professor M.R.G. Conzen have been discussed further by Jeremy Whitehand (ed., 1981) and developed by Terry Slater, and in particular the systematic examination and metrological analysis of burgage plots has yielded dividends which were only dimly perceived in 1976 (Slater, 1980, 1981a, b, 1990; Scrase, 1989). A more historical approach to medieval towns has been taken by Susan Reynolds (1977). Medieval houses in London have been discussed by John Schofield (1994). Amongst individual medieval towns, Winchester has received the most detailed treatment in three magisterial volumes in the *Winchester Studies* series (Biddle, 1976; Keene, 1985).

Changes in towns in the early post-medieval period have been explored in two collections of essays and local studies edited by Peter Clark (1981, 1984). For the later post-medieval period Jonathan Brown (1986) provides a useful summary. The Royal Commission on Historical Monuments (England) has published model surveys of a seventeenth-century industrial suburb in Frome (Leech, 1981), of the late seventeenth-century port of Whitehaven (Collier, 1991) and of the railway town of Swindon (Cattell & Falconer, 1995). Important contributions to the study of post-medieval urban and industrial housing have been made by Stefan Muthesius (1982), M.J. Daunton (1983), John Burnett (1986) and Martin Doughty (ed., 1986). The character and history of suburbs has been examined by Arthur Edwards (1981). Guides to urban documentary records are provided by John West (1983) and Stephen Porter (1990). The aesthetics of townscapes have been covered by a number of writers, including David Lloyd (1984), Mark Girouard (1990) and Alec Clifton-Taylor (1978, 1981, 1984).

We now need to take a more European perspective. The first steps towards this were provided by a collection of essays on urban archaeology edited by Maurice Barley (1977). Another valuable collection of essays on the archaeology of sub-Roman and early medieval towns in Europe has been provided by Richard Hodges & Brian Hobley (1988), while the Viking contribution is analysed by Helen Clarke & Bjorn Ambrosiani (1991). A more historical approach is taken in Longman's series *A History of Urban Society in Europe*, under the general editorship of Robert Tittler (Nicholas, 1997a, 1997b; Friedrichs, 1994).

Bibliography

ADDYMAN, P. V. (1974)   York: The Anatomy of a Crisis in Rescue Archaeology, in RAHTZ, P. A. (ed.) *Rescue Archaeology*, pp. 153-62 (Harmondsworth).

ADDYMAN, P. V. and BIDDLE, M. (1965)   Medieval Cambridge: Recent Finds and Excavations, *Proceedings of Cambridge Antiquarian Society*, Vol. LVIII, pp. 74-137.

ADDYMAN, P. V. and HILL, D. H. (1968)   Saxon Southampton: A Review of the Evidence.   Part i: History, Location, Date and Character of the Town, *Proceedings of Hampshire Field Club*, Vol. XXV.

ADDYMAN, P. V. and HILL, D. H. (1969)   Saxon Southampton: A Review of the Evidence.   Part ii: Industry, Trade and Everyday Life, *Proceedings of Hampshire Field Club*, Vol. XXVI.

ADDYMAN, P. V. and RUMSBY, J. H. (1971)   The Archaeological Implications of Proposed Development in York: A report to the Council for British Archaeology and the Yorkshire Philosophical Society.

ALCOCK, L. (1968-70)   Excavations at South Cadbury Castle, *Antiquaries Journal*, Vols. XLVIII-L.

ALCOCK, L. (1971)   *Arthur's Britain: History and Archaeology, A.D. 367-634* (Harmondsworth).

ALCOCK, L. (1972)   *'By South Cadbury is that Camelot . . .' Excavations at Cadbury Castle, 1966-70*, esp. pp. 131-58 (London).

ALDSWORTH, F. and HILL, D. (1971)   The Burghal Hidage—Eashing, *Surrey Archaeological Collections*, Vol. LXVIII, pp. 198-201.

ARLOTT, J. (ed.) (1953)   *John Speed's England*, 4 vols (London).

ASHWORTH, W. (1954)   *The Genesis of Modern British Town Planning: A study in Economic and Social History of the Nineteenth and Twentieth Centuries* (London).

ASTON, M. and ROWLEY, R. T. (1974)   *Landscape Archaeology: An Introduction to Fieldwork Techniques on Post-Roman Landscapes*, esp. pp. 90-116 (Newton Abbot).

BAKER, A. (1968)   Viroconium: A Study of the Defences from Aerial Reconnaissance, *Transactions of Shropshire Archaeological Society*, Vol. LVIII, pt. iii.

225

BALCHIN, W. G. V. (1954)   *The Making of the English Landscape: Cornwall*, esp. pp. 77–94 (London).

BANNISTER, T. (1950)   The First Iron-Framed Buildings, *Architectural Review*, Vol. CVII (April, 1950), pp. 231–46.

BARKER, P. A. (1961)   Excavations on the Town Wall, Roushill, Shrewsbury, *Medieval Archaeology*, Vol. V, pp. 181–210.

BARKER, P. A. (1973)   *Excavations on the Site of the Baths Basilica at Wroxeter (Viroconium Cornoviorum), 1966–1973: An Interim Report* (Birmingham).

BARLEY, M. W. (1974)   *A Guide to British Topographical Collections*, Council for British Archaeology (London).

BARLEY, M. W. (forthcoming)   Town Defences in England and Wales, in BARLEY, M. W. (ed.)   *The Plans and Topography of Medieval Towns in England and Wales*, Council for British Archaeology (London).

BARLEY, M. W. and STRAW, I. F. (1969)   Nottingham, *Historic Towns Atlas*, Vol. I (London).

BEAVER, S. H. (1964)   The Potteries: A Study in the Evolution of a Cultural Landscape, *Transactions of the Institute of British Geographers*, Vol. XXXIV, pp. 1–31.

BELL, C. and BELL, R. (1969)   *City Fathers: The Early History of Town Planning in Britain* (Harmondsworth).

BENSON, D. and COOK, J. (1967)   *City of Oxford Redevelopment: Archaeological Implications*, Oxford City and County Museum.

BENTON, J. F. (ed.) (1968)   *Town Origins: The Evidence from Medieval England* (Boston, U.S.A.).

BERESFORD, M. W. (1957)   *History on the Ground: Six Studies in Maps and Landscapes* esp. pp. 125–50 and pp. 151–84 (London).

BERESFORD, M. W. (1959)   The Six New Towns of the Bishops of Winchester, 1200–55, *Medieval Archaeology*, Vol. III, pp. 187–215.

BERESFORD, M. W. (1967a)   *New Towns of the Middle Ages: Town Plantation in England, Wales and Gascony* (London).

BERESFORD, M. W. (1967b)   Prosperity Street and Others, in BERESFORD, M. W. and JONES, G. R. J. (eds)   *Leeds and its Region*, British Association for the Advancement of Science, pp. 186–97 (Leeds).

BERESFORD, M. W. (1971)   The Back-to-Back House in Leeds, 1787–1937, in CHAPMAN, S. D. (ed.)   *The History of Working-Class Housing: A Symposium*, pp. 93–132 (Newton Abbot).

BERESFORD, M. W. (1974)   The Making of a Townscape: Richard Paley in the East End of Leeds, 1771–1803, in CHALKLIN, C. W. and HAVINDEN, M. A. (eds)   *Rural Change and Urban Growth, 1500–1800*, pp. 281–320 (London).

BERESFORD, M. W. and ST JOSEPH, J. K. (1958)   *Medieval England: An Aerial Survey* (Cambridge).

BEST, G. (1968)   The Scottish Victorian City, *Victorian Studies*, Vol. XI.

BIDDLE, M. (1963–75)   Excavations at Winchester, Interim Reports, *Antiquaries Journal*, Vols XLIII–LV.

BIDDLE, M. (1968) Archaeology and the History of British Towns, *Antiquity*, Vol. XLII, pp. 109–16.

BIDDLE, M. (1970) *The Old Minster: Excavations near Winchester Cathedral, 1961–1969* (Winchester).

BIDDLE, M. (1972) The Winton Domesday, in BESCH, W., *et al. Die Stadt in der Europaischen Geschichte: Festschrifte Edith Ennen*, pp. 36–43 (Verlag, Bonn).

BIDDLE, M. (1974) The Future of the Urban Past, in RAHTZ, P. A. (ed.) *Rescue Archaeology*, pp. 95–112 (Harmondsworth).

BIDDLE, M. (forthcoming) The Evolution of Towns: Planned Towns Before 1066, in BARLEY, M. W. (ed.) *The Plans and Topography of Medieval Towns in England and Wales*, Council for British Archaeology (London).

BIDDLE, M. and HILL, D. (1971) Late Saxon Planned Towns, *Antiquaries Journal*, Vol. LI, pt. i, pp. 70–85.

BIDDLE, M. and HUDSON, D. (1973) The Future of London's Past: A Survey of the Archaeological Implications of Planning and Development in the Nation's Capital, *Rescue Publication*, no. 4.

BIDDLE, M., LAMBRICK, H. T. and MYRES, J. N. L. (1968) The Early History of Abingdon, Berkshire, and its Abbey, *Medieval Archaeology*, Vol. XII, pp. 26–69.

BILSON, J. (1928) Wyke upon Hull in 1293, *Transactions of East Riding Antiquarian Society*, Vol. XXVI, pp. 37–105.

BOND, C. J. (1973) The Estates of Evesham Abbey: a preliminary survey of their medieval topography, *Vale of Evesham Historical Society*, Vol. IV, esp. pp. 44–50—'Urban Ventures'.

BOON, G. C. (1957) *Roman Silchester* (London).

BOON, G. C. (1974) *Silchester, the Roman Town of Calleva* (Newton Abbot).

BOWEN, H. C. and TAYLOR, C. C. (1964) The Site of Newton (*Nova Villa*), Studland, Dorset, *Medieval Archaeology*, Vol. VIII, pp. 223–6.

BRANDON, P. (1974) *The Making of the English Landscape: The Sussex Landscape*, esp. pp. 208–47 (London).

BROOKS, N. (1964) The Unidentified Forts of the Burghal Hidage, *Medieval Archaeology*, Vol. VIII, pp. 74–90.

BROWN, R. A., COLVIN, H. M. and TAYLOR, A. J. (1963) *The History of the King's Works*, 2 Vols (H.M.S.O. London).

BUCHANAN, C. (1963) *Traffic in Towns* (Harmondsworth).

BUCHANAN, C. (1968) *Bath: A Study in Conservation* (H.M.S.O. London).

BUCKLAND, P. and DOLBY, M. (1972) Doncaster, *Current Archaeology*, No. 33 (July 1972), pp. 273–8.

BURGESS, L. A. (1964) The Origins of Southampton, *University of Leicester Dept. of English Local History, Occasional Papers*, No. 16.

BURGESS, L. A. (1974) The Southampton Terrier of 1454, *Southampton Record Series* 15.

BURKE, G. (1971) *Towns in the Making* (London).

BURROWS, G. S. (1968) *Chichester: A Study in Conservation* (H.M.S.O. London).

BUTLER, L. (forthcoming) The Evolution of Towns: Planned Towns after 1066, in BARLEY, M. W. (ed.) *The Plans and Topography of Medieval Towns in England and Wales*, Council for British Archaeology (London).

BUTLER, R. M. (1972) A Late-Seventeenth-Century Plan of York, *Antiquaries Journal*, Vol. II, pt. ii, pp. 320–9.

BUTT, J. (1971) Working-Class Housing in Glasgow, 1851–1914, in CHAPMAN, S. D. (ed.) *The History of Working-Class Housing: A Symposium*; pp. 55–92 (Newton Abbot).

CAMDEN, W. (1586) *Britannia* (Newton Abbot). First English edition 1610.

CAMPBELL, J. (1975) Norwich, *Historic Towns Atlas*, Vol. II (London).

CARTER, A. (1972) The Norwich Survey: Excavations in Norwich 1971: An Interim Report, *Norfolk Archaeology*, Vol. XXXV, pt. iii.

CARTER, A. (1975) Norwich, *Current Archaeology* No. 48 (Jan. 1975), pp. 8–15.

CARTER, A. and ROBERTS, J. P. (1973) Excavations in Norwich 1972— The Norwich Survey—2nd Interim Report, *Norfolk Archaeology*, Vol. XXXV, pt. iv.

CARTER, H. (1965) *The Towns of Wales: A Study in Urban Geography* (Cardiff).

CARTER, H. (1968) Phases of Town Growth in Wales, in DYOS, H. J. (ed.) *The Study of Urban History*, pp. 231–52 (London).

CARTER, H. (1969) Caernarvon, *Historic Towns Atlas*, Vol. I (London).

CARTER, H. (forthcoming) The Town in its Setting: The Geographical Approach, in BARLEY, M. W. (ed.) *The Plans and Topography of Medieval Towns in England and Wales*, Council for British Archaeology (London).

CARUS-WILSON, E. M. and LOBEL, M. D. (1975) Bristol, *Historic Towns Atlas*, Vol. II (London).

CARVER, M. O. H. and WILLS, J. (1974) *Shrewsbury: The Buried Past: The Threatened Archaeology of Shrewsbury and its Recovery*, Shrewsbury Archaeological Unit.

CHALKLIN, C. W. (1961) A Seventeenth-Century Market Town: Tonbridge, *Archaeologia Cantiana*, Vol. LXXVI (1961), pp. 152–62.

CHALKLIN, C. W. (1974a) *The Provincial Towns of Georgian England: A study of the Building Process, 1740–1820*, Studies in Urban History, No. 3 (London).

CHALKLIN, C. W. (1974b) The Making of some New Towns, c. 1600–1720, in CHALKLIN, C. W. and HAVINDEN, M. A., *Rural Change and Urban Growth, 1500–1800*, pp. 229–52 (London).

CHAMBERS, J. D. (1945) *Modern Nottingham in the Making* (Nottingham).

CHAMBERS, J. D. (1952) *A Century of Nottingham History, 1851–1951* (Nottingham).

CHAMPION, S. (1973) *Andover—The Archaeological Implications of Development*, Andover and District Excavation Committee.

CHANDLER, G. and HANNAH, I. C. (1949) *Dudley: As it was and as it is today* (London).

CHAPLIN, R. (1972) Discovering lost New Towns of the Nineteenth Century, *Local Historian*, Vol. X, No. 4, pp. 186–95.

CHAPLIN, R. (1973) The Rise of Royal Leamington Spa, *Warwickshire History*, Vol. II, No. 2, pp. 13–29.

CHAPLIN, R. (1974) New light on the Origins of Royal Leamington Spa, *Transactions of Birmingham and Warwickshire Archaeological Society*, Vol. LXXXVI, pp. 148–66.

CHAPMAN, S. D. (1963) Working-Class Housing in Nottingham during the Industrial Revolution, *Transactions of Thoroton Society*, Vol. LXVII.

CHAPMAN, S. D. (ed.) (1971) *The History of Working-Class Housing: A Symposium*, incl. Working-Class housing in Nottingham during the Industrial Revolution, pp. 133–63 (Newton Abbot).

CHATWIN, A. (1975) *Cheltenham's Ornamental Ironwork* (Cheltenham).

CLARKE, B. F. L. (1938) *Church Builders of the Nineteenth Century: A Study of the Gothic Revival in England* (Newton Abbot).

CLIFFORD, E. M. (1961) *Bagendon: A Belgic Oppidum* (Cambridge).

CLIFTON-TAYLOR, A. (1972) *The Pattern of English Building* (London).

CLUNN, H. (1936) *The Face of the Home Counties* (London).

COAD, J. G. (1969) Chatham Ropeyard, *Post-Medieval Archaeology*, Vol. III, pp. 143–65.

COLLINGWOOD, R. G. and RICHMOND, I. (1969) *The Archaeology of Roman Britain*, revised edition, esp. pp. 95–132 (London).

COLVIN, H. M. (1947) The Bastards of Blandford, *Archaeological Journal*, Vol. CIV, pp. 178–95.

COLVIN, H. M. (1954) *A Biographical Dictionary of English Architects, 1660–1840* (London).

COLYER, C. (1975) *Lincoln: The Archaeology of an Historic City*, Lincoln Archaeological Trust.

CONZEN, M. R. G. (1960) Alnwick, Northumberland: A Study in Town Plan Analysis, *Institute of British Geographers*, No. 27 (London).

CONZEN, M. R. G. (1968) The Use of Town Plans in the Study of Urban History, in DYOS, H. J. (ed.) *The Study of Urban History*, pp. 113–30 (London).

CORDER, P. (1955) The Reorganisation of the Defences of Romano-British Towns in the Fourth Century, *Archaeological Journal*, Vol. CXII, pp. 20–42.

COURT, W. H. B. (1938) *The Rise of the Midland Industries, 1600–1838* (Oxford).

COX, R. C. W. (1973) The Old Centre of Croydon: Victorian Decay and Redevelopment, in EVERITT, A. (ed.) *Perspectives in English Urban History*, pp. 184–212 (London).

CRAMP, R. (1967) Anglian and Viking York, *Borthwick Papers*, No. 33, University of York Borthwick Institute of Historical Research.

CRAWFORD, O. G. S. (1933) An English Hill-Top Town (Stow-on-the-Wold), *Antiquity*, Vol. VII, pp. 347–50.

CRAWFORD, O. G. S. (1942) Southampton, *Antiquity*, Vol. XVI, pp. 39–47.

CRUMMY, P. (1974) *Colchester. Recent Excavations and Research*, Colchester Excavation Committee (Colchester).

CULLEN, G. (1961a) *The Concise Townscape* (London).

CULLEN, G. (1961b) *Townscape* (London).

CUNLIFFE, B. (1962) The Winchester City Wall, *Proceedings of Hampshire Field Club*, Vol. XXII, Pt. ii, pp. 51–81.

CUNLIFFE, B. (1964) *Winchester Excavations, 1949–1960*, Vol. I (Winchester).

CUNLIFFE, B. (1974) *Iron Age Communities in Britain. An Account of England, Scotland and Wales from the Seventh Century B.C. until the Roman Conquest* (London).

DALE, A. (1947) *Fashionable Brighton, 1820–1860* (London).

DALE, A. (1967) Regency Brighton, *Transactions of the Ancient Monuments Society* New Series, Vol. XIV, pp. 23–38.

DARBY, H. C. (ed.) (1963) *Historical Geography of England before 1800* (Cambridge).

DARLINGTON, I. and HOWGEGO, J. (1964) *Printed Maps of London, Circa 1553–1850* (London).

DAVISON, B. K. (1967) The Late Saxon Town of Thetford: An Interim Report on the 1964–6 Excavations, *Medieval Archaeology*, Vol. XI, pp. 189–208.

DAVISON, B. K. (1972) The Burghal Hidage Fort of Eorpeburnan: a suggested identification, *Medieval Archaeology*, Vol. XVI, pp. 123–7.

DE BOER, G. (1973) The Two Earliest Maps of Hull, *Post-Medieval Archaeology*, Vol. VII, pp. 79–87.

DEFOE, D. (1724–6) *A Tour Thro' the Whole Island of Great Britain*, 3 Vols (London).

DICKINSON, T. M. (1974) Cuddesdon and Dorchester-on-Thames, Oxfordshire: two early Saxon 'princely' sites in Wessex, *British Archaeological Reports*, No. 1.

DILKS, T. B. (1933, 38, 45, 48), DUNNING, R. W. and TREMLETT, T. D. (1971) Bridgwater Borough Archives 1200–1485, *Somerset Record Society*.

DOE, V. (1974) Later Urban Landscapes, in ROGERS, A. and ROWLEY, R. T. (eds) *Landscapes and Documents*, pp. 63–74 (London).

DRURY, P. (1973) Chelmsford, *Current Archaeology*, No. 41 (Nov. 1973), pp. 166–76.

DYOS, H. J. (1955) Railways and Housing in Victorian London, *Journal of Transport History*, Vol. II, No. 1.

DYOS, H. J. (1961) *Victorian Suburb. A Study of the Growth of Camberwell* (Leicester).

DYOS, H. J. (1967) The Slums of Victorian London, *Victorian Studies*, Vol. XI, No. 1.

DYOS, H. J. (ed.) (1968) *The Study of Urban History* (London).

EDWARDS, M. (ed.) (1966) *Scarborough, 966–1966*, Scarborough and District Archaeological Society.

EDWARDS, P. (1898) *London Street Improvements 1855–1897* (London).

ESHER, Viscount (1968) *York: A Study in Conservation* (H.M.S.O. London).

EKWALL, E. (1954) *Street Names of the City of London* (Oxford).

ELLIS, C. D. B. (1948) *History in Leicester 55 B.C.–A.D. 1900* (Leicester).

EMERY, F. (1974) *The Making of the English Landscape: The Oxfordshire Landscape*, esp. pp. 190–216 (London).

EVERITT, A. (1973) The English Urban Inn, 1560–1760, in EVERITT, A. (ed.) *Perspectives in English Urban History*, pp. 91–137 (London).

FASHAM, P. J. (1972) The Archaeological Implications of Redevelopment in Banbury, *Cake and Cockhorse* (Banbury Historical Society), Summer 1972.

FASNACHT, R. (1954) *A History of the City of Oxford* (Oxford).

FAULKNER, P. A. (1967) Medieval Undercrofts and Town Houses, *Archaeological Journal*, Vol. CXXIII, pp. 120–35.

FEACHEM, R. W. (1963) *Prehistoric Scotland* (London).

FINBERG, H. P. R. (1955) *The Making of the English Landscape: Gloucestershire* (London).

FINBERG, H. P. R. (1957) The Genesis of the Gloucestershire Towns, in FINBERG, H. P. R. (ed.) *Gloucestershire Studies*, pp. 52–88 (Leicester).

FLEMING, O. (1900) *Working Class Dwellings: the Rebuilding of the Boundary Street Estate*.

FORDHAM, A. (1965) Town Plans of the British Isles, *Map Collectors' Series*, No. 22.

FORSTER, C. A. (1972) Court Housing in Kingston-upon-Hull. An Example of Cyclic Processes in the Morphological Development of Nineteenth-Century Bye-Law Housing, *University of Hull Occasional Papers in Geography*, No. 19.

FOWLER, P. J. (1971) Hillforts, A.D. 400–700 in JESSON, M. and HILL, D. (eds) *The Iron Age and its Hill Forts*, pp. 203–13 (Southampton).

FRERE, S. S. (1962) Excavations at Dorchester-on-Thames, 1962, *Archaeological Journal*, Vol. CXIX.

FRERE, S. S. (1966) The End of Towns in Roman Britain, in WACHER, J. S. (ed.) *The Civitas Capitals of Roman Britain*, pp. 87–100 (Leicester).

FRERE, S. S. (1967) *Britannia. A History of Roman Britain*, esp. pp. 239–63 (London).

FRERE, S. S. (1970) The Roman Theatre at Canterbury, *Britannia*, Vol. I, pp. 83–113.

FRERE, S. S. (1972) Verulamium Excavations, Vol. I, *Society of Antiquaries Research Committee Report*, XXVIII.

FULLBROOK-LEGGATT, L. E. W. O. (1946) *Roman Gloucester* (**Glevum**) (Gloucester).

FULLBROOK-LEGGATT, L. E. W. O. (1952) *Anglo-Saxon and Medieval Gloucester* (Gloucester).

GARMONSWAY, G. N. (ed.) (1953) *The Anglo-Saxon Chronicle* (London).

GARRETT, C. W. F. (1972)   Bewdley and the Stinking Ditch: An Exposition, in SNELL, L. S. (ed.) *Essays towards a History of Bewdley* (Birmingham).

GELLING, M. (1967)   English Place Names derived from the compound *Wicham*, *Medieval Archaeology*, Vol. XI, pp. 87–104.

GILBERT, E. W. (1939)   The Growth of Inland and Seaside Health Resorts in England, *Scottish Geographical Magazine*, Vol. LV, pp. 16–35.

GILBERT, E. W. (1954)   *Brighton* (London).

GOODER, E. (1967)   Coventry's Town Wall, *Coventry and North Warwickshire, History Pamphlets*, No. 4.

GOULD, J. (1967–9)   First and Third Reports on the Excavations at Tamworth, Staffordshire, 1967–8, *Transactions of Lichfield and South Staffordshire Archaeological and Historical Society*, Vol. IX–X.

GRANVILLE, A. B. (1841)   *The Spas of England, and Principal Sea-Bathing Places*, 3 Vols (reprint, Newton Abbot).

GREEN, B. and YOUNG, R. M. R. (1972)   *Norwich: The Growth of a City*, City of Norwich Museums (1st edn 1963).

GREEN, H. J. M. (1961)   Early Medieval Godmanchester, *Proceedings Cambridgeshire Antiquarian Society*, Vol. LIV.

GRIMES, W. F. (1968)   *The Excavation of Roman and Medieval London* (London).

HADFIELD, C. (1966)   *The Canals of the West Midlands* (Newton Abbot).

HANCOCK, C. V. (1951)   Stourport—A Georgian Inland Port, *Country Life*, 10th August, 1951, p. 414.

HARBOTTLE, B. (1969)   The Town Wall of Newcastle-on-Tyne: Consolidation and Excavation in 1968, *Archaeologia Aeliana*, Ser. 4, Vol. XLVII, pp. 71–95.

HARLEY, J. B. (1963)   The town plans and small-scale maps of England and Wales, *Amateur Historian*, Vol. V, No. 8, pp. 251–9.   Reprinted, in HARLEY, J. B. and PHILLIPS, C. W. *The Historian's Guide to Ordnance Survey Maps* (London, 1964).

HARLEY, J. B. (1967)   Maps and plans of towns, *Local Historian*, Vol. VII, No. 6, pp. 196–207.   Reprinted, in HARLEY, J. B.   *Maps for the Local Historian: A Guide to the British Sources* (London, 1972).

HARVEY, A. (1911)   *The Castles and Walled Towns of England* (London).

HARVEY, J. H. (1969)   *William Worcestre Itineraries* (Oxford).

HARVEY, P. D. A. (1969)   Banbury, *Historic Towns Atlas*, Vol. I (London).

HASSALL, T. G. (1969–74)   Excavations at Oxford, 1968–74, Interim Reports, *Oxoniensia*, Vol. XXXIV–XXXIX.

HASSALL, T. G. (1972)   *Oxford: The City beneath your Feet. Archaeological Excavations in the City of Oxford, 1967–72*, Oxford Archaeological Excavation Committee.

HASSALL, T. G. (1974)   Urban Surveys: Medieval Oxford, in ROGERS, A. and ROWLEY, R. T. (eds)   *Landscapes and Documents*, pp. 49–62 (London).

HAY, G. D. (1974)   Houldsworth's Cotton Mill, Glasgow, *Post-Medieval Archaeology*, Vol. VIII, pp. 92–100.

HEIGHWAY, C. M. (ed.) (1972)   *The Erosion of History: Archaeology and Planning in Towns*, Council for British Archaeology (London).

HEIGHWAY, C. M. (1974) *Archaeology in Gloucester: A Policy for City and District* (Gloucester).

HILL, D. (1967a). The Burghal Hidage—Southampton, *Proceedings of Hampshire Field Club*, Vol. XXIV, pp. 59–61.

HILL, D. (1967b) The Burghal Hidage—Lyng, *Proceedings Somerset Archaeological and Natural History Society*, Vol. III, pp. 64–6.

HILL, D. (1969) · The Burghal Hidage—the estabishment of a text, *Medieval Archaeology*, Vol. XIII, pp. 84–92.

HILL, D. (1970) Late Saxon Bedford, *Bedfordshire Archaeological Journal*, Vol. V, pp. 96–100.

HILL, J. W. F. (1948) *Medieval Lincoln* (Cambridge).

HILL, J. W. F. (1956) *Tudor and Stuart Lincoln* (Cambridge).

HILL, J. W. F. (1966) *Georgian Lincoln* (Cambridge).

HODGETT, C. A. J. (1971) The Cartulary of Holy Trinity, Aldgate, *London Record Society*.

HOLMES, M. (1966) An Unrecorded Map of London, *Archaeologia*, Vol. C, pp. 105–28.

HOOKER, J. (1919) The Description of the Citie of Excester, *Devon and Cornwall Record Society* (1919–47).

HOPE, W. H. ST J. (1909) The ancient topography of the town of Ludlow, *Archaeologia*, Vol. LXI.

HOSKINS, W. G. (1949) The Origin and Rise of Market Harborough, *Transactions of Leicestershire Archaeological and Historical Society*, Vol. XXV. Reprinted, in HOSKINS, *Provincial England* (1963), pp. 53–67 (London).

HOSKINS, W. G. (1953a) The Rebuilding of Rural England, 1570–1640, *Past and Present*, Vol. IV, Nov. 1953, pp. 44–59. Reprinted, in HOSKINS, *Provincial England* (1963), pp. 131–48 (London).

HOSKINS, W. G. (1953b) The Landscape of Towns: I The Planned Town, II The Open-Field Town, III The Market Town, *The Listener*, XLVIII, pp. 457–8, 499–500, 539–40, 555.

HOSKINS, W. G. (1955a) *The Making of the English Landscape*, esp. pp. 210–30 (London).

HOSKINS, W. G. (1955b) An Elizabethan Provincial Town: Leicester, in PLUMB, J. H. (ed.) *Studies in Social History: A Tribute to G. M. Trevelyan*. Reprinted, in HOSKINS, *Provincial England* (1963), pp. 86–114 (London).

HOSKINS, W. G. (1956) English Provincial Towns in the Early Sixteenth Century, *Transactions of Royal Historical Society*, 5th Ser., Vol. VI. Reprinted, in HOSKINS, *Provincial England* (1963), pp. 68–85.

HOSKINS, W. G. (1957) *The Making of the English Landscape: Leicestershire*, esp. pp. 67–85 (London).

HOSKINS, W. G. (1959) *Local History in England*, esp. pp. 71–92 (London).

HOSKINS, W. G. (1960) *Two Thousand Years in Exeter* (Chichester).

HOSKINS, W. G. (1967) *Fieldwork in Local History*, esp. pp. 24–29 and pp. 65–73 (London).

HOWARD, E. (1902) *Garden Cities of Tomorrow* (1st edn 1898: *Tomorrow: A Peaceful Path to Land Reform* (London).

HURST, H. (1972–4) Excavations at Gloucester, Interim Reports, *Antiquaries Journal*, Vol. LII, pt. i, LIV, pt. i.

HUTTON, K. (1969) Streets called 'Gate', *Local Historian*, Vol. VIII, No. 8.

HYDE, J. K. (1966) Medieval Descriptions of Cities, *Bulletin of the John Rylands Library, Manchester*, Vol. XLVIII, Spring 1966, No. 2, pp. 308–40.

INSALL, D. W. (1968) *Chester: A Study in Conservation* (H.M.S.O. London).

ISON, W. (1948) *The Georgian Buildings of Bath from 1730 to 1830* (Bath).

ISON, W: (1952) *The Georgian Buildings of Bristol* (London).

JESSON, M. (1973) *The Archaeology of Churches*, Council for British Archaeology, London.

JESSON, M. and HILL, D. (eds) (1971) The Iron Age and its Hill Forts: Papers Presented to Sir Mortimer Wheeler, *University of Southampton Monograph Series*, No. 1.

JOHNS, E. (1965) *British Townscapes* (London).

JONES, E. (1966) *Towns and Cities* (Oxford).

JONES, E. L. (1968) The Reduction of Fire Damage in Southern England, 1650–1850, *Post-medieval Archaeology*, Vol. II, pp. 140–9.

JONES, F. M. (1968) The Aeshetics of the Nineteenth Century Industrial Town, in DYOS, H. J. (ed.) *The Study of Urban History* (London).

JONES, P. N. (1969) Colliery Settlement in the South Wales Coalfield, 1850 to 1826, *University of Hull Occasional Papers in Geography*, No. 14.

JOWITT, R. L. P. and JOWITT, D. (1971) *Discovering Spas* (Tring, Herts).

KEENE, D. J. (1972) Some Aspects of the History, Topography and Archaeology of the North-Eastern Part of the City of Winchester, with special reference to the Brooks area (University of Oxford D.Phil. thesis, unpublished).

KEENE, D. J. (forthcoming) Suburban Growth, in BARLEY, M. W. (ed.) *The Plans and Topography of Medieval Towns in England and Wales,* Council for British Archaeology (London).

KELLETT, J. R. (1968) *The Impact of Railways on Victorian Cities* (London).

KELLETT, J. R. (1969) Glasgow, *Historic Towns Atlas*, Vol. I (London).

KELSALL, A. F. (1974) The London House Plan in the later 17th Century, *Post-Medieval Archaeology*, Vol. VIII, pp. 80–91.

KENYON, K. (1948) Excavations at the Jewry Wall Site, Leicester, *Society of Antiquaries Research Committee Reports*, XV.

KIDSON, P., MURRAY, P. and THOMPSON, P. (1965) *A History of English Architecture* (Harmondsworth).

LAITHWAITE, M. (1973) The Buildings of Burford: A Cotswold Town in the Fourteenth to Nineteenth Centuries, in EVERITT, A. (ed.) *Perspectives in English Urban History*, pp. 60–90 (London).

LANCASTER, J. (1974) Coventry, *Historic Towns Atlas*, Vol. II (London).

LATTEY, R. T., PARSONS, E. J. S. and PHILIP, I. G. (1936) A Contemporary Map of the Defences of Oxford in 1644, *Oxoniensia*, Vol. I.

LEE, F. (1954) A New Theory of the origins and early growth of Northampton, *Archaeological Journal*, Vol. CX (1954), pp. 164–74.

LINDSAY, I. G. (1973) *Georgian Edinburgh* (Edinburgh).

LEWIS, E. A. (1912) *The Medieval Boroughs of Snowdonia* (Cardiff).

LOBEL, M. D. (1935) *The Borough of Bury St Edmunds. A Study in the Government and Development of a Monastic Town* (Oxford).

LOBEL, M. D. (1969) Hereford, *Historic Towns Atlas*, Vol. I (London).

LOBEL, M. D. (1974) Cambridge, *Historic Towns Atlas*, Vol. II (London).

LOBEL, M. D. and TANN, J. (1969) Gloucester, *Historic Towns Atlas*, Vol. I (London).

LONDON SURVEY COMMITTEE (1900 onwards) *Survey of London* Parish volumes, continuing (London).

LOYN, H. R. (1961) Boroughs and Mints, A.D. 900–1066, in DOLLEY, R. H. M. (ed.) *Anglo-Saxon Coins*, pp. 122–135 (London).

MACIVOR, I. (1965) The Elizabethan Fortifications of Berwick-upon-Tweed, *Antiquaries Journal*, Vol. XLV, Pt. i.

MAHANY, C. (1968) Stamford, *Current Archaeology*, No. 10 (Sept. 1968), pp. 266–70.

MANBY, T. (1971) Urban Archaeology in Yorkshire, *Current Archaeology*, No. 27 (July 1971), pp. 111–2.

MARSHALL, J. D. (1968) Colonisation as a Factor in the Planting of Towns in North-West England, in DYOS, H. J. (ed.) *The Study of Urban History*, pp. 215–30 (London).

MARTIN, G. H. (ed.) (1963) The English Borough in the Thirteenth Century, *Transactions of Royal Historical Society*, Vol. XIII, 5th ser., pp. 123–44.

MARTIN, G. H. (ed.) (1973) *The Ipswich Recognizance Rolls, 1294–1327*, Suffolk Record Society.

MERRIFIELD, R. (1965) *The Roman City of London* (London).

MIDWINTER, E. (1971) *Old Liverpool* (Newton Abbot).

MILES, D. and FOWLER, P. (1972) *Tewkesbury: The Archaeological Implications of Development*, Tewkesbury Archaeological and Architectural Committee.

MILLWARD, R. (1955) *The Making of the English Landscape: Lancashire*, esp. pp. 66–103 (London).

MILLWARD, R. (1974) The Cumbrian Town between 1600 and 1800, in CHALKLIN, C. W. and HAVINDEN, M. A. *Rural Change and Urban Growth, 1500–1800*, pp. 202–28 (London).

MORGAN, J. B. and PEBERDY, P. (eds) (1968) *Collected Essays on Southampton* (Southampton).

MORRIS, A. E. J. (1972) *History of Urban Form: Prehistory to the Rennaissance* (London).

MORRIS, C. (ed.) (1947) *The Journeys of Celia Fiennes* (London).

MORRIS, J. (1973) *The Age of Arthur: A History of the British Isles from 350 to 650* (London).

MORRIS, R. J. (1971) The Friars and Paradise: an essay in the building history of Oxford, 1801–1861, *Oxoniensia*, Vol. XXXVI, pp. 72–98.

MUMFORD, L. (1961) *The City in History* (Harmondsworth).

NEALE, F. (ed.) (forthcoming) William Worcestre's Bristol, *Bristol and Gloucestershire Archaeological Society, Record Section.*

NEALE, R. (1974) Society, Belief and the Building of Bath, 1700–1793, in CHALKLIN, C. W. and HAVINDEN, M. A. *Rural Change and Urban Growth, 1500–1800*, pp. 253–80 (London).

NEWTON, R. (1972) *The Making of the English Landscape: The Northumberland Landscape*, esp. pp. 144–211 (London).

NOBLE, F. (1964) Medieval Boroughs of West Herefordshire, *Transactions of Woolhope Field Club*, Vol. XXXVIII, pp. 62–70.

NORTON, J. E. (1950) Guide to the National and Provincial Directories of England and Wales, excluding London, published before 1856, *Royal Historical Society.*

OLSEN, D. J. (1964) *Town Planning in London: the Eighteenth and Nineteenth Centuries* (London).

O'NEIL, B. H. ST J. and STEPHENS, W. E. (1945) A Plan of the Fortifications of Yarmouth in 1588, *Norfolk Archaeology*, Vol. XXVIII.

ORDNANCE SURVEY (1966) *Map of Britain in the Dark Ages* (2nd edn, Chessington).

ORDNANCE SURVEY (1973) *Britain before the Norman Conquest* (Southampton).

PALLISER, D. M. (forthcoming) Sources for Urban Topography: Documents, Building and Archaeology, in BARLEY, M. W. (ed.) *The Plans and Topography of Medieval Towns in England and Wales*, Council for British Archaeology (London).

PANTIN, W. A. (1947) The Development of Domestic Architecture in Oxford, *Antiquaries Journal*, Vol. XXVII, pp. 120–50.

PANTIN, W. A. (1963) Medieval English Town-house Plans, *Medieval Archaeology*, Vol. VI–VII, pp. 202–39.

PANTIN, W. A. (1963) Some Medieval English Town Houses: A Study in Adaptation, in FOSTER, I. LL. and ALCOCK, L. *Culture and Environment*, pp. 445–78 (London).

PARKER, V. (1970) The English House in the Nineteenth Century, *Historical Association.*

PARKER, V. (1971) *The Making of Kings Lynn* (Chichester).

PEVSNER, N. *et al.* (1951 onwards) *The Buildings of England:* County volumes (Harmondsworth).

PLATT, C. (1973) *Medieval Southampton: The port and trading community, A.D. 1000–1600* (London).

PLATT, C. (forthcoming) The Evolution of Towns: Natural Growth, in BARLEY, M. W. (ed.) *The Plans and Topography of Medieval Towns in England and Wales*, Council for British Archaeology (London).

PORTEOUS, J. D. (1968) Urban Genesis and Development: the case of canal-created river-ports of the English industrial revolution (University of Hull Ph.D. thesis, unpublished).

PORTEOUS, J. D. (1969) The Company Town of Goole: An Essay in Urban Genesis, *University of Hull Occasional Papers in Geography*, No. 12.

PORTEOUS, J. D. (1970) The nature of the Company Town, *Transactions of Institute of British Geographers*, Vol. LI, pp. 127–42.

PORTMAN, D. (1966) *Exeter Houses, 1400–1700* (Exeter).

RADLEY, J. (1971) Economic Aspects of Anglo-Danish York, *Medieval Archaeology*, Vol. XV, pp. 37–57.

RADLEY, J. (1972) Excavations in the Defences of the City of York: an early medieval stone tower and the successive earth ramparts, *Yorkshire Archaeological Journal*, Vol. XLIV.

RAHTZ, P. A. (1960) Caistor, Lincolnshire, 1959, *Antiquaries Journal*, Vol. XL.

RAHTZ, P. A. (1968) Hereford, *Current Archaeology*, No. 9 (July 1968) pp. 242–46.

RAHTZ, P. A. and FOWLER, P. J. (1972) Somerset, A.D. 400–700, in FOWLER, P. J. (ed.) *Archaeology and the Landscape*, pp. 187–221 (London).

RAISTRICK, A. (1970) *The Making of the English Landscape: West Riding of Yorkshire*, esp. pp. 152–75.

RALEGH RADFORD, C. A. (1958) The Medieval Defences of Shrewsbury, *Transactions Shropshire Archaeological Society*, Vol. LVI, pt. i, pp. 15–20.

RALEGH RADFORD, C. A. (1970) The Later Pre-Conquest Boroughs and their Defences, *Medieval Archaeology*, Vol. XIV, pp. 83–103.

RALEGH RADFORD, C. A. (1973) Excavations at Cricklade, 1948–1963, *Wiltshire Archaeological & Natural History Magazine*, Vol. LXVII, pp. 61–111.

RAWNSLEY, J. E. (1970) *Wales: The Second Part of Speed's Atlas* (Wakefield).

REDDAWAY, T. F. (1940) *The Rebuilding of London after the Great Fire* (London).

REECE, R. and CATLING, C. (1975) Cirencester: The Development and Buildings of a Cotswold Town, *British Archaeological Reports*, No. 12 (Oxford).

REEDER, D. A. (1968) A Theatre of Suburbs: Some Patterns of Development in West London, 1801–1911, in DYOS, H. J. (ed.) *The Study of Urban History* (London).

REES, J. F. (1957) *The Story of Milford* (Cardiff).

RICHMOND, I. A. and CRAWFORD, O. G. S. (1949) The British Section of the Ravenna Cosmography, *Society of Antiquaries*.

RIMMER, W. G. (1961) Working Men's Cottages in Leeds, 1770–1840, *Thoresby Society*, Vol. XLVI, pp. 165–99.

RIPON CIVIC SOCIETY (1972) *Ripon: Some Aspects of its History* (Clapham).

RIVET, A. L. F. (1958) *Town and Country in Roman Britain*, esp. pp. 72–98 (London).

RIVET, A. L. F. (1970) The British Section of the Antonine Itinerary, *Britannia*, Vol. I.

ROCQUE, J. and DURY, A. (1764) *A Collection of Plans of the Principal Cities of Great Britain and Ireland* (London).

RODWELL, K. (ed.) (1975) *Historic Towns in Oxfordshire: A Survey of the New County*, Oxfordshire Archaeological Unit.

RODWELL, K. and ROWLEY, R. T. (eds) (1975)   Small Towns of Roman Britain, *British Archaeological Reports*, No. 15.

ROGERS, A. (ed.) (1965)   *The Making of Stamford* (Leicester).

ROGERS, A. (1970)   *The Medieval Buildings of Stamford* (University of Nottingham).

ROGERS, K. H. (1969)   Salisbury, *Historic Towns Atlas*, Vol. 1 (London).

ROPER, J. S. (1962)   Dudley: The Medieval Town, *Dudley Public Libraries Transcript*, No. 3.

ROPER, J. S. (1963)   Dudley: The Town in the Sixteenth Century, *Dudley Public Libraries Transcript*, No. 4.

ROPER, J. S. (1965)   Dudley: The Seventeenth Century Town, *Dudley Public Libraries Transcript*, No. 5.

ROPER, J. S. (1968)   Dudley: The Town in the Eighteenth Century, *Dudley Public Libraries Transcript*, No. 12.

ROWLEY, R. T. (1972)   *The Making of the English Landscape: The Shropshire Landscape*, esp. pp. 173–206 (London).

R.C.H.M. (1910 onwards)   *Royal Commission on Historical Monuments: County Inventories* (H.M.S.O. London).

R.C.H.M. (1939)   *Royal Commission on Historical Monuments: City of Oxford* (H.M.S.O. London).

R.C.H.M. (1959a)   Wareham West Walls: Excavations by the Royal Commission on Historical Monuments (England), *Mediaeval Archaeology*, Vol. III, pp. 120–38.

R.C.H.M. (1959b)   *Royal Commission on Historical Monuments: City of Cambridge* (H.M.S.O. London).

R.C.H.M. (1962)   *Royal Commission on Historical Monuments: Roman York*, (H.M.S.O. London).

R.C.H.M. (1964)   *Royal Commission on Historical Monuments: Newark-on-Trent, Civil War Siegeworks* (H.M.S.O. London).

R.C.H.M. (1972)   *Royal Commission on Historical Monuments: City of York*, Vol. II—The Defences (H.M.S.O. London).

R.C.H.M. (1973)   *Royal Commission on Historical Monuments: City of York, South-West* (H.M.S.O. London).

RUSSELL, P. (1960)   *A History of Torquay* (Torquay).

RYE, W. (ed.) (1903–15)   A Calendar of Norwich Deeds, *Norfolk & Norwich Archaeological Society*.

SAINT, A. (1970)   Three Oxford Architects, *Oxoniensia*, Vol. XXXV, pp. 53–102.

ST. JOSEPH, J. K. (1966)   The contribution of aerial photography, in WACHER, J. S. (ed.) *The Civitas Capitals of Roman Britain*, Ch. 1 (Leicester).

SALTER, H. E. (1960, 1969)   *Survey of Oxford*, ed. W. A. PANTIN, *Oxford Historical Society*, New Series, Vol. XIV, XX.

SAVAGE, W. (1952)   *The Making of Our Towns* (London).

SCARFE, N. (1972)   *The Making of the English Landscape: The Suffolk Landscape* (London).

238

SCOLE COMMITTEE (1973) *Ipswich: The Archaeological Implications of Development* (Ipswich).

SHARP, T. (1968) *Town and Townscape* (London).

SHEPHERD, T. (1829) *London and its Environs in the Nineteenth Century, illustrated by a Series of Views from Original Drawings* (London).

SHERCLIFF, W. H. (1960) *Manchester: A Short History of its Development* (Manchester).

SHERIDAN, K. (1972–3) Sixth and Seventh Reports of Excavations at Tamworth, Staffordshire, 1960, 1971, *Transactions of South Staffordshire Archaeological & Historical Society*, Vol. XIV, pp. 32–44.

SHOESMITH, R. (1972). Hereford, *Current Archaeology*, No. 33 (July 1972), pp. 256–58.

SHOESMITH, R. (1974) *The City of Hereford—Archaeology and Redevelopment*, West Midlands Rescue Archaeology Committee.

SIMPSON, C. (1973) *Wallingford: The Archaeological Implications of Development*, Oxfordshire Archaeological Unit.

SIMPSON, G. G. (ed.) (1972) *Scotland's Medieval Burghs—An archaeological heritage in danger*, Council of Society of Antiquaries of Scotland.

SIMPSON, W. D. (1946) Brough under Stainmore, *Transactions of Cumberland & Westmorland Antiquarian & Archaeological Society*, New Series, Vol. XLVI, pp. 229–32.

SKELTON, R. A. (1952) Tudor Town Plans in John Speed's 'Theatre', *Archaeological Journal*, Vol. CVIII.

SKELTON, R. A. (ed.) (1966) Braun and Hogenberg: *Civitates Orbis Terrarum, 1572–1618*, 3 vols (London).

SKEMPTON, A. W. and JOHNSON, H. R. (1962) The First Iron Frames, *Architectural Review*, Vol. CXIX, pp. 175–86 (March 1962).

SLADE, C. F. (1969) Reading, *Historic Towns Atlas*, Vol. I (London).

SMAILES, A. E. (1953) *The Geography of Towns* (London).

SMAILES, A. E. (1955) Some Reflections on the Geographical Description and Analysis of Townscapes, *Transactions of Institute of British Geographers*, Vol. XXI, pp. 99–115.

SMITH, B. S. (1964) *A History of Malvern* (Leicester).

SMITH, J. T. (1953) Shrewsbury: Topography and Domestic Architecture to the Middle of the Seventeenth Century (University of Birmingham M.A. thesis, unpublished).

SMITH, T. P. (1970) The Medieval Town Defences of Kings Lynn, *Journal of British Archaeological Association*, Vol. XXXIII, pp. 57–88.

SQUIRES, T. W. (1928) *In West Oxford: Historical Notes and Pictures concerning the Parish of St. Thomas the Martyr, Oxford* (London and Oxford).

STANFORD, S. C. (1971) Credenhill Camp, Herefordshire: An Iron Age Hill-Fort Capital, *Archaeological Journal*, Vol. CXXVII, pp. 82–129.

STANFORD, S. C. (1974) *Croft Ambrey* (Leominster).

STEANE, J. M. (1974) *The Making of the English Landscape: The Northamptonshire Landscape*, esp. pp. 130–59, and pp. 247–80 (London).

STEDMAN, M. B. (1958)   The Townscape of Birmingham in 1956, *Transactions of Institute of British Geographers*, Vol. xxv.

STENTON, F. M. (1934)   Norman London, *Historical Association*.

STEVENSON, W. H. (ed.) (1890)   *Rental of all the Houses in Gloucester, A.D. 1455* (Gloucester).

STOW, J. (1598)   *A Survey of London: Conteyning the Originall, Antiquity, Increase, Modern Estate, and Description of that City*, etc. (ed. C. L. KINGSFORD, 1908) (London).

STUBBS, W. (ed.) (1887–9)   *Willelmi Malmesbiriensis Monachi de Gestis Regum Anglorum, Rolls Series*, 2 vols (London).

SUMMERSON, J. (1945)   *Georgian London* (B.L. Service).

SUMMERSON, J. (1949)   *John Nash, Architect to King George IV* (London).

TAMWORTH RESEARCH COMMITTEE (1971)   *Tamworth Development: The Archaeological Implications*, Tamworth Museum.

TARN, J. N. (1966)   The Peabody Donation Fund: The Role of a Housing Society in the Nineteenth Century, *Victorian Studies*, Vol. VII, pp. 7–38.

TARN, J. N. (1971)   Working Class Housing in Nineteenth Century Britain, *Architectural Association*, Paper No. 7.

TAYLOR, C. C. (1969)   The Origins of Lichfield, Staffordshire, *Transactions South Staffordshire Archaeological and Historical Society*, Vol. X, pp. 43–52.

TAYLOR, C. C. (1970)   *The Making of the English Landscape: Dorset*, esp. pp. 173–201 (London).

TAYLOR, C. C. (1973)   *The Making of the English Landscape: The Cambridgeshire Landscape*, esp. pp. 245–69 (London).

TAYLOR, H. M. and TAYLOR, J. (1965)   *Anglo-Saxon Architecture*, 2 vols (Cambridge).

TAYLOR, I. C. (1970)   The Eighteenth-Century Origin of the Liverpool Slum, *Transactions of Historical Society of Lancashire and Cheshire*, Vol. CXXII.

TAYLOR, M. V. (ed.) (1912)   *Liber Luciani de Laude Cestrie, Record Society of Lancashire and Cheshire*, Vol. LXIV, pp. 45–7.

TAYLOR, R. (1974)   Town Houses in Taunton, 1500–1700, *Post-Medieval Archaeology*, Vol. VIII, pp. 63–79.

TEMPLE, N. (1963)   *Farnham Buildings and People* (Farnham).

THOMPSON, F. H. and WHITWELL, J. B. (1973)   The Gates of Roman Lincoln, *Archaeologia*, Vol. CIV, pp. 129–207.

THORPE, H. (1951)   The City of Lichfield: A Study of its Growth and Function, *Staffordshire Historical Collections* (1950–1), pp. 139–211.

TODD, M. (1969)   The Roman Settlement at Margidunum: The Excavations of 1966–68, *Thoroton Society*, Vol. LXXIII.

TODD, M. (1970)   The Small Towns of Roman Britain, *Britannia*, Vol. I, pp. 114–30.

TOMS, E. (1962)   *The Story of St. Albans* (London).

TOULMIN SMITH, L. (ed.) (1907–10)   *The Itinerary of John Leland* (London).

TOUT, T. F. (1918)   Medieval Town Planning, *Bulletin of the John Rylands Library*, Vol. IV, pp. 26–58.

TURNER, H. L. (1971) *Town Defences in England and Wales: An Architectural and Documentary Study, A.D. 900–1500* (London).

URBAN HISTORY NEWSLETTER (1963 onwards).

URRY, W. (1967) *Canterbury under the Angevin Kings* (London).

VERE HOLE, W. (1965) The Housing of the Working Classes in Britain, 1850–1914: A Study of the Development of Standards and Methods of Provision (University of London Ph.D. thesis, unpublished).

VICTORIA COUNTY HISTORY (1900 onwards), County volumes (London).

WACHER, J. S. (1962) A Survey of Romano-British Town Defences of the Early and Middle Second Century, *Archaeological Journal*, Vol. CXIX.

WACHER, J. S. (ed.) (1966) *The Civitas Capitals of Roman Britain* (Leicester), incl. WACHER, J. S.: Earthwork Defences of the Second Century, pp. 60–69.

WACHER, J. S. (1974) *The Towns of Roman Britain* (London).

WALKER, D. (1971) Bristol in the Early Middle Ages, *Historical Association*.

WARD, D. (1962) The Pre-Urban Cadaster and the Urban Pattern of Leeds, *Annals of Association of American Geographers*, Vol. LII.

WARD, P. (ed.) (1968) *Conservation and Development in Historic Towns and Cities:* A Report of a Conference at York in 1968.

WEBBER, R. (1969) *Covent Garden: Mud Salad Market* (London).

WEBSTER, G. (1966) Fort and Town in Early Roman Britain, in WACHER, J. S. (ed.) *The Civitas Capitals of Roman Britain*, pp. 31–45 (Leicester).

WEBSTER, G. and WOODFIELD, P. (1966) The 'Old Work' at the Roman Public Baths at Wroxeter, *Antiquaries Journal*, Vol. XLVI, pp. 229–39.

WELCH, E. (1964) Southampton Maps from Elizabethan Times, *Southampton Record Society*.

WEST, T. H. (1963) *A History of Architecture in England* (London).

WHEELER, R. E. M. and WHEELER, T. V. (1936) Verulamium: A Belgic and two Roman Cities, *Society of Antiquaries Research Committee Report*, XI.

WHEELER, R. E. M. (1943) Maiden Castle, Dorset, *Society of Antiquaries Research Committee Report*, XII.

WHEELER, R. E. M. (1954) The Stanwick Fortifications, *Society of Antiquaries Research Committee Report*, XVII.

WHYMAN, J. (1973) A Hanoverian Watering-Place: Margate before the Railway, in EVERITT, A. (ed.) *Perspectives in English Urban History*, pp. 138–60 (London).

WIGLEY, E. (1972) Hayle: A New Industrial Town of the West, in TODD, A. C. and LAWS, P. *Industrial Archaeology of Cornwall*, pp. 86–102 (Newton Abbot).

WILKES, L. and DODDS, G. (1964) *Tyneside Classical: The Newcastle of Grainger, Dobson and Clayton* (London).

WILLIAMS, J. (1974) Northampton, *Current Archaeology*, No. 46 (Sept. 1974), pp. 340–48.

WINSTONE, R. (1960) *Bristol in the 1890's* (Bristol).

The Landscape of Towns

WISE, M. J. (1949)   The Evolution of the Jewellery and Gun Quarters in Birmingham, *Transactions Institute of British Geographers*, Vol. xv.
WITHERICK, M. E. (1967)   The Medieval Boroughs of Cornwall: An Alternative View of their Origins, *Southampton Research Series in Geography* No. 4.
WOHL, A. S. (1966)   The Housing of the Artisans and Labourers in Nineteenth Century London, 1815–1914 (Brown University Ph.D. thesis, unpublished).
WOHL, A. S. (1971)   The Housing of the Working Classes in London, 1815–1914, in CHAPMAN, S. D. (ed.) *The History of Working-Class Housing: a Symposium*, pp. 13–54 (Newton Abbot).
WOLEDGE, G. (1944)   The Medieval Borough of Leeds, *Thoresby Society, Miscellany* xxxvii, pt. iii, p. 288.
WOOD, P. D. (1962)   Frontier Relics in the Welsh Border Towns, *Geography*, Vol. xlvii, pt. i, pp. 54–62.
WORSKETT, R. (1969)   *The Character of Towns: An Approach to Conservation* (London).
YOUNGSON, A. J. (1966)   *The Making of Classical Edinburgh* (Edinburgh).

BIBLIOGRAPHY SINCE 1975

BARLEY, M.W. (ed., 1977) *European Towns: their Archaeology and Early History* (London)
BIDDLE, M. (ed., 1976) *Winchester in the Early Middle Ages: an Edition and Discussion of the Winton Domesday* (Oxford)
BLAIR, J. (1988) 'Minster Churches in the Landscape', in HOOKE, D. (ed.), *Anglo-Saxon Settlements* (Oxford), pp. 35–58
BROWN, J. (1986) *The English Market Town: a Social and Economic History, 1750–1914* (Ramsbury)
BURNETT, J. (1986) *A Social History of Housing, 1815–1985* (2nd edn, London)
BURNHAM, B.C. & WACHER, J. (1990) *The 'Small Towns' of Roman Britain* (London)
CARVER, M. (1987) *Underneath English Towns: Interpreting Urban Archaeology* (London)
CATTELL, J. & FALCONER, K. (1995) *Swindon: the Legacy of a Railway Town* (RCHME, London)
CLARK, P. (ed., 1981) *Country Towns in Pre-Industrial England* (Leicester)
CLARK, P. (ed., 1984) *The Transformation of English Provincial Towns, 1600–1800* (London)
CLARKE, H. & AMBROSIANI, B. (1991) *Towns in the Viking Age* (Leicester)
CLIFTON-TAYLOR, A. (1978) *Six English Towns* (London)
CLIFTON-TAYLOR, A. (1981) *Six More English Towns* (London)
CLIFTON-TAYLOR, A. (1984) *Another Six English Towns* (London)
COLLIER, S. (1991) *Whitehaven, 1660–1800* (RCHME, London)

DANIELLS, M.J., HALL, R.A. & YORK, R.N. (1978) *Two Thousand Years of York: the Archaeological Story*

DAUNTON, M.J. (1983) *House and Home in the Victorian City: Working-Class Housing, 1850–1914* (London)

DE LA BÉDOYÈRE, G. (1992) *Roman Towns in Britain* (London)

DOUGHTY, M. (ed., 1986) *Building the Industrial City* (Leicester)

EDWARDS, A.M. (1981) *The Design of Suburbia: a Critical Study in Environmental History* (London)

EVERITT, A. (1974) 'The Banburys of England' *Urban History Yearbook*

FRIEDRICHS, C.R. (1994) *The Early Modern City, 1450–1750* (London & New York)

GIROUARD, M. (1990) *The English Town* (New Haven, USA)

GOOD, G.L., JONES, R.H. & PONSFORD, R.H. (eds, 1991) *Waterfront Archaeology: Proceedings of the third international conference, Bristol, 1988* (CBA Research Report no. 74)

HASLAM, J. (ed., 1984) *Anglo-Saxon Towns in Southern England* (Chichester)

HILL, D. & RUMBLE, A.R. (eds, 1996) *The Defence of Wessex: the Burghal Hidage and Anglo-Saxon Fortifications* (Manchester)

HODGES, R. (1982) *Dark Age Economics: the Origins of Towns and Trade, AD 600–1000* (London)

HODGES, R. & HOBLEY, B. (1988) *The Rebirth of Towns in the West, AD 700–1050* (CBA Research Report no. 68)

KEENE, D. (1985) *Survey of Medieval Winchester* (2 vols, Oxford)

LEECH, R. (1981) *Early Industrial Housing: the Trinity Area of Frome* (RCHME Supplementary series no. 3, London)

LLOYD, D. (1984) *The Making of English Towns: 2000 Years of Evolution* (London)

LOBEL, M.D. (ed., 1991) *The City of London from Prehistoric Times to c. 1520* (British Atlas of Historic Towns, Vol. III, Oxford)

MORTON, A.D. (ed., 1992) *Excavations at Hamwic, Vol. 1* (CBA Research Report no. 84)

MUTHESIUS, S. (1982) *The English Terraced House* (New Haven, USA)

NICHOLAS, D. (1997a) *The Growth of the Medieval City, from Late Antiquity to the Fourteenth Century* (London & New York)

NICHOLAS, D. (1997b) *The Later Medieval City, 1300–1500* (London & New York)

OTTAWAY, P. (1992) *Archaeology in British Towns, from the Emperor Claudius to the Black Death* (London)

PLATT, C. (1976) *The English Medieval Town* (London)

PORTER, S. (1990) *Exploring Urban History: Sources for Local Historians* (London)

REYNOLDS, S. (1977) *An Introduction to the History of English Medieval Towns* (Oxford)

RCHME. (1975) *An Inventory of Historical Monuments in the City of York, Vol. IV: Outside the City Walls, East of the Ouse* (London)

RCHME. (1977) *The Town of Stamford* (London)

RCHME. (1980) *Ancient and Historical Monuments in the City of Salisbury, Vol. I* (London)

RCHME. (1981) *An Inventory of Historical Monuments in the City of York, Vol. V: The Central Area* (London)

RCHME. (1982) *Beverley: an Archaeological and Architectural Study* (Supplementary Series no. 4, London)

RCHME. (1985) *An Inventory of Archaeological Sites and Churches in Northampton* (London)

RCHME. (1993) *Salisbury: the Houses of the Close* (London)

SCHOFIELD, J. (1994) *Medieval London Houses* (New Haven, USA)

SCHOFIELD, J. & DYSON, T. (eds, 1980) *The Archaeology of the City of London*

SCHOFIELD, J. & LEECH, R. (eds, 1987) *Urban Archaeology in Britain* (CBA Research Report no. 61)

SCHOFIELD, J. & PALLISER, D. (eds, 1981) *Recent Archaeological Research in English Towns* (CBA, London)

SCHOFIELD, J. & VINCE, A. (1994) *Medieval Towns* (Leicester)

SCRASE, A.J. (1989) 'Development and change in burgage plots: the example of Wells', *Journal of Historical Geography*, Vol. 15, pp. 349–65

SLATER, T.R. (1980) 'The analysis of burgages: three case studies from the West Midlands', *West Midlands Archaeology*, No. 23 (1980), 57–9

SLATER, T.R. (1981a) 'The analysis of burgage patterns in medieval towns', *Area*, No. 13 (1981), pp. 211–16

SLATER, T.R. (1981b) 'Urban genesis and medieval town plans in Warwickshire and Worcestershire', in SLATER, T.R. & JARVIS, P.J. (eds), *Field & Forest: an Historical Geography of Warwickshire and Worcestershire* (Norwich), pp. 173–202

SLATER, T.R. (1990) 'English medieval new towns with composite plans: evidence from the Midlands', in SLATER, T.R. (ed.) *The Built Form of Western Cities* (Leicester) pp. 60–82

SLATER, T.R. & ROSSER, G. (eds, 1998) *The Church in the Medieval Town* (Aldershot)

SOULSBY, I. (1983) *The Towns of Medieval Wales* (Chichester)

WEST, J. (1983) *Town Records* (Chichester)

WHITEHAND, J.W.R. (ed.) *The Urban Landscape: Historical Development and Management* (Institute of British Geographers, Special Publication no. 13)

WOODIWISS, S. (ed., 1992) *Iron Age and Roman Salt Production and the Medieval Town of Droitwich* (CBA Research Report no. 81)

Index

NOTE—All place-names are followed by the name of the modern county in which they are situated.